The Inside Story of
TV's First Black Superstar

KEVIN COOK

VIKING

VIKING
Published by the Penguin Group
Penguin Group (USA) Inc., 375 Hudson Street,
New York, New York 10014, USA

USA | Canada | UK | Ireland | Australia | New Zealand | India | South Africa | China

Penguin Books Ltd, Registered Offices: 80 Strand, London WC2R 0RL, England
For more information about the Penguin Group visit penguin.com

Frontispiece: Reproduced with permission of *Time* magazine. Copyright © 1972.
Page xi: Photograph courtesy of Cookie Mackenzie

LIBRARY OF CONGRESS CATALOGING-IN-PUBLICATION DATA
Cook, Kevin, 1956–
Flip : the inside story of TV's first Black superstar / Kevin Cook.
    pages   cm
Includes bibliographical references and index.
ISBN 978-0-670-02570-1 (hardback)
1. Wilson, Flip. 2. Comedians—United States—Biography.   3. African American comedians—Biography.
4. Television personalities—United States—Biography.   5. African American television personalities—United
States—Biography.   I. Title.
PN2287.W477C66 2013
792.702'8092—dc23
[B]
2012039994

Printed in the United States of America
10 9 8 7 6 5 4 3 2 1

Book design by Carla Bolte

To Lily and Cal

and always for Pamela

CONTENTS

LIBERTY

◈

Flip Wilson's favorite picture of himself as a child.

Killer Ride

◈ He can't wait to finish his bows. Flip Wilson, a compact man in a bespoke suit and pink tie, faces an adoring studio audience in Burbank, California. "Goodnight!" he says, bowing with his manicured hands on his knees, letting the applause wash over him. His name sparkles behind him in letters ten feet high: *FLIP.*

Winking at the camera that's sending his smile to twenty million viewers, he looks like the happiest man in America. But the moment the camera's red light blinks out, his smile disappears. His lively eyes dim. He's out of there.

He greets a few front-row fans on his way offstage. Loosening his tie, he pats his producer on the back. "Bob, good work tonight." Moving on, he slaps hands with one of the show's writers, Richard Pryor. "See you Monday, motherfucker."

Pryor bows. "Yassuh, massa."

Flipping Pryor the bird, Flip strides through the soundstage to a loading bay behind the studio. Light spills from the loading-bay door to the hood of his car, a sky-blue Rolls-Royce Corniche convertible, top down. Flip's two-ton road yacht has a 250-horsepower engine and a top speed of 115. Its license plates read KILLER. Its glove box holds a bag of pot and a vial of cocaine. Tossing his jacket onto the front seat along with a yellow legal pad, a script, and a paperback joke book, he climbs behind the wheel and peels out, saluting the guard at the NBC gate as he heads up Olive Avenue to the Ventura Freeway.

He barrels east through the last clots of rush-hour traffic, through Glendale and Pasadena to the Barstow Freeway, dry wind shooting dust and bits of sand up the hood and over the windshield. He reaches up to feel the wind through his fingers. It feels like freedom. Another ninety-hour workweek done, another show in the can.

North of San Bernardino the freeway climbs four thousand feet to Cajon Pass, a notch between the San Gabriel and San Bernardino mountains. This is where covered wagons struggled west from Utah to Southern California a century before. The wagon trains averaged a mile per hour on a good day. Flip kicks the Rolls past ninety and pokes an eight-track tape into the dashboard, Herb Alpert and the Tijuana Brass. Stars emerge in the blue-black desert sky. The road flattens out, arrowing through the cactus-studded Mojave. He drives to the rhythm of the music, rolling from right lane to left and back. Several hours out of L.A. he reaches for the amber vial in the glove box. He taps a pair of white dashes onto the back of his hand and sniffs up the powder. Now the stars look a shade brighter.

Just outside Needles he pulls into a truck stop, giving the attendant fifty dollars to fill the tank. "Keep the change."

The attendant says, "Hey, aren't you—"

"Nope. He's taller."

There's a bar nearby, a honky-tonk with beer signs flashing in the window. Flip parks, grabs his script and legal pad, and steps inside. He sees American flags at both ends of the bar, pinball games along the wall, and hears Johnny Cash on the jukebox. Three years ago he would have thought twice about coming in here, but fame changes everything. A couple guys at the bar, good ole boys in jeans and flannel shirts, check out the new arrival. The black new arrival. One of them elbows the other. *No shit?!* They know him.

Flip asks the bartender, "What's on tap?"

One of the drinkers says, *"What you see is what you get!"*

He takes a Schlitz to a corner booth and opens next week's script. Soon he's humming, alone with his show at last. He mumbles punch lines, underlines a few, crosses out others, jots notes in the margins. Reaching for his legal pad, he writes the setup for a sketch: *GDINE=1ST LADY??* He's getting a little tired of Geraldine, but what's he supposed to do? She's his meal ticket. He works and reworks the sketch until it's a crosshatched, scrawled-up mess, just the way he likes it.

Two big-haired women hurry in, buzzing about the Rolls. A minute later they're crowding his table. "Say something funny," one says.

"Sorry. I'm off duty."

"Do Geraldine."

Flip drops a twenty on the table. "I'm a professional entertainer. I don't do my act in booths in bars. I'll sign autographs if you'd like."

"C'mon, do Geraldine. *The devil made me buy this dress!*"

He slips out the door as she says it again and again.

Kingman, Seligman, Ash Fork, Flagstaff—Arizona towns fly by like the credits at the end of the show. Near the border of Arizona and Utah, just north of Bitter Springs, a side road leads to a high-desert gorge almost as deep as the Grand Canyon. This is his spot, a mile off the highway, 525 miles from the NBC lot. He found it on a previous drive when he took a wrong turn and almost drove into space two thousand feet over the Colorado River.

He parks at the barricade where the road dead-ends, a few yards from the canyon's edge. Worn out by the show, the drive, the coke, the beer, and the weight of the choice he's about to make, he stretches out in the front seat with his feet on the dash, looking up at the night sky, waiting. It won't be long now.

RAGS

1

Jersey City Runaway

◈ The spotlight stung his eyes. Clerow Wilson groaned. He twitched. Lying on a stretcher on the gymnasium stage, Clerow was playing a soldier in the school play at P.S. 14, a redbrick hulk on a trash-strewn block in Jersey City, New Jersey. He had no lines in the play; in fact he was lucky to be in it at all. Mrs. Davis, the director, had chosen a blond-haired white girl to play the heroine, Civil War nurse Clara Barton, and filled out the cast with older children. "Sorry, Clerow," she'd said. "You didn't make it."

"*Pleeeeeze*, Miz Davis. I'll play a tree," he'd said. "Or a dead guy."

She relented. Little Clerow, the smallest, jumpiest kid in his class, got to play a wounded soldier, basically a prop. His job was to lie on his stretcher wrapped in ketchup-stained bandages while Clara pranced around talking about tourniquets and the Battle of Bull Run. But under Clerow's bandages lay sixty pounds of ham. During dress rehearsal he moaned, rolled over and loudly, foot-shakingly, died.

"Thank you for that heartfelt contribution," Mrs. Davis said. "Please remember that our play is called *Clara Barton of the Red Cross*, not *Wounded Soldier*."

Clerow didn't answer. He was still twitching and winking, getting laughs from the kids.

The next night, with more than a hundred parents, teachers, and students waiting for the curtain, the girl playing Clara got stage fright. She couldn't move or speak. Mrs. Davis was about to send everyone home when Clerow piped up. "I can do her part!" Lying on his stretcher during rehearsals, he had memorized the whole play.

They found a blond wig. Eight-year-old Clerow put it on along with Clara's white smock, bonnet, and high-button shoes, and, as he remembered years later, "Clara Barton became a little black chick. People laughed when they saw me, so I started ad-libbing. *Hello, Manassas!*" That night's crowd caught the first public glimpse of Clerow "Flip" Wilson, who would grow up to be one of America's favorite comedians. His journey out of a Jersey City slum would take him to Air Force bases in the South Pacific, nightclubs on the segregated Chitlin' Circuit, and Johnny Carson's *Tonight Show* in its heyday; from drug dens and flophouses to his own top-rated TV show, the pinnacle of pop culture. It started that night in 1942, in a smelly gym at P.S. 14.

"That was my first gig—playing a girl. The play became a comedy, and it was a smash."

Clerow Wilson Jr. was born on December 8, 1933, a drab day in Jersey City, New Jersey, across the Hudson River from New York. Like Frank Sinatra twenty years before him, Clerow could look across the river at the Manhattan skyline and dream of making it there. Like Sinatra before him, he saw the Statue of Liberty standing at the mouth of the Hudson with her back to New Jersey. Unlike Sinatra, who grew up in working-class Hoboken, the next town to the north, Clerow couldn't afford a ferry ticket to Liberty Island.

His parents—Clerow Sr., a handyman and janitor, and his wife, Cornelia—shared a four-room apartment in The Hill, one of the poorest parts of a deteriorating city, with their fast-growing family. The Wilsons' windows looked out at the funeral home across Clinton Avenue, a street few white citizens walked except by accident.

Clerow Sr. and Cornelia had had nine children before Clerow came along. Soon there were two more, making him the tenth of a dozen Wilson kids spilling into streets jammed with trolley cars and buses, soldiers and sailors, church bells, glad and angry and prayerful voices, soapbox evangelists, flying Spaldeens, dogs, cats and rats, junkies and numbers runners. In an era when light skin meant status and many blacks dreamed of passing for white, Clerow Jr. had the darkest skin in the family. "You're black as burnt toast. Black as a bad banana," his father said. "I ought to throw you out with the garbage." Clerow was ashamed to be so black until he decided it made him special. When Mrs. Davis at P.S. 14 pointed out the window at the Statue of Liberty and said, "If one of you lazybones ever did something worthwhile, maybe she'd turn back around this way," he thought he might be the one.

At the age of seven or eight Clerow fell for a girl from "the neatest family on the block." Her name was Geraldine. Her skin, as he remembered it, was "so black it was almost blue." Her mother dressed Geraldine in starched pink dresses and rubbed her legs with Vaseline to make them shine. "I asked her to be my girlfriend, but Geraldine said no because I was a ragamuffin. Then she said she *might* be my girl if I got her some fake fingernails at Woolworth's." Without a penny in his pocket, he shoplifted the nails. They were the wrong size. He sneaked back into the store only to get caught in the act, "and then Geraldine wouldn't talk to me because I was a criminal."

One day he went home to find his brothers and sisters huddling in an empty apartment. Their mother was gone. "She ran off with a man. Took my baby brother and all the furniture, too. My pops went to the bank and his money was gone. She'd been there with a certificate of his death and withdrawn it." Unable to pay rent, Clerow Sr. lost the apartment. He herded his kids into a coal cellar, where they huddled on the floor while he slept sitting up on the stairs. After they got kicked out of there, Clerow Sr. spent his nights in other basements or tool sheds while the children fended for themselves. Some wound up in foster homes. Clerow Jr. moved in with his older sister Eleanor, who had married a long-haul truck driver. Eleanor and her husband had three children of their own. "They always ate first," he remembered. "I had to wait. I got what their kids didn't eat, and they resented me being there, so they'd slop their food around and play with it, just to show me who was who."

Life in Jersey City's slums was chaotic and often violent. When a relative raped one of the Wilsons' cousins, a girl of eleven, nobody reported it. When a man pitched his wife out a second-story window, she spent a night in the hospital and then climbed back up the stairs to her husband. Clerow's sister Eleanor slept with other men when her husband was on the road. When her man came home, she hosted house parties for him and his trucker friends, charging the other truckers a couple dollars' admission at the door. The men drank and gambled straight through to breakfast. They were used to driving through the night. One night Eleanor's husband amused his friends by having little Clerow serve as their craps table. The boy sat in a kitchen chair with the dice board on his lap. He had to sit up straight so they could use his stomach as a backstop for the dice. Clerow stayed up long after Eleanor's kids went to bed, holding still while the truckers threw dice and money, hooting and yelling. He was earning his keep: "I had to stay awake or get out." If he nodded off, Eleanor's husband, a street fighter known for knocking men out by head-butting them, leaned over and banged heads with him.

"There's your wake-up call," he'd say.

Clerow stayed in touch with his father, who haunted The Hill looking for any work he could get as a janitor, painter, carpenter, plumber, or handyman. His pops would stand on the curb for hours in all weather, wearing his work boots, tool belt, and canvas gloves, waiting for someone to hire him. He'd work a plug of Red Man tobacco in his cheek for hours, spitting the juice into a paper cup. Men with steady jobs earned fifty cents an hour in those days; Pops settled for less. He hauled trash for restaurants and food stands, and sometimes the proprietors let him keep some of their unsold fruits and vegetables. He'd sit in a restaurant basement with Clerow, dividing the contents of a string bag full of apples, bananas, potatoes, carrots, onions, cabbages, and heads of lettuce, half of it spoiled. They cut out the rotten parts and ate the rest.

After the sun went down, Pops rode Jackson Avenue bar stools. He introduced Clerow to drinkers and bartenders as "my boy, the one named after me, and I'm very proud of him." Nobody remarked on the fact that Clerow Jr. was darker-skinned than Clerow Sr., closer to the skin tone of another man who took an interest in him. Leroy Taylor, who drank in the same taverns as Pops, was a friend of the family, an old boyfriend of Cornelia's. A high-school graduate, Taylor was the first black electrical foreman in Jersey City, highly regarded up and down the avenue. "Come here, my boy," Taylor would say, calling Clerow down to his bar stool. "You working hard in school? You got enough to eat?" Taylor gave the boy more money than his pops did. Why?

"Why?" Eleanor thought that was funny. "Because he's your real father. Pops don't even know," she said.

Taylor took him for a drive in his Model T Ford, Clerow's first ride in a car. They went to the zoo and the circus and one day to a stage show at the grand old Mosque Theater in Newark. After Count Basie and His Barons of Rhythm played a set, a comedian came out. Dressed in spats, a top hat, and white gloves, the comic performed an old blackface routine called "Open the Door, Richard." Playing a drunk pitched out of a fine restaurant, he said, "I'm goin' keep drinkin' to everybody's health until I ruin my own."

Wobbling back to the restaurant, he bawled, "Open the dooo-oo-oor, Richard!" Clerow would never forget the laughter and cheers that filled the theater. "I thought, 'Wow, they all *love* that guy. That's what I want to do. That's what I want to be.'"

Watching the world wobble around him, Clerow saw grown-ups lie, cheat, and steal while their kids went hungry. Eleanor cheated on her husband. She picked her boyfriends' pockets while they were sleeping. She demanded money from Pops for Clerow's "room and board" and used it to play the numbers. But of all the double-dealing adults in the world, Clerow thought, his mother was the worst. "What a dirty trick—this woman has a son by her boyfriend and names it Clerow. Her husband's name! And then she leaves us, but she takes my baby brother with her. Why not take me, too?"

Sitting on the curb with his cuckolded pops, he parroted the word that Pops, Eleanor, Leroy Taylor, and probably Frank Sinatra all used to name his mother. *Bitch.* And that gave him an advantage when the neighborhood boys played the dozens.

The dozens was a talking game. You insult another kid, and he insults you back, harder. The game's name dated back at least a century to slave auctions when the "worst" slaves, broken down by hard labor or rape, some with hands or limbs cut off for disobedience, were sold in lots, twelve at a time. They were cheaper by the dozen. Nothing was more insulting. By Clerow's time the insults were strictly verbal, often describing in detail how fat or ugly somebody's mother was. As in rap battles of later decades, the attacks escalated until somebody lost his train of thought or his nerve.

"I fucked your momma."

"A gang of guys fucked your momma."

"A *busload* of guys fucked yours, and the bitch was so fat the bus got a flat."

Most boys had limits. When dogs and leprechauns, Captain

Marvel and mule teams of double-dicked donkeys started fucking people's mommas, they backed off. Not Clerow. "I always won. I could beat anybody talking that shit because they couldn't hurt my feelings about my momma. I hated the bitch."

Not long after Clerow's stage debut as Clara Barton, a neighbor filed a complaint about the Wilson kids running the streets. The New Jersey Board of Children's Guardians rounded them up and placed them in foster homes. Clerow wound up with a black family in Bayonne, just south of Jersey City. The Lewises, devout Catholics who prayed morning and night, kissing the shiny black beads of their rosaries, had two other foster children as well as a son of their own. The state gave them sixty dollars a month plus a ration of canned milk for each foster child, a tidy sum at a time when a loaf of bread cost a dime and gas was fifteen cents a gallon. As at Eleanor's apartment, the "real" family ate first. Clerow sat in a corner watching the Lewises' real son drink the milk the state sent for Clerow, watching the boy smile and wipe off his milk mustache.

Clerow began wetting his bed. He was nervous. Homesick. "Mrs. Lewis woke me up every morning and beat my ass for wetting the bed. I'd change clothes and watch them eat breakfast."

He played alone in the Lewises' backyard. The white kids next door watched through a knothole in the fence, jeering at him. "Nigger! Look at the little nigger. *Eeny meeny miny moe, catch a nigger by the toe, if he hollers let him go . . .*" It stopped when Clerow poked a rake handle through the knothole and hit one of them in the eye.

The neighbor kid's mother complained, and Mrs. Lewis whipped Clerow with a belt. That night he ran away. It was seven miles from the Lewis house back to Jackson Avenue. Picking his way through a garbage dump, he found a weather-beaten wooden sled. He'd always wanted a sled. He was dragging it behind him when the police picked him up, laughing to see a boy pulling a sled in June.

"Don't send me back," he pleaded with them. "That lady beats me." But the cops said they had no choice. They took him back to Mrs. Lewis, who smiled and thanked them and whipped him as soon as they left. Between blows he distracted himself by hatching a plan: he would keep running away until the Board of Children's Guardians sent him to reform school, where his brother Clifford was.

He ran away eight times in a year. The social workers responded by transferring him from one foster home to another. One was lorded over by a loud, theatrical preacher, a finger-snapping, slide-stepping, Cadillac-driving reverend who would serve as the model for one of Flip Wilson's most popular characters. Clerow ran away. Another foster family ran a turkey farm where the skinny eight-year-old, not much taller than the poultry, vaccinated the birds by the hundred, giving each one a shot in its plump, mottled thigh. He fed them, too, tossing grain from a bucket while the turkeys mobbed him. They liked him so much that they gobbled like crazy the night he ran away, almost foiling his escape.

Finally the state gave up on him. The Board of Children's Guardians assigned Clerow Wilson to the New Jersey Reform School at Jamesburg, forty miles southwest of Jersey City. He was eight and a half.

Surrounded by fences topped with barbed wire, the notorious Jamesburg school provided beds and a rudimentary education for more than four hundred boys deemed too wild for the foster-care system. The barracks were crowded, discipline strict, meals sloppy and cold. Clerow loved the place. "I was the smartest kid there. And Sundays we got tapioca pudding." Before dawn one morning a couple of guards drove him to a clinic where a doctor took his tonsils out and circumcised him. Armed with two bags of ice, Clerow was back at the reformatory in time for lunch.

A white teacher named Alice Jones felt sorry for the nervous runt who talked a blue streak once you got him going on about his favorite stuff: jokes, radio serials, clean clothes, rhythm and blues music, penny candy, tapioca, comic books. Mrs. Jones gave him Bugs Bunny and Little Orphan Annie comics. Clerow loved wise guy Bugs and plucky Annie, saved from an orphanage by wealthy Daddy Warbucks, though some of Orphan Annie's stories upset him. He skipped the parts where Annie got bullied or kidnapped, and picked up where she got rescued.

Mr. Herman, Jamesburg's night watchman, ate his lunch at midnight. Every night, just before opening the waxed-paper bag his wife had packed, he woke Clerow. "We need to stop you from wetting the bed," he said. "Go pee." After the boy peed and washed and rewashed his hands, they shared Mr. Herman's lunch—a jar of peaches and a sandwich. Soon the watchman was bringing a late lunch for Clerow, too. They sat up late talking about what a boy could do with his life if he stayed out of trouble and worked hard every day, like being a lawyer or an airplane pilot, or even a man in a top hat entertaining cheering crowds at the Mosque Theater in Newark.

With World War II roaring in Europe and the South Pacific, Little Orphan Annie and a band of cartoon kids called the Junior Commandos collected newspapers and scrap metal to aid the war effort. One of the Junior Commandos was black, which led some newspapers to drop the comic strip. President Roosevelt announced gasoline rationing to aid the war effort as the Air Force bombed Germany and Italy, and physicist Enrico Fermi split atoms in a cyclotron under the football field at the University of Chicago, the first step toward an atomic bomb. Clerow Wilson celebrated his ninth birthday in December 1942. Mrs. Jones and Mr. Herman, two white grown-ups who owed him nothing, sang "Happy Birthday." "It's my happiest memory of childhood," he remembered. "They gave me the first birthday presents I ever got—a can of shoe polish and a box of Cracker Jack."

* * *

After six months at Jamesburg, he was reunited with three of his older brothers and sisters in a foster home near Atlantic City. His new foster father worked as a chef in a hotel on the boardwalk. The hotel threw out the heels of bread loaves, so the man brought home bags full of them. His wife, a fortune teller, fed them the heels with hot tea. In the evenings they all sat around a tall wooden radio listening to serials—*The Green Hornet, The Shadow,* the scary *Inner Sanctum.* In the mornings Clerow helped his teenage brother Clifford with his newspaper route, which he inherited when Clifford moved on to burglary and armed robbery. After that, Clifford was always in trouble. One day he took Clerow along on one of his mandatory visits to the police station, figuring his probation officer wouldn't hit him if his little brother was standing there. He was wrong. "The probation officer made Clifford lie on a bench. He whipped his ass with a rubber hose. Then he looked over at me. He said, 'Look here, little nigger, I want to show you what happens if you do like your brother.' He picked me up, slammed me against some lockers, and hit me a couple times with the rubber hose. That was 'just in case,' he said."

The chef's house was comfortable enough, but the arrangement ended when social workers discovered that the lady of the house was reading palms and holding séances. The Wilson kids were transferred to all-black Whitesboro, New Jersey. Their new foster parents, the Townsends, were members of the Sanctified Church, a black revivalist congregation that looked down on radio dramas, movies, jokes, dancing, and comic books. To fit in, Clerow agreed to be saved. Dressed in a brand-new suit and tie, he stood up in church, raised his arms, spun around, and swore he'd let Jesus into his heart. Soon he was the Townsends' favorite, testifying at churches all over South Jersey. Every weekday before school, Mrs. Townsend gave the children sweet potatoes right out of the oven;

on cold mornings they warmed their hands with them while they waited for the school bus, then ate them when the bus arrived. After he was saved, Clerow was given an extra sweet potato.

While the children vied for "Mother" Townsend's attention, she made money off them. Clerow and the other boys got summer jobs working on nearby farms, making ten dollars a week. She took eight and left them two dollars apiece. "On Saturdays she'd take us to an amusement park. We'd spend a dollar on rides, but you had to keep something back for the church collection, and you had to buy a gift for Mother. Once I spent my whole two dollars on a great big card for her." Years later he could still recite the verse on the card: *Mother—to one who bears the sweetest name and adds luster to the same, who shares my joys and tears when sad, the greatest friend I ever had, no other could take the place of my mother.* "And that made me her pet, but it made me mad. I was resentful of women, starting with my real mother. I never saw how she could leave me, or why my sister fucked around and stole, or how Mrs. Lewis could give my milk to her kid, or how Mrs. Townsend could take her sixty dollars a month from the state and still cheat us—chicks always *using* motherfuckers for their money." He could almost understand why his pops started wearing a gold chain around his neck after Clerow's mother left him. When he asked about the chain, Pops said he wore it because of his runaway wife. If he saw her again, he said, he'd take off that chain and strangle her with it.

Clerow told himself he could do without a mother. He had eyes that saw everything going on around him, and a mind that spun so fast sometimes it scared him. If he could hold on until he was old enough to fend for himself, he'd find his way out of the lying, cheating, stealing, ass-whipping world he was born into.

He kept running away from foster homes—thirteen times in all—until the state sent him back to The Hill to live with Pops. Still a runt at fourteen, Clerow bore scars on his bottom from beatings his last foster mother had given him with a double loop of copper electrical wire. He was thrilled to be back with Pops, who was working as custodian of a building in a white neighborhood. As a perk of the job, he got a four-room apartment in the building, rent-free. They shared the place with a shifting set of relatives, including Lemuel Brown, who found the whole world amusing. A brother of Clerow's mother, Uncle Lemuel was a bartender and painter. Some of his paintings sold for $100 and up, including a few that got him arrested: vivid oils of boxing champ Joe Louis in action, naked, swinging a heavyweight penis any man would be proud of.

When Clerow brought his first girlfriend around, Uncle Lemuel whistled. "That's a cute gal you got there."

"Thank you, Unc," Clerow said.

"You get her little fruit cup yet?"

"C'mon, Unc, don't talk like that to my girl."

"And you call yourself a Wilson!" Uncle Lemuel laughed. "Let me tell you something about the Wilsons. If a Wilson man meets a girl on Wednesday, he gets her little fruit cup by Tuesday—the day *before.*"

Clerow liked living with Pops and Uncle Lemuel in postwar Jersey City, attending Henry Snyder High School and working as a pinsetter in a bowling alley. Sometimes his capacity for happiness surprised him. Walking home from the bowling alley with the Statue of Liberty at his back, he'd whistle and do a dance step across the sidewalk. His spirits ebbed when he saw how people looked right through him. Whites and blacks alike paid no attention to the raggedy boy in patched pants, secondhand shoes, and shirts that were missing buttons. He was ashamed of his clothes, natty hair, empty pockets, and even his rear end. When his first girlfriend agreed to play doctor, he chickened out. "I didn't want her to see the scars on my butt," he confessed to Uncle Lemuel.

"So don't show her the butt," his uncle said. "Give her the flip side!"

Leroy Taylor and his Model T Ford were out of the picture by now. Clerow never knew what became of his biological father, but he learned a lot about his pops in the years they lived together, including his strange sleeping habits. "From the time my mother left, he never slept in a bed. Always in a chair by the kitchen stove, sitting up." Pops would drink himself to sleep, sitting up in a stiff-backed chair as if waiting for his wife to come home, then stand up, stretch, and go to work in the morning, fixing the white tenants' squeaky doors and leaky toilets, cleaning up their messes. Clerow loved his pops but he didn't want to live like that. He wasn't cut out to be a trucker like Eleanor's husband, or a bartender like Uncle Lemuel. And while he had no idea how the blackface comics at the Mosque Theater got started, he was pretty sure it wasn't by wasting their time on what he later called "slum nigger shit."

In the winter of 1949, the year Clerow turned sixteen, his pops lugged a heavy cardboard carton up the stairs and said, "Looky here." He sliced the box open. It held six quart bottles of bourbon. "We are about to have a very merry Christmas."

Clerow's big brother Lem, their uncle's namesake, was sleeping over at the time. A boxer and semipro football player, Lem saw himself as a tough guy. He boasted that he could drink more of that whiskey than Pops. Drink him right under the kitchen table.

"Oh no, you can't," Pops said.

"Hundred says I can." Lem carried a showy bankroll of twenty-dollar bills, which he began peeling off.

"Five hundred," Pops said. More than he made in a month.

They made Clerow hold the stakes: a thousand dollars in twenties, tens, and a handful of Pops's crinkly fivers and singles. The two men sat at the kitchen table, each with a quart of bourbon and a tall water glass in front of him. Pops filled his glass and drained it. Lem took longer to empty his. Pops poured another. After three big glasses, his whiskey bottle was dry. Lem, still working on his second glass, gave up. He snatched a handful of bills from Clerow and started for the door. Pops went after him. Clerow froze. The men reached the door at the same time. Pops kicked it shut, grabbed for the money with one hand and got a handful of Lem's hair with the other. Lem got loose and ran through the apartment, Pops chasing him, twenty-dollar bills flying, Lem shutting doors and Pops shoving them open. At some point Pops came up with a hatchet. Lem slammed the bedroom door and began shoving furniture against it, cussing and hollering insults and threats, but he forgot the door behind him. Pops rushed in, waving the hatchet, and Lem threw the money at him and ran for his life.

When it was over, Clerow was breathing as hard as his pops. He didn't know where he belonged, if anywhere, but it wasn't here.

2

He Flippeth!

◈ He lied his way out of town.

Clerow and one of Eleanor's sons, Ray, went sauntering one spring day in 1950. Ray was one of the kids who played with his food while motherless Clerow waited his turn. Up Hudson Boulevard they went, skipping over the abandoned rails of the old trolley line toward Journal Square. Being Eleanor's son made Ray Clerow's nephew, despite the fact that he was a year older and several inches taller. "Got some mixed-up relations in our family," Clerow said about that. "Some of us probably older than ourselves." Ray called him "Unc" while playfully kicking him and flicking a finger off the side of his head.

Journal Square thrummed with commerce. Billboards for Coca-Cola, Ruppert beer, Schenley and Philadelphia whiskeys, Camel cigarettes, and the Ringling Brothers circus loomed over six lanes of traffic. The boys weaved around newsstands, shoeshine stands, ice-cream vendors, a baton-twirling cop, and a used-book salesman who flashed French postcards when the coast was clear. Moviegoers streamed in and out of the grand State and Loews Jersey movie theaters, and the even grander Stanley with its electric billboard and all-brass marquee. Studebaker limousines purred outside the seven-story Hotel Plaza, a brown-brick landmark at the corner of the square. Clerow and Ray passed the hotel, and the rose- and honeysuckle-scented premises of Theodore the Florist, before reaching a storefront with an Uncle Sam poster in one window and a fighter-plane poster in the other. "C'mon," Ray said.

Next thing he knew, sixteen-year-old Clerow was telling a man in a pristine white uniform, "Yes, sir, I'm seventeen." The Air Force recruiter nodded. He had a quota to fill. Enlistment age was eighteen, he said, "or seventeen with parental consent."

Clerow knew his pops wouldn't want him getting shot at. He said, "I'm an orphan. My big sister looks after me." Ray ran home and brought back his mother. Eleanor wouldn't cooperate at first, but as soon as Clerow promised her some of the ninety-five dollars a month he'd be making, she signed as his legal guardian. The recruiter stamped the date, June 16, 1950, under her signature, and Clerow was in the Air Force.

"I wasn't patriotic, just tired of being ashamed of my clothes," he recalled years later. "And the thought of getting paid ninety-five dollars a month—I didn't know what I'd do with all that money."

With World War II over he wasn't worried about getting shot at. The Air Force sounded like a dream come true: free clothes, hot food, and a chance to fly. Clerow couldn't wait to start flying planes. He took a free train ride, his first trip out of New Jersey, to Lackland Air Force Base in Texas, where a sergeant informed the new recruit that he was something less than pilot material. The Air Force wasn't putting ninth-grade dropouts at the controls of its million-dollar aircraft. Only college graduates went to flight school. Airman Wilson, assigned to the Seventy-eighth Food Service Squadron, could expect to control a potato peeler. Unless he got sent to fight—which became a distinct possibility when the Korean War began nine days after Clerow Wilson enlisted.

Boot camp was a breeze for lean little Clerow, except for the time he almost killed himself. Hearing a bunch of paratroopers discussing the proper technique for landing a jump, the raw recruit who'd never been higher than seven floors up said he knew how to do it. (He'd seen it in movies.) The paratroopers said the impact at the end of a jump felt like a twenty- or thirty-foot fall. Clerow bet his paycheck that he could jump off the two-story barracks building, smile, and walk away.

Throwing down their tens and twenties, the paratroopers whistled and clapped rhythmically—"one, two, three, go, one, two, three, *go*"—as he climbed a ladder and sat on the barracks roof, thirty feet up.

"I was pretty sure I knew how to land. You come down on your toes, bend your knees, and roll. So I jumped. But I came down wrong. I landed in a squatting position, and all of a sudden I'm like one of those cartoon characters that fall and hit, turn into a statue, and then shatter into a million pieces. I almost passed out. I heard guys yelling, 'He said he'd smile and walk away.'" The smile was the hardest part. "I forced a kind of sick smile, got the money, and limped to my bunk. I couldn't move for about five days."

He limped through a second round of training at Hamilton Air Force Base in San Rafael, California, where Clerow, the youngest recruit, was also the lone black airman among more than three hundred in his barracks, a peppercorn in a pot of mashed potatoes. He'd learned to keep his mouth shut and his head down around the few whites he encountered in Jersey City. The only whites he'd really known at all, the kind teacher and night watchman at the Jamesburg reform school, had treated him better than his own family. Now an MP welcomed him to Hamilton AFB with, "Nigger, step out of line once, and you're going to the guardhouse."

Airman Wilson kept to himself. Other recruits razzed him at mail call: *Why don't the colored boy get any mail?* He deflected the question with a joke. "My cheapskate relatives only write collect." On the morning that duty assignments came through, he found himself stationed at a typewriter while other Food Service Squadron members grated cheese, peeled potatoes, and mopped kitchen floors.

"You're a clerk now, Wilson," his commanding officer said. Clerow snapped off a salute. Lonely or not, military life had its pluses: he had a pay stub in the pocket of his crisp khakis, new shoes with a mirror shine, and a belly full of government-issue bacon, eggs, and biscuits. His CO, Major Lloyd Llewellyn Lancaster Lynn, a drawling Tennessean, sent the new clerk to typing classes and told him they'd get on just fine as long as he worked his Negro tail off. "You'll practice your typing every morning," Lynn instructed, "and I'll check your progress in forty-five days." Clerow practiced until he could type fifty words a minute without a mistake. After six weeks, Major Lynn handed him a letter to type. Clerow banged it out, fingers zipping over the keys. If he couldn't be a pilot, at least his fingers could fly.

"You're not done," Lynn said. The left margin was nine spaces rather than ten. "Type it again." This went on until Clerow had typed the letter more than twenty times, with the major pointing out an error on each one—a misplaced comma, a short dash instead of a long one, a smudge. Finally the letter was perfect. They worked that way every day until Wilson was the Van Cliburn of his Remington keyboard, the best typist in the office if not on the whole base. Major Lynn protected him from bigots in the barracks—"Nobody can touch you," he said—and when the Hamilton AFB clerks were all tested for typing, spelling, and grammar, both men were proud of Clerow's perfect score. The test won him a promotion to corporal as well as a transfer to base headquarters.

At HQ he clerked for the director of personnel, helping him implement orders, some straight from the Pentagon. Many of the documents crossing the director's desk required judgment calls: Which servicemen on the base should go to pilot school? Which deserved hardship discharges? Before long the director was letting Clerow sift through personnel records and make recommendations. "That's how much regard he had for me," Clerow recalled. "I was a whiz at memorizing regulations and quotas and the men's records. I studied every report. After a couple months, he'd sign anything I drew up for him." The base ran better than ever until Clerow stepped out of line. After breakfast, running late for duty, he discovered that he was out of clean shirts. He couldn't report to the director's office like a ragamuffin, so he took a shirt from another man's locker. *Just for today,* he thought. *I'll get it laundered and slip it back.* He was tying his tie when his first sergeant strode up behind him. "You misappropriated that shirt," the sergeant said.

"But Sarge, I—"

"Nigger, I don't want to hear it. Come with me."

Busted from corporal back to airman, the outfit's only black clerk spent two weeks in the guardhouse, long enough to nurse a grudge. No white corporal would have gone to the brig for "misappropriating" a shirt. The shame of it burned like a fever. He would have borrowed a shirt if he'd had one friend in the outfit, but he didn't, so here he sat, the director's right-hand man, jailed for two weeks like some Jersey City vagrant.

The moment his sentence was up, he applied for a transfer. "Wilson, you're not going anywhere. I need you here," the director said. But for each transfer application his boss wadded up and tossed in the trash, Clerow filled out another. To him, the Air Force was just the latest family to betray him, one more rotten phony home to escape.

"You're dead set on getting out of here," the director said.

"Yes, sir."

"Type it up again, then. And good luck to you," the director said. "God knows you'll need it."

Clerow boarded a troop ship out of San Francisco, headed west. As the ship shoved off he hurried to the rail to see the Golden Gate Bridge pass overhead and puked into San Francisco Bay. It was his first time on a boat of any kind, and the thought of the voyage ahead, 5,800 miles across the Pacific to Andersen Air Force Base on Guam, made him pine for his hungry, bed-wetting, butt-whipped days in New Jersey. "I was seasick for three days," he recalled. "They kept me belowdecks because I wanted to jump over the side." Throwing up in the head didn't always relieve his nausea. If he leaned down to puke into a urinal at the wrong time, when the ship was climbing a wave, the piss in the bowl sloshed into his face.

"I finally got my sea legs on the fourth day. I went up on deck and saw the sky and the sea rolling off to the end of the world, so beautiful I never forgot it."

Some of the men went carousing while the ship refueled in Hawaii. They told Clerow to stay behind for his own safety, warning, "Hawaiians don't like coloreds." He spent the evening walking laps around the deck, admiring the moonlight on Honolulu Harbor, wondering what lay ahead.

Guam lay 1,500 miles east of the Philippines. Thirty miles long and four miles wide, ringed by coral reefs and shallows the color of Aqua Velva, the island was a U.S. territory, seized from Japan in 1944. Three thousand Americans died in the World War II Battle of Guam. Japan's Imperial Army, trained never to surrender, lost almost twenty thousand men. (One Japanese soldier, Shoichi Yokoi, escaped into the jungle, where he lived alone in a cave for twenty-seven years. Discovered wearing pants made of tree bark, he was shipped home to Tokyo in 1972—the second season of *The Flip Wilson Show*.) Seven years after the battle, Guam's Andersen AFB served as a base for B-29s bombing targets in Korea. Clerow gawked at the island's white sand beaches, waterfalls, banana trees, bougainvillea, and topless Chamorro women. If he wound up getting killed in this war, he thought, at least he'd seen paradise first.

Assigned as a clerk to Captain Henry Spiker of the motor pool, his latest white CO, Airman Wilson earned special privileges in no time. The captain liked his sense of humor. One morning Spiker invited the teenage clerk into his office. Pushing a copy of the military newspaper *Stars and Stripes* across his desk, he said, "Wilson, read me the paper. Give me your interpretation." Clerow read aloud, ad-libbing comments on the latest rules and regs, blunders by the Army and Navy, and pompous pronouncements by "our doo-doo-ly elected civilian leaders." He could make Harry Truman sound like a blackface comedian. Or a turkey. Before long he was goofing on *Stars and Stripes* or the *Guam Daily News* every morning with Captain Spiker, who told him, "When we're in this room, you can call me Hank." Clerow handled his other duties with ease, typing, filing, requisitioning. But when Spiker said he deserved a promotion, Clerow shook his head. "No, sir," he said. "I don't want a promotion. I'm going to serve my time and get out."

"And why is that?"

"I want to make it on my own."

"Well, son, if I can't promote you, what should I do with you?"

Clerow said, "Hank, let me think about that."

Ever since his first nights in the all-white barracks in Texas, he'd fought loneliness by reading. The PXs sold used books for nickels and dimes. His favorite was a dog-eared copy of Max Eastman's *Enjoyment of Laughter*, a 1936 tome on the theory and practice of comedy (*Be Interesting . . . Be Effortless . . . Be Sudden*). As months passed at Air Force bases in Texas, California, and Guam, he filled his footlocker with books on an array of topics, including another favorite, sex. Clerow was no virgin—sex was as common as hunger where he came from—but he was a novice with scars. He still had marks on his bottom from his last foster mother's beatings, and he bore emotional scars from his childhood abuse and abandonment. He wasn't sure what to think of sex. Some of the young airmen in his barracks told one dirty joke after another. Some lay in their bunks holding a nude pinup with one hand, jerking off with the other. Clerow never jerked off. He claimed he never had, not in his loneliest nights in foster homes, not in Pops's apartment, and not on any of the bases where he'd served, trying to sleep in barracks full of snoring, farting, occasionally masturbating men. Clerow wanted to control his impulses. And to help control the strongest impulse, he read and observed. He read Freud and the Kinsey Report. He watched the men in his unit flirt with Chamorro girls who milled around outside the base, and wondered why these brown girls pulled white airmen into the bushes but wouldn't kiss a black man.

He watched a dozen men line up outside a Quonset hut on payday. One by one they handed money to a sergeant and then waited, shooting the breeze until it was their turn to go inside and screw the sergeant's wife. The sergeant earned more than a thousand dollars a month this way.

Clerow watched other men blunt their sex drives by getting wasted. Every payday the five black airmen in his outfit chipped in to buy a case of wine apiece. There were six half-gallon bottles in a case. That gave them thirty half-gallon jugs of wine, one for every night till the next payday. They sat at the edge of what they called "the boonies," the jungle, sharing one of the bottles. (Japanese soldier Soichi Yokoi was hiding in the boonies somewhere, eating grubs and tree bark in the seventh year of his 27 years in hiding.) Some of the men boasted about their wives and girlfriends, but Clerow was more struck by the sob stories. "Every mail call brought a couple more Dear John letters," he remembered. "They're six thousand miles from home, they get a letter, and their wife says she wants a divorce. Or their girl got engaged. These tall, strong men sat there and cried." Clerow was glad he didn't have a girl to cry over. He was happy to be a world away from Jersey City, sitting under a coconut palm enjoying the wine and a hit off the joint his new friends passed around. Sharing dope was the least they could do, since they smuggled joints around the base in books Clerow ordered from the library and the PX. Two of the smokers promised him a taste of something better.

One night they said, "Our package got here. C'mon."

He followed them to the baseball field at a far end of the base. The field was deserted at this time of night. They sat on a bench in one of the dugouts.

One of the men unwrapped a paper packet. He stuck his nose into it, sniffed, and stepped back as if a gust of wind had hit him. "Your turn," he said, lifting the packet of toast-colored powder to Clerow's upper lip.

Almonds. It smelled like almonds. He sniffed, and the offerer pulled it back and said, "Too much!" and laughed, rewrapping the packet, adding, "You'll feel that." Clerow felt a wave of electric bile stream from his sinuses to his gut to his gullet. He threw up, but afterward, "I felt better. Better than better. Very, very alert. The stars were out on a starry, starry night. We were soaked with perspiration from the heroin and the heat, so we took off all our clothes and went out and lay down on the bases. One of us on first base, one on second, me on third, looking up at the sky. I kept thinking, *What if someone comes out here and sees us, with our balls out to the stars?* What do I say, 'Bases loaded'?"

The smack smugglers let him pay thirty dollars for a cut of the next package. When it came he snorted a pinch and hid the rest in his footlocker. He lay on his bunk with his mind rolling back to the day he found his brothers and sisters hugging in an empty rowhouse apartment. He saw his pops at the bank, asking for money. There was no money. He saw Pops pushing a mop. He saw the telephone numbers of his foster homes moving across the barracks ceiling.

"Wilson. *Wilson!*" One of the wine drinkers had a hand on his foot, shaking it. "Gomez says you're holding," the guy said. "Please let me cop some, please please please."

Clerow nodded, nodding off. "Footlocker," he said. "Leave me some."

In the morning he found $75 in the locker, with enough powder left to light him up two or three more times. The "please please" junkie was honorable, even generous. Clerow sucked up a hit, bought a $100 stake in the next "package from home," sold half of that package for $300 and snorted the rest. He bought more books, including one on addiction. The book called heroin "the devil's bait." Clerow was afraid to get hooked, and after three months of dealing and using, he could feel the drug start to claw at him. A hit brought three hours of bliss followed by four sleepless, constipated, Jekyll-and-Hyde days in which he thought about nothing but his next hit. Nothing was funny anymore. "That's when I knew I had to stop. I was losing my funny."

He quit investing in smack and turned his eye to what passed for entertainment on Guam.

Packs of wild dogs roamed the island, chasing feral pigs and rats, romping around the base's perimeter, baying at the lights, and stealing scraps from the trash dump behind the mess hall. Some of the men fed the mangy "boonie dogs," treating them almost as pets. And when the female boonie dogs came in heat, a couple of airmen captured three or four of them. They leashed the bitches to palm trees and benches in the base's central courtyard, sealed it off, and went around asking the men, "You gonna come watch the dogs fuck?" They didn't charge admission; the show was what they called "a public service." "Just bring beer," they said. Around eight P.M., when searchlights came on over the courtyard, the men opened a gate and loosed a pack of fifty to sixty male dogs on the leashed females. The males, catching the scent, split into groups surrounding them. Airmen crowded the courtyard fence, laughing, cracking open cold beers, making bets on which bitches would mate willingly with which dogs and which would get snowed under. Clerow had a hard time watching the spectacle and instead watched the men, some of whom looked madder than the animals. Something about sex unhinged them. A few threw their heads back and howled at the moon.

After the dog-fucking spectacle, he trudged back to his bunk and fished a few books from his footlocker. He made notes in the margins of books by Freud (*We all want to be motherfuckers?*) and Kinsey (*We're 10% fags!*). He read about sex in animals—dogs, cats, insects, and elephants, with special attention to species native to Guam, like the giant coconut crab. A banana and coconut eater, the voracious tree-climbing crab weighed in at fifteen to twenty pounds, with leg spans of a meter and pincers capable of cracking coconuts or human fingers. During mating season the male crab sidles up to a female and without so much as a back-scratch, flips her over and attaches a spermatophore, a sperm ball, to her stomach.

To a budding comedian whose main competition would be motor-pool announcements, VD filmstrips, and dog-pack sex, it sounded like killer material.

Once a month the brass held a Troop Information Meeting hosted by an information officer who read duty announcements off a clipboard and screened a filmstrip. The men stayed away in droves. Clerow thought he could do better. He marched into the captain's office and said, "Hank, I know how we can increase attendance at Troop Information Meetings. Let me give a talk."

Captain Spiker said, "A talk?"

"A lecture. On the sex habits of the coconut crab."

He stapled notices on bulletin boards all over the base: SEX AND THE COCONUT CRAB. His lecture drew the biggest Troop Information crowd yet, more than four hundred men starved for laughs.

Airman Wilson cleared his throat. "Some of you men know a lot about crabs," he said, giving his crotch a scratch. "You may even have given your girl some inside information." He heard a few laughs. "But how much do you know about the *coconut* crab?" he asked. "Did you know he ventures up to thirty miles inland looking for food? *Way* inland. But the coconut crab only mates in the water. And he's *slow*. To make it with his lady crab he's gotta crawl back to the beach, carrying a sticky ball of sperm. You've gotta want it bad to crawl thirty miles! And finally there he is, dead tired, back on the beach with his lady. She's showing off a little segmented leg. He says, 'Come here, honey, and let me apply this sperm ball to your thorax.' And she says, 'Oh no, you don't! I am *not* that kind of a crab!'"

The men cheered. They thumped him on the back when he finished, repeated his laugh lines, bought him drinks. Clerow's talk was such a hit that Captain Spiker arranged for him to deliver it at Army and Navy compounds all over the island. At each gig he added a few lines, a new bit or two. Crab sex never failed, but Airman Wilson didn't stop there. He added new lines, including a Shakespeare bit spoofing a dog-eared book in his footlocker, *Julius Caesar*.

Dressed in a parachute toga, popping the wide, expressive eyes that would help make him a TV star, he joked about "chowing-eth downeth" and "goingeth to hecketh," finally working his way from "lend me your rears" to a proclamation about an ancient Roman fruit cup. "I come not to bury Caesar," he declared, "but to seize your wife's berry!"

More cheers. Clerow saluted. The whistles and applause felt better than sex or dope. He'd heard a sound like this a decade before at the Mosque Theater in Newark. Now the cheers were for him. He bowed. He did a quick sidestep in his toga. An airman in the hooting crowd shouted, "He flippeth his lid!"

And the nickname stuck. *Flip* Wilson.

3

Look at the Lights

◈ Dressed in freshly shined shoes and a brass-buttoned suit, he dropped a suitcase in front of the swank Manor Plaza Hotel in San Francisco. His hair was conked—straightened with caustic lye—in the fashion of the day, carefully combed and shiny with pomade. Bowing, he extended a gloved hand to the Sunday-dressed woman. "Right this way, beautiful lady."

She put a quarter in his hand.

"Thank you very very," said the hotel's new bellhop. It wasn't the kind of work he'd dreamed of when he finished his Air Force hitch, but Clerow's forty-dollar-a-week paycheck was more than a lot of guys had in a job market overflowing with returning servicemen.

Honorably discharged in January 1954, he'd ridden a troop ship from Guam back to the West Coast, under the Golden Gate Bridge to San Francisco, where he stayed. "There was nothing for me in Jersey City," he recalled decades later. He stuck his discharge papers in a duffel along with his clothes, books, and a letter from Captain Spiker. The letter praised Airman Wilson as a popular entertainer, expert typist, and credit to his people. After dragging his belongings uphill through a winter fog, twenty-year-old Clerow found that *typist* was his most useful credit so far. Nobody was hiring comics to lecture about crabs, coconut or otherwise. But the Manor Plaza needed office help. "So I bellhopped from eight in the morning till four in the afternoon, then worked in the office from six to ten at night." His room in a Fillmore boardinghouse cost twenty dollars a week, leaving him enough in pay and tips to sample the nightlife.

This wasn't the flowers-in-your-hair San Francisco of the sixties. The integrated, syncopated Fillmore District of the 1950s, often called the Harlem of the West, featured Charlie Parker, Ella Fitzgerald, and Dizzy Gillespie headlining at the Fillmore Auditorium; Dexter Gordon and John Coltrane raising the roof at Bop City; and Billie Holiday singing the blues at the New Orleans Swing Club. In 1954 the Manor Plaza's downstairs showroom featured another top headliner, Louis Jordan and His Tympany Five. Jordan, a sax player and singer with a pencil mustache over his Pepsodent smile, was a veteran star of the Chitlin' Circuit, a string of nightclubs and music halls catering to black Americans that stretched from Chicago, Detroit, and New York through the dangerous Deep South to Texas. Along with Duke Ellington and Count Basie, Jordan ranked among the top black bandleaders of his time, and with 78-rpm hits like "G.I. Jive," "Choo Choo Ch'Boogie," and "Is You Is or Is You Ain't My Baby?" he outranked them by one measure. Fans and critics hailed Jordan as the monarch of a popular new machine: he was "King of the Jukebox."

Jordan was an innovator. His tight Tympany Five, cheaper to pay and take on tour than Ellington's and Basie's sixteen-piece orchestras, helped bridge the mid-century gap between the big-band era and the rise of rock and roll. His promotional film clips, called "soundies," filled segregated movie theaters with Jordan's silky singing voice, which one critic compared to peach brandy. Jordan's soundies predated music videos by thirty years. His patter about cute "chicks" introduced the term as a synonym for "girl," and his "Saturday Night Fish Fry" used "rockin'" in a new sense, to mean danceable music rather than sex—another reason Jordan is enshrined in the Rock and Roll Hall of Fame as the "Grandfather of Rock."

Back in 1940 one of Jordan's young rivals, bandleader Walter Barnes, had led his Royal Creolians through a one-nighter at one of the Chitlin' Circuit's homeliest dives, a converted hardware store at the edge of a swamp in Natchez, Mississippi. Workers boarded up the windows to keep gawkers from seeing the show for free, then decorated the rafters with dry Spanish moss and spritzed the moss with flammable Flit bug spray to keep mosquitoes away. Hours later, when a stray match set the room ablaze, more than two hundred dancers crowded the only exit. "Keep calm! Be cool," Barnes told them. Lifting his alto sax to his lips, Barnes led his band into the song "Marie" while flames climbed the walls. According to Chitlin' Circuit chronicler Preston Lauterbach, "With the final breath of his life, trumpeter Paul Stott blasted a note just as the inferno gulped the remaining oxygen, collapsing the tin roof and walls. . . . The flaming ceiling slumped onto the stage like a fiery curtain descending on Walter Barnes." The Natchez fire, memorialized in songs by Cab Calloway, John Lee Hooker, and others, led Chitlin' Circuit performers to shy away from small-town firetraps in favor of safer, more lucrative urban venues. During a gig at San Francisco's Golden Gate Theater in 1948, Louis Jordan and His Tympany Five grossed an unheard-of $70,000 in two weeks. (President Eisenhower worked all year to make $100,000.) Six years later the Jukebox King was forty-five, wearing a hernia truss under his lavender suit but still light on his feet as he stepped from his chauffeur-driven car to the curb at 930 Fillmore Street, where a young bellhop hustled Jordan's bags to the door.

"Welcome to the Manor Plaza, Mister Jordan."

"Thank you kindly, son." Jordan gave Clerow a silver dollar. Their hands touched and Clerow felt a spark, a *click*. Jordan was already past him, scanning the lobby for photographers and swooning young chicks, or better yet women who were, say, twenty-five to thirty-five, like the majority of his wives—he'd had five so far—grown women who knew more than chicks knew of the arts of companionship. Jordan glided through the lobby with Clerow a step behind, forgotten, until the kid bellhop hurried ahead and told the puzzled bandleader his name.

"They call me Flip. Flip Wilson. I'm a comedian," he said.

Most people didn't call him much of anything during the days he split twelve-hour workdays between the bell stand and a manual typewriter in the hotel office. Women of all ages ignored him, but he didn't mind. He figured chicks would come after him if he could get famous like Jordan, and at that point he'd deserve them. After work he slipped downstairs to the Manor Plaza's showroom to hear Jordan's brandy-smooth quintet. The crowd, well-dressed black couples with a salting of bohemian whites, danced to the jump blues of "Ain't Nobody Here But Us Chickens" and "Let the Good Times Roll," the music floating up to neon Fillmore Street and beyond, sounding sweeter the longer Clerow nursed a glass of wine. The only lull came a little after one A.M., when the band took a breather and the lights came up. The spell was broken, stains on the carpet and ceiling revealed, the crowd milling around the bandstand, waiting. Each night a few bored couples wandered upstairs to see what was doing at street level and didn't return.

Clerow cornered the manager, Willie McCoy, an expensively dressed, conk-headed skinflint who kept tabs on every free drink and salted peanut in the place. "Let me go on during the break," he said.

McCoy said, "Go on and do what?"

"Talk."

"Talk?" That struck McCoy as funny. "Talk's not an act. *I* can talk."

Baby-faced Clerow grinned. "You'll sell more drinks. Give me five minutes."

"Five minutes." They shook on it, and the next morning Clerow risked fifteen dollars on a big, floppy stovepipe hat and a Salvation Army tuxedo. *Everybody loves a drunk*, he thought, remembering the Mosque Theater comic bawling "Open the door, Richard!" While Jordan and his band finished their first set, Clerow sipped white port wine with a dash of lemon juice, the Fillmore District drink of the moment. When Jordan bowed and led his Tympany Five off the bandstand, Clerow counted to ten. *No hurry*, he thought. *Let it happen*. With no introduction he stepped into the spotlight. Shielding his eyes, he said, "Bad day. I had a bad day today." Pause. "Almost as bad as you all look."

That got the patrons' attention. As bad as *they* looked? They weren't sure if this rumpled fellow was part of the show or just a lush on his way to the bathroom. He bumped into a drum set; customers smiled and pointed. Despite the wine buzz his mind raced, turning over which lines he might say next. At the same time he felt his gorge rise like he might throw up. Eyes on him, people snickering—it turned his stomach. Would they love him? Hate him? He avoided their eyes by looking at the stage lights. There was safety there, a clean white like the spotlight on Clara Barton at P.S. 14, and for the first time he could remember, he felt at home.

"Had cornflakes for breakfast," he said suddenly, "but I ran out of milk. What's worse than that? Do you eat a little half bowl with a normal milk level, or one big soggy bowl with dry flakes up the sides?"

Scattered laughs.

"This chick I'm going out with, we're rockin' and rollin', you know what I mean, and she yells out, 'Oh, Ray, I loves you!'" He looked miserable. "Ray's my brother. Bad day."

More laughter. Laughs from paying customers, not joke-starved servicemen. Now flying on more than the wine, he dropped the stage-drunk act and spoke as himself, riffing on what he'd seen riding the bus around town—the fog, the cable cars, the drunken sailors, the junkies and bums. "I was so turned on," he remembered years later. "I couldn't wait for them to shut up laughing so I could say the next thing." When the Tympany Five lined up to return to the stage, he ignored them. He did ten minutes more, snapping his fingers and adding a shuffle step when a line worked. Manager McCoy waved his arms, pointing at the royally irked Jukebox King. Still Flip talked. The crowd laughed and applauded. At last McCoy strode onstage, clamped his hand around the bellhop's wrist, and marched him out of the spotlight.

"Watch who you're grabbin'!"

"Watch who you're upstagin'," McCoy said, nodding toward Jordan. "That's ten thousand dollars a week." The band kicked into an up-tempo number while customers patted Clerow's shoulder or pulled his sleeve, saying, *Good job!* and *Bad day!* and asking, *What's your name?* McCoy yanked him toward the stairs, warning, "They like you. But pull more shit like that and you're done here."

Flip shook him off. "You can't 'done here' me. I quit."

His exile lasted twenty-four hours. He was pacing the sidewalk the next day, talking to himself, when McCoy pulled up in a long black car, rolling the window down. "People are asking after you," he said. "You can do the break every night. Ten minutes, all yours."

"Fifteen," Flip said, and kept walking.

In 1954 "Flip" Wilson—his first name rendered in quotation marks—began appearing for fifteen minutes six nights a week at the Manor Plaza. Each night he got a little looped on white port before he went on. He recycled his bad-day and dry-cornflakes bits, adding new riffs as he learned which lines needed a slide step or finger snap, which ones should be shouted, which whispered. "Pretty soon I'm observing the crowd, looking out the corner of my eye at different people," he recalled, "wondering why one guy's laughing and the person next to him isn't. And it broke my concentration. That's when I figured something out. It wasn't about them, it was about *me*." He realized that the customers weren't there to evaluate the performers. They just wanted to have a good time. All he had to do to win them over was give them the confident, infectiously likable performer the airmen on Guam flipped for. "From that night on I just looked at the lights. It was like talking to a mirror. Totally relaxed, giving off that *I'm good* vibe. *I'm good and I know it*. Because that relaxed, confident guy, Flip, he's someone the audience would like to be their friend. Be their friend, and they'll love you forever."

After two weeks, Jordan and his Tympany Five moved on, ceding the Manor Plaza's stage to a colorful dance act. Joe DeCosta's troupe wore bright feathered outfits that called for several costume changes in the course of the show. During their breaks, DeCosta's five-piece band played rhythm and blues. Manor Plaza manager McCoy lengthened the breaks to make time for the fledgling comedian, who was starting to draw a few fans of his own. Flip described Joe DeCosta as "a gay cat, an elaborate dresser" who invited him to join the act on the road. Flip couldn't resist. *I don't owe this place anything*, he thought, and off he went, squished into the backseat of a rusty green convertible with DeCosta's band. They followed the troupe's other vehicle, a matching green convertible, across the Bay Bridge, through Oakland and hilly green Contra Costa County to Pittsburg, California, a coal-mining town, population fifteen thousand, mostly poor and black. Settling in for a three-night engagement at the dingy Black Jack Club, they checked into a hotel that charged three dollars a night for a bed, a lamp, a nightstand, a Gideon Bible, and a toilet down the hall. It sounded cheap enough until Flip lined up behind the dancers and the band after Friday night's show.

"Five, six," DeCosta said, counting dollar bills into the piano player's hand. "Six dollars and sixty-seven cents." Next he paid the sax player. "Six dollars, sixty-seven cents."

Finally it was Flip's turn. "Ninety, ninety-five," DeCosta said. "One dollar."

"That's it?"

"The dancers are guaranteed, dear. The band, too. I pay them first. You get a cut of what's left of the door." DeCosta shrugged. "But don't fret. Don't sweat. Tomorrow's Saturday." Saturday was better. Flip's cut came to $1.05. He got ninety-five cents after Sunday's show, leaving him with an even three dollars for three nights to go with a nine-dollar hotel bill. The dancers and musicians had made up to twenty dollars apiece but had blown it on food, drink, and drugs. They gathered in Flip's second-floor room, griping about the hotel and the Black Jack Club, and decided to skip town. One by one they climbed out the window to the fire escape, dropped their bags into the green convertible, and jumped. DeCosta and piano player Charles Calloway caught their luggage in the alley below and stowed it in the convertibles' trunks. Flip, as usual, went last. He dropped his Air Force duffel bag to DeCosta, sat on the edge of the fire escape, and scooted into empty space. He came down in the backseat of one of the convertibles—a perfect landing—and they peeled out of Pittsburg, laughing all the way.

Stockton, California, was a farm town with a Navy base. Its black farmhands, cowboys, and off-duty sailors spent their paychecks in Goat Valley, a dirt-road neck of town where a woman named Lucille ran an after-hours club beside a tomato field. A three-hundred-pound six-footer in a calico dress, Lucille sported a proud, curly, natural hairdo that barely fit through doorways. She paid her entertainers nothing. She put them up in rattletrap rooms, fed them in the club's steamy kitchen—heaps of fried chicken, oxtails, greens, fried tomatoes, and corn on the cob with pitchers of sweet iced tea—and let them pass the hat after their shows. DeCosta's dancers paraded their plumage around Lucille's faded-linoleum stage, and Flip did his thing during intermissions. He got laughs, but now there were silences, too, dead air in spots where the Manor Plaza crowd had laughed. After a Saturday show, he smoked Pall Malls and sipped white port with DeCosta's piano player, Charles Calloway, while a wrinkly, shirtless old man mopped the floor. Calloway was in his forties, elderly in Flip's eyes, with long, graceful fingers and elegant creases on his face. He had a family back east but was no more faithful to his wife than most road musicians, as Flip learned while trying to sleep on nights when Calloway entertained women in the next room.

"Young Flipper," Calloway said, blowing a smoke ring. "You never been out on the road, have you?"

"No, Charles. It's my first time," Flip replied, expecting romantic advice.

"Professionally speaking, you're an amateur. You do a joke, these people sit there like dumb animals. Same joke killed 'em in Frisco. Why? Because these is yokels. You're in the sticks. You go a little louder in the sticks."

"Louder?"

"Not louder louder. *Bigger.* Moderate and modulate. Look at me. I might prefer to tap the keys à la *Prelude in C Sharp Minor,* but I don't. In Frisco it's more like "Round Midnight,' and in a place like this"—he looked around at the peeling walls and warped floorboards—"it's 'Camptown Races.'" Flip knew what he meant. He'd noticed that Calloway played Lucille's honky-tonk upright louder than the piano at the Manor Plaza, or at least *bigger,* hitting the same notes a hair harder, holding them an instant longer, and singing a weepier blues for the Goat Valley crowd. "It's the tones, not the tunes," Calloway said. "You give 'em what they already like."

"Well, that's just it. I don't want to do that. I'm just gonna be me."

Calloway chuckled. "Simon Pure, that's you. Working for corn on the cob."

"Keyboard Cal," Flip said. "Selling out for corn on the cob."

"Touché, young Flipper, and I'll drink to that."

Flip and Calloway got on so well that they worked up a two-man bit. Between dance numbers, while DeCosta's dancing girls changed costumes, Calloway played and sang a brokenhearted blues tune. When he got to the chick who done him wrong, Flip flounced on-stage in a blond wig and tight skirt. Nervous laughter from the crowd as Calloway played on, wailing about his girl leaving him for a man with a bigger bankroll. Now Flip gave the piano a bump with his hip.

"Wasn't just his bankroll was bigger, honey!"

The crowd roared. Before long DeCosta gave them two spots a night. Word of the funny duo spread around Stockton, and Lucille's club was soon packed every weekend. Before long the manager of Club Four, an upscale nightspot on Main Street, came to see the new arrivals. He offered Flip and Calloway a gig of their own, three shows a week, seven dollars apiece every show. Twenty-one dollars a week was a shade under Clerow's Air Force pay, but it beat room and board at Lucille's. Still he wondered: How could they just ditch DeCosta?

"Easy," Calloway said. "When he's got a mouthful of Tom, Dick, or Dick, we decamp."

Flip said no. "What did he do to hurt us?" Instead he went to the dance impresario and told him everything.

"You know what?" DeCosta said, nodding as if he'd expected this visit. "It's cool. I took you from Willie McCoy. Next guy takes you from me. That's business. You take what you can, when you can, long as you can. You'll drop Calloway, too."

"I will?"

"And you'll be right to. You won't need him. You're the real thing,

Wilson. So go on and do good." DeCosta reached into his pocket. He stuck out a manicured hand.

Flip looked at the coins in DeCosta's palm. "What's this?"

"Back pay."

Ninety-five cents.

Black men in jackets and ties, gold watches glistening under their sleeves, danced with chopstick-thin women in shimmery dresses. Club Four smelled of sweat, cologne, cigarette smoke, sex, and celebration. Calloway crooned, *"Baby, give me back that wig I bought you."*

Flip flounced onstage, brushing blond-wig bangs off his forehead. *"You mean my golden tresses?"*

"Don't roll yo' bloodshot eyes at me, girl."

Flip shook his fist. *"I'll give your blood a shot!"*

He and Calloway spent almost a year at Club Four in Stockton, selling out the room three nights a week. Flip's pay rose from seven dollars a night to fifteen and finally twenty-five a night—seventy-five dollars a week, more than triple his Air Force salary. More than he could spend. He sent ten- and twenty-dollar money orders home to Jersey City, addressed to his sister Eleanor, the family member with a permanent address, always adding a note saying, *For Pops.*

Flip's hip-shaking blond chick, unnamed so far, proved so popular that he worried about getting pegged as a drag queen. "We need another character," he told Calloway. Toward the end of their year in Stockton he introduced a rabble-rousing preacher modeled on one of his foster fathers. "The Rev," Flip called him. The Rev waved shivery hands toward heaven and swore that God helps them that help themselves. Accordingly he helped himself to the lion's share of the weekly collection, reminding his flock that today, just as in gladiatorial times, the lion's share sure beat the Christians' share.

"Rev," Calloway called out, "we got a big blue Cadillac blocking the church door!"

"Don't I know it? The Lord smiled down on me in last week's raffle!"

The Rev kept his shoulders low and knees bent as if he might abscond any second. Bouncing on the balls of his sneaky cat feet, he mimed the first step of a sprint. "The dash," he called that pose. And it caught on. Soon half of black Stockton was mimicking the kid comic's sneaky preacher. Men posed like sprinters, doing the dash. Women and kids, too. "For the first time," Flip said, "I saw something I did catch on."

Another surprise: One night he rolled into his cramped hotel room, kicked the door shut, and jumped halfway out of his skin. A girl was waiting for him. Not just any girl—a stripper from another club on Main Street. She was slim-hipped, in a tight skirt and a scoop-neck top that showed plenty of cleavage. Her fake eyelashes were almost as long as her crimson fake nails, and she was sitting on his bed. If this was his groupie, Flip thought, he could do worse.

"I want to tell you something," she said. "About your dick."

His eyes must have bulged because she smiled. She stood up, looked him level in the eye.

"It's your worst enemy." She nodded. "You see, I don't like men, but I see a great talent in you, a great future. Unless you let some girl fuck it up. So take some good advice while you can, Flip Wilson. Don't fall in love, not until you make it big. And then you can do anything you want." With that she turned and left him alone with his worst enemy.

4

Circuit Rider

◈ After a year in Stockton, he'd heard enough advice. "Time for me to be a solo act," Flip told Calloway. They played a final Saturday-night set, had a couple rounds of drinks, and said their goodbyes. They shook hands. They hugged. Flip was getting choked up when Calloway reminded him who was ditching whom. Flip's last view of his first and only performing partner was of tall, dignified Calloway crossing Main Street in the middle of the night. Reaching the curb on the other side, Calloway turned and posed like a sprinter, doing the dash.

Flip rode buses north to Eureka and Redding, south to L.A., Long Beach, and San Diego, talking his way into occasional gigs, filling in for comics who got sick or skipped town, working for a cut of the door that might be counted in coins. After the relative comfort of Stockton, he found himself bumming cigarettes and joints and filling his belly with kitchen scraps, the leftover salads and quarter-sandwiches busboys saved for him. He ranged as far east as Las Vegas, a boomtown where blacks labored as waiters, cooks, maids, and porters in the new, sawdust-floored hotel-casinos on the Strip, but could not eat or rent a room there. Even black headliners at the Flamingo and the Sands were barred from staying there. In fifties Las Vegas, Nat King Cole and Lena Horne had to use the service entrance to enter and leave the hotel-casinos where they performed. They got to the stage by way of the kitchen. Between sets they were required to wait outside, often standing around the swimming pool. When Dorothy Dandridge, the first black woman to be nominated for a Best Actress Oscar, took a dip in the pool at the Frontier, the hotel's manager promptly drained it. Horne was occasionally—secretly—allowed to stay at the Flamingo, but after she checked out, her towels and bedsheets were burned.

Unknown Flip Wilson got nowhere near the big hotels' spotlights. He trudged from the bus depot to West Las Vegas, the neighborhood some folks called "darktown," lugging a satchel festooned with glitter. The Stockton stripper who believed in him had used glitter and glue to write a message on the satchel: *If I can't make you laugh, you got no business laughing.* Now it shed glitter flakes with every step he took.

Billed as quotation-marked "FLIP" WILSON on hand-lettered signs and mimeographed flyers—except for the time a typo made him "FILP"—he ad-libbed all but a few old reliables like "bad day" and "dry cornflakes." He'd pop his eyes, twist his rubbery features and get laughs without saying a word. During the late fifties he learned when to riff on current events or Shakespeare (the first show of the evening), when to talk dirty (later, when customers are drunk), and how to deal with hecklers. Depending on the all-black crowd's mood he might humor a heckler: "Have another cocktail, sir, and try not to soil yourself." Or attack: "You loud, ugly, shit-faced motherfucker." Or go local: "Right here's the dimmest bulb in Vegas." Or racial: "You know, brother, when we take over, we're gonna have to kill some of *us*, too."

He'd left Stockton with a bankroll of twenty-dollar bills wrapped around tens and fives. Dollar bills he kept in another pocket to use as tips. After three months on the road, his roll was a twenty over a thumb-thick sheaf of fives and singles. After six months, it was all fives and singles, until the night he emptied his pockets at a Greyhound ticket counter. His worldly possessions added up to a little less than ten dollars, a crumpled cigarette, and several matches. A bus ticket cost twelve dollars. He hitchhiked to the next town, where he worked for a chance to pass the hat. "That's how you get the best lesson, which is how to be funny when you don't feel funny. When you feel shitty," he recalled. That night, in a drab, smoky basement in some dot on the map, he killed. A crowd of a dozen or so whistled and hooted. Flip bowed and waved. He passed the hat, and the hat came back without a single bill in it. Pocketing the silver, he left the pennies behind. *I'm not that low yet.* Then he went back for the pennies, thinking, *Who am I to turn down Mr. Lincoln?*

"I wasn't too proud to scrounge. I had a goal that kept me going," he recalled. "Greyhound had a deal where you could ride anywhere in the country for ninety-nine dollars. If I could get to a point where I always had a hundred dollars, I'd never be stranded. So that was my goal, a hundred dollars in my pocket."

The glitter had by now fallen off his satchel, leaving the stripper's boast outlined in dry glue. He carried it with pride anyway. Flip knew he was funny, and people who heard him during the years he called his endless wanderings thought so, too. Flip got laughs in big-city jazz clubs where the patrons sipped cognac and in dives where performers passing the hat were lucky to get the hat back. He got laughs in a waterfront bar he claimed was so tough "they frisked everyone at the door, and if you didn't have a knife, they gave you one." He said he didn't need a knife, just a fork and a little brisket.

Once, when a cop rousted him off a bus station bench, Flip saw snow falling outside. Rather than sleep in a blizzard he spent a dime to escape into a pay toilet, and slept curled up in the stall. In the morning he found the local post office, where he sent a dollar home for his father care of Eleanor. He sent money home every month, but never heard from Pops or Eleanor.

"Hungry guys make the best prizefighters and comedians," he liked to say. A little hunger, or even a lot, wouldn't kill him, and neither would a few months alone on the road. "I'd spent my whole life among strangers. Many nights I'd be out by the highway, hitchhiking. There were hours when no cars went by. I'd lay down beside a tree and look up at the stars. I had a ball." When a car appeared, he'd scramble to the shoulder of the road and stick out his thumb. When black drivers—never a white one—gave him a lift, he'd get them talking and laughing, and as often as not the driver took him home for dinner. The bright-eyed, round-faced young man was just plain likable. "They'd ask if I'd eaten that day. I'd say no, and they'd drive me home and feed me, introduce me to the wife or their friends, nice people. Then they'd drive me where I was going and say, 'Here's a couple dollars for cigarettes.' This happened again and again. People want to help you if you let them."

He worked his way from Greyhound's western stations to clubs on the slightly better-paying Chitlin' Circuit, cadging meals and free drinks. Many black musicians and comics thought of the circuit as the big time, but many of its venues were run by greedy hustlers. "You'd play on a stage as big as a sofa, with drunks hollering and throwing bottles," recalls Merald "Bubba" Knight, who sang backup for his sister Gladys in firetraps where "the fights got scary." When a brawl spilled onto the stage one night in Lithonia, Georgia, he and his fellow backup singers, the Pips, lifted teenage Gladys on their shoulders and carried her to safety. "And we didn't get paid. You could pack the house and not get paid. The promoter shrugs and says, 'I didn't make no money,' so you don't get your ten or fifteen dollars. We played clubs where the people threw coins on the stage if they liked you. Then the owner sends a guy from the kitchen with a brown paper bag to pick up the coins, and you're beat again."

In the Deep South, Flip slept in "Colored" waiting rooms at bus stations where candy stands sold gumballs, lemon drops, and licorice dots called nigger babies. When he could afford a ticket, the fledgling comic in the rumpled corduroy jacket rode in the back of the bus with other blacks. Even after Rosa Parks and the twenty-six-year-old pastor of Montgomery, Alabama's Dexter Avenue Baptist Church, the Reverend Martin Luther King, staged a successful boycott of segregated buses in 1955, Flip gave up his seat to any white rider who wanted it. He didn't want any trouble, particularly with police who might find the weed in his jacket pocket.

Months became years as he crisscrossed a country that seemed to be holding its breath, poised between atomic jitters and hula hoops. While Russia's H-bombs quickened the nuclear arms race, Wham-O's plastic hoops became the craze of 1958. The toymaker sold more than 100 million of them, making the $1.98 hula hoop twice as popular as another new toy of the time, Barbie. The U.S. nuclear submarine *Nautilus* made history by cruising under the North Pole ice pack that summer, three weeks before Reverend King sat at Blumstein's Department Store in Harlem signing copies of his first book, *Stride Toward Freedom*. A black woman named Izola Curry leaped from the crowd and stabbed him with a letter opener. King lay still for three hours, the blade sticking out of his chest, so close to his heart that doctors were afraid to touch it. "If you'd sneezed during those three hours, you'd be dead," a surgeon told him after they finally removed the letter opener. King survived the attack and forgave Izola Curry, which was more than Flip could do for a future King from the Deep South.

Elvis Presley, twenty-four, a year younger than Flip, was on the radio around the clock. His 1956 appearance on TV's *Ed Sullivan Show* had jump-started the rock-and-roll era. This was the now-famous performance that Sullivan's cameras cut off at the belt. One account has Sullivan saying they shot above Elvis's swiveling pelvis because "he's got some kind of device in his pants, so when he moves back and forth you can see the outline of his cock . . . I think it's a Coke bottle." Like plaid-jacketed Bill Haley, whose "Rock

Around the Clock" had upended the pop charts two years earlier, Presley took music pioneered by Louis Jordan and other black artists, watered it down, and resold it to millions of white record buyers. "Jungle music" borrowed from Chitlin' Circuit players carried Elvis out of Tupelo, Mississippi, to the Sullivan show and on to a Las Vegas debut at the Frontier. Presley was the opening act for Borscht Belt comic Shecky Greene in the hotel's Venus Room, where Elvis was billed as "The Atomic-Powered Singer." That gig proved to be one of the few hiccups of his early career. The *Las Vegas Sun* dismissed him: "For teen-agers, the long, tall lad is a whiz; for the average Vegas spender or showgoer, a bore. His musical sound is uncouth." Presley wouldn't play Vegas for another decade, which was fine with Flip, who wondered when the country would finally embrace an entertainer who didn't have to pretend to be black. The same year Elvis drove Ed Sullivan's audience wild, Flip had sat in a cramped motel room fiddling with the controls of a black-and-white TV, watching *The Nat King Cole Show,* the first network variety program with a black star. Cole's fifteen-minute program lasted fifteen months. Southern stations refused to carry it, and NBC never found a single national sponsor for it. American TV, Cole said, was "afraid of the dark."

Screw NBC, Flip thought. *And screw Elvis.*

Four years into his career Flip was still ad-libbing, riffing on life on the road, relying on the inborn talent he called "the funny" and on preshow hits of professional-grade weed. His pot dealer in one southern stop did double duty, managing a nightclub when he wasn't selling dope. Flip lit up as usual before his performance and told the audience about it. "Feelin' fine tonight," he said, miming a puff. "I partook of some fine local shit, and the authorities are none the wiser." The crowd laughed. The manager didn't. When Flip came offstage, the fuming man marched him upstairs to his office and lectured him about performing stoned, baiting the cops, "disrespecting this establishment." Flip thought that was funny. Chicken-necking and mimicking the man—"dis-*spect*ing the '*stab*lishmint!"—he returned to the club for a drink and a smoke.

The next day, feeling guilty, he went back to apologize. A thick-necked fellow blocked the stairs in the empty club. "Where you going?" the man said.

"To see the manager."

Thick Neck shook his head. Flip heard a commotion in the manager's office. Thumps. Glass breaking. A minute later two men as brawny as the first bounded downstairs and out the door. The sentinel followed them. Flip found the manager on the floor upstairs, in a bloody heap beside his desk, beaten to a pulp. He must have owed them money, Flip thought. I *hope* he owed them money. Or maybe it had to do with a woman. It couldn't have anything to do with comics disrespecting the club or the cops or the local dope distributor, could it? "I'm sorry," he told the moaning manager, reaching for the phone. Then he stopped. The police might be the last people he wanted to talk to.

Helping the manager sit up, Flip peered into his battered, swollen eye. The one that was still open. "I'm sorry!" he said again, and fled.

Flip looked at his own bloodshot eyes in a gas-station mirror, the kind of mirror that was plain metal because glass wouldn't last a week in such a place. He saw a not-so-young man who liked getting high and making people laugh. Was that so bad? Yes, he thought. Because it was easy. Because it wasn't enough. On his next bus ride he reached into his satchel for his tattered copy of Max Eastman's *Enjoyment of Laughter*. The book's crinkly pages broke off at the edges like dead skin. He'd already circled, checked, and underlined bits of Eastman's advice on almost every page. Now he read and reread. *There is a science to humor*, Eastman wrote. Flip believed it, but his approach had been all instinct. Because it was easy. *When we are in fun, a peculiar shift of values takes place*, Eastman wrote. That rang true. Flip would never think of talking to a stranger about sex or drugs or race, but a *roomful* of strangers waiting for a joke—that changed the equation. Audiences wanted comics to surprise them. The very essence of comedy—*We are in fun*—gave the comic power. He could talk about anything.

Yet here was Flip after three years alone on the road, ad-libbing about his breakfast. If nobody laughed he'd act drunk or tell about his Air Force years and the sex lives of tree-climbing crabs. The more he thought about it, the less he liked his own act. Van Cliburn didn't just show up and play, did he? He practiced. Jim Brown crashed the line in weekday workouts when the stands were empty. Jackie Robinson and Mickey Mantle took batting practice, but Flip Wilson had done the last thing a black man in fifties America had any business doing. He'd gotten lazy.

At the next bus stop, he bought his first yellow legal pad. He wrote down his thoughts on leading comics. "I analyzed them to find out what made them great," he recalled, "and found that most of them had one special characteristic. With Bob Hope, it was his timing. With Jerry Lewis, his dynamics—the way he moved. George Burns was effortless. Rochester and Butterfly McQueen had unique voices." Like many a convert, he expected everyone else to share his new religion. "I tried discussing the laws of humor with other comics in those Chitlin' Circuit joints, but they'd say, 'Hey, you better cut it out. If you think too much, you'll lose your funny.' I thought, *Bullshit*."

The new Flip filled legal pads with notes to himself. *Rev raffle. Wife shopp spree . . . DEVIL did it! Voice . . . ?* He wondered how "black" he should sound onstage. Was he a specifically black comic, or was funny color-blind? It was hard to tell playing to all-black audiences on the Chitlin' Circuit. He decided that funny was funny, at least for now. He could learn to entertain white crowds if he ever got the chance. And he decided to give it fifteen years. If he wasn't famous by 1973, after fifteen years of study and practice, he'd quit. Meanwhile he intended to outthink and outwork all the guys who just liked to get high and make people laugh.

He considered quitting smoking weed. That lasted a few hours. Total sobriety made him feel thick and slow. (Maybe Calloway was right: "It turns you white.") But now, instead of just enjoying the high, he consciously put it to use the way musicians did, letting his musicality come out. For the first time he counted out the meter of his punch lines, and on good nights he could hear the difference— a more percussive laugh from crowds that reacted all at once as if on cue. Watching comedians on TV or from the back row of big-city clubs, he heard the same thing. The best comics didn't just entertain crowds, they played them.

Night by night Flip built his act around bits that got big, fast laughs, writing everything down, making his way east through Mississippi, Alabama, and Georgia. Most nights he worked for "five dollars and a meal, beans and greens." The pay was far better in the music halls farther north: the Howard Theatre in Washington, D.C., the Uptown in Philadelphia, the Fox in Detroit, the Regal in Chicago, and the Circuit's crown jewel, the grand Apollo Theater in Harlem, where Billie Holiday swooned at the stand-up microphone and the club's hard-fought Amateur Night competition launched the careers of Ella Fitzgerald, Lena Horne, James Brown, Marvin Gaye, and, later, Jimi Hendrix, the Jackson Five, and Mariah Carey. But the Apollo seemed worlds away in the years Flip shared cow-town stages with jugglers, banjo players, "exotic shake dancers," and old-time vaudeville duos with names like Buck and Wing, Jake and Bake, and Hap'n'Stance. Club owners swung a greedy rake at the door, building fist-thick bankrolls and driving Cadillacs while the comics' stomachs growled. Still, the mid-century Chitlin' Circuit, owned and managed by black businessmen, was a vast upgrade over the nightclub chain that preceded it. The white-owned-and-operated Theater Owners Bookers Association (TOBA) had ruled southern black clubs in the twenties and thirties, treating the talent almost like slaves. Black comics blackened their faces with burnt-cork makeup and set off their lips with white greasepaint to play stage darkies with names like Sambo, Shine, and Zip Coon. Even headliners worked for whatever TOBA owners chose to give them. Performers joked that the chain's name stood for "Tough On Black Asses." When Bessie Smith complained about her pay to Charles P. Bailey, the white owner of the 81 Theater in Atlanta's so-called Darktown, Bailey beat her up and called the police, who threw her in jail.

Flip had an easier row to hoe. He club-hopped through the South and Midwest, scribbling on legal pads by the light of off-brown bulbs on all-night buses, and along the way he found his voice.

One day he stepped off a bus in a midwestern town—Kansas City or St. Louis, or maybe Cincinnati. He could never remember which town it was, but he never forgot the black soldier stepping off the same Greyhound to meet his happy family. A girl who must have been the soldier's sister threw her hands up and cried, "Mama, here come Willie back from the Army! Show Mama how you march, Willie. *Hup*, two, three, four!" Flip liked the chime of the teenage girl's voice so much that he went around imitating it for days, mostly under his breath, to amuse himself, but sometimes loud enough to startle passersby. *"Here come Willie!"* Neither a squeal nor a trill, it was happier and prouder than just about any voice he'd ever heard. Bossier, too. *"Show Mama how you march, Willie!"* Flip tried it in his act when he needed a female voice. A girl rebuffing a kiss—formerly the reluctant female crab in his Air Force routine—now chimed, *"Listen up!* You don't *know* me that well," in the voice of the soldier's sister. Audiences loved her. Men hooted and stamped their feet while their dates hid their laughs behind their hands. Almost twenty years after his stage debut as Clara Barton at P.S. 14, three years after Flip in a blond wig hip-checked Calloway's piano, his boisterous girly voice was killing in mid-level black clubs. That made sense according to Eastman's theories about humor, incongruity, and double meanings, but as entertainers from Sophocles and Shakespeare to Tony Curtis and Jack Lemmon, then starring in *Some Like It Hot*, had proved, there was a simpler factor at work: drag was just *funny*.

It got even funnier when Flip paired his girly voice with another trope he'd used before: giving history a new spin. On Guam he'd turned *Julius Caesar* into a toga party. Now he imagined a mash-up of schoolboy history and drag comedy. What if Queen Isabella of Spain had sounded like Willie's sister?

It started with the voice. "Chris" Columbus needed royal backing for his expedition. Flip became "Queen Isabelle Johnson," who threw her hands up and squealed, "That's a lot of money, honey! You want me to hock my crown jewels?" Switching back to Columbus, Flip swore his journey would be worth any cost. If he didn't discover America, there'd never be a Benjamin Franklin or "Star-Spangled Banner."

"No 'Star-Spangled Banner'!" said Queen Isabelle Johnson. "Oh say, you *can't* see!"

Though audiences cheered the queen, the bit didn't feel finished. Flip wrote lists of American things—roller coasters, apple pie, milkshakes, duckpin bowling, Little Orphan Annie, double plays, Thanksgiving—and tried them out.

"No Thanksgiving? No, thanks!"

The bit improved when he added what Eastman would call a logical consequence. Now Queen Isabelle ticked off the supplies Columbus would need, a list inflected by Flip's military service: "Three used ships, two pair of fatigues, some shades, two chicken sandwiches, three cans of Vienna sausages, five cases of Scotch, a small 7UP, and a rag to tie his head with." She paid Chris by traveler's check. As the fifties waned, Flip honed the routine onstage and between shows, sitting in hotel rooms, coffeehouses, barbers' chairs, bus stations, and on park benches, filling legal pads with lines and observations.

"No Snickers?" Queen Isabelle Johnson asked one night. That got more laughs than Thanksgiving or "The Star-Spangled Banner." Partly because "Snickers" was a funny word, Flip thought, and partly because it was less predictable. Surprise was a comedian's best friend. "Snickers" was also more of a piece with sassy Isabelle's city-girl sound. Eastman would have called it contextual: "Snickers" beat "Thanksgiving" because urban blacks could be pictured grabbing a candy bar more readily than gathering for turkey and stuffing. Flip was thinking for himself, closing in on a principle Eastman never mentioned. He realized that he needed congruity as well as incongruity. He needed a line that fit the character in a perfectly surprising way. And when you stop to think about it, Queen Isabelle Johnson wouldn't cry over spilled duckpins or milkshakes. She wouldn't hock her jewels for a turkey dinner. What did she *treasure*? Flip racked his brain until it hit him.

One night he looked up at the stage lights, waiting for the laughs to ebb as Chris Columbus made his case. Using his own voice as Chris, he threatened a catastrophe. If he didn't discover America, he said, nobody'd ever hear of the man who sang "I Got a Woman" and "What'd I Say."

Switching from Chris to Isabelle, Flip froze. He took a beat. He popped his eyes and said, "You gonna find him? He in *America*?"

Sure is, Chris said.

Queen Isabelle Johnson did a dance step. She raised her hands to heaven. "Take *all* the money, honey!" she said. *"Chris gonna find Ray Charles!"*

5

Miami Vise

◈ Miami was tightly segregated in the fifties and early sixties. Black people were supposed to stay in Overtown, a sweltering inland neighborhood popularly known as Colored Town. In the rest of the city they faced a sundown curfew that sent them hurrying home to Overtown every evening from Miami Beach, Coral Gables, and other white enclaves. Nightclub performers and hotel employees got special passes. If the police stopped Ella Fitzgerald on her way to Overtown after a show at the Fontainebleau Hotel, the First Lady of Song could either produce a pass or face arrest.

After arriving in the late 1950s, Flip kept his head down in Overtown, where rooms rented for five dollars a night. He could always find a twenty-five-cent plate of biscuits and gravy or a nickel bag of weed within walking distance of the Sir John Hotel, where he worked as an emcee and got a few stand-up sets. A low-slung, L-shaped stucco landmark with a pool, patio bar, and downstairs showroom, the Sir John loomed over Overtown the way the Fontainebleau dominated Miami Beach. Nat Cole, Count Basie, and Louis Armstrong stayed at the Sir John when they were in Miami. Baseball's recently retired Jackie Robinson chatted in the lobby with former heavyweight champ Joe Louis and octogenarian author and critic W.E.B. Du Bois, a founder of the NAACP. Then they headed downstairs to a showroom called the Knight Beat, a few steps below street level. Sometimes the celebrities stepped around Flip, who sat in the smoky stairwell writing notes to himself. One of his notes paraphrased Eastman: *Things can be funny only when we are in fun.* He took that to mean he should avoid political material of the sort Lenny Bruce was doing to wild applause, booing, and occasional death threats. Flip's style was less confrontational, particularly when the subject was race. Setting a long fuse, he called it. Adding to his Chris Columbus routine, he had Columbus discover America only to find dark-skinned "native types" already there.

"We don't wanna be discovered," hollered an Indian maid, sounding suspiciously like Queen Isabelle. "You better discover your ass away from here!" Chris sailed home vowing to get even with those hostile Indians. He said, "We'll make a map and give it to the Pilgrims. Let the Pilgrims fix their ass."

Sometimes Flip looked down from the Sir John's stage lights and spotted a famous face at a front table. He was delighted when heavyweight Sonny Liston and pint-sized Sammy Davis Jr. came to meet him offstage on separate nights and said, "Little man, you're funny!" and "Well done, big guy," respectively. Flip's work at the Sir John kept him flush while it lasted, but touring acts took up most of the schedule at the Knight Beat. Sometimes he slept outdoors. Eventually he lucked into a gig at a racially mixed club outside Overtown, his first appearance at a "white club." As at all but the biggest venues, there was no curtain. Taking the stage in a freshly pressed suit, he waited a beat, unlit in the momentary blackout before the emcee introduced him. One night a white heckler brayed, "Smile so I'll know where you're at!" As soon as the lights came up, Flip nodded at the man and said, "Your sister found me okay." The line got the first laugh of a night when everything clicked. The heckler loved him as much as the rest of the crowd. Columbus and Isabelle went over so well that Flip got impatient during the laughter, counting *one-two-three* to slow himself down before launching the next bit. At the end he bowed through two curtain calls—on-off blinks of the lights—before making his way to the bar. Audience members crowded around. A white man with a gold watch and a fat cigar squeezed the back of his neck. "Flip Wilson," the man said, "you're going to be big."

"Thank you, Mister . . ."

Herbie Shul stuck out his hand. "Shul, rhymes with 'no bull.'" He described himself as a businessman, connoisseur of comedy, and friend of the colored man. Flip allowed that he could use a friend; he'd been sleeping on car hoods lately. Over the next few weeks he kept seeing Shul around town, even in Overtown, where he treated Flip to lunch or coffee. They talked about life, comedy, race, women. Shul said comedy talent was "like beachfront property. There's never enough to go around. So, Wilson, what can I do for you?"

"I could use a place to sleep."

"Suppose I gave you fifty a week, no strings attached."

Fifty dollars was more than Flip earned in a good week or a lousy month. "I'm listening."

"All you have to do is get better. Get famous, make me look like a genius. Maybe someday you pay me back. What do you say?"

Flip said thanks. He spent some of Shul's first check on drugs and the rest on a used typewriter. Rolling in a page, setting the margins with military precision, he began work on what he would call "Flip's Laws of Comedy." One of the first was *Be interesting, be effortless.* Another: *To be effortless may require 25 years of effort.* Over the years he would type and edit hundreds of pages, crossing out all but a handful of lines he came to think of as comedy facts or rules. One of them would shape his stage persona for the rest of his life. Its wording varied as he filled and edited a loose-leaf folder labeled FLIP'S LAWS, honing the rule the way he trimmed and sharpened his act, until it was as tight as he could get it: *Make them remember Flip Wilson as a self-confident man of the world, projecting an "I Don't Care if You Laugh" attitude.*

* * *

Shul had connections in the Bahamas. He considered Nassau's resort hotels a training ground for young comics. "Don't thank me. Just go and do," he said, handing over a cabin-class ticket to Nassau. The next thing Flip knew, he was married.

Flip never spoke publicly about his brief marriage in the Bahamas, but years later he told his closest friends the basics. His wife's name was Lovenia Patricia, but everybody called her Peaches. She danced onstage at Nassau's jazzy Cat and Fiddle Club, outshining the other dancers with her straightened hair, full lips, and bedroom eyes. Petite Peaches saw the five-foot-six American comic as a bit of a big shot, blowing kisses to him from the stage. Before long she was serving him breakfast in bed. Flip, enjoying the island life, Peaches' cooking, and nightly sex, pretended to be entranced by Peaches' backstage gossip and talk of growing up in the Bahamas. "I kept saying how interesting she was," he told Richard Pryor a decade later. "That's a lie every bitch believes." He and Peaches had practically nothing in common, right down to their dancing styles—she was limber and loose while Flip, for all his quick-stepping virtuosity onstage, never loosened up on the dance floor. Still, he married his adorable dancer in Nassau in 1959. After a month, they both knew it was a mistake. They bickered about everything from his unwillingness to dance to her unwillingness to quit dancing and move to Florida with him. After six months, he returned to Miami alone, with divorce papers in the back of his notebook. Peaches went on to wed a Bahamian bandleader, and Flip told himself that his guardian stripper was right all along: women ain't worth it.

After losing momentum in Nassau, he worked double-time, performing every chance he got, writing all night, littering his boardinghouse room with wadded-up pages of discarded routines. Some of his new material featured funny-sad junkies like the ones Pryor would make famous fifteen years later. Flip knew junkies who were musical geniuses, others who managed to hold down steady jobs, and still others who slept on cardboard strips under locust trees in Overtown's Henry Reed Park. Recalling the taste of the heroin he sampled on Guam, he typed the tragicomic essence of addiction on a notebook page: *Gonna get straight. Tomorrow.* In his act, drug jokes and his dead-on impressions of junkies drew surefire laughs. Flip thought he knew why: they sounded hip to every crowd. Black audiences could feel he was talking "just between us," while whites thought they were getting a peek at life on the dark side of the tracks. He reacquainted himself with heroin's almond tang, thinking of it as research, sharing his high with a young tough-guy actor who went on to win an Academy Award. But smack still made Flip irritable, unfunny, and constipated. He preferred the weed that fueled all-night writing and editing sessions in which he tightened his Chris-and-Isabelle routine into seven minutes until every syllable counted. He also expanded on the "Rev" character he'd based on one of his foster fathers, giving the Rev a name and a constituency. Now the finger-snapping, flock-fleecing Reverend Leroy parked his Eldorado at the Church of What's Happening Now.

A storyteller in the vaudeville tradition rather than a rim-shot jokester, Flip built routines by adding to them, stretching stories to seven or eight minutes, sometimes longer. Soon Reverend Leroy had a wife who burned through his hard-hustled cash, a wife with a perfect excuse for her spending sprees. "I didn't wanna buy this dress," she'd say. "The *devil* made me buy this dress!" Demonstrating how she'd stiff-armed Satan, she went on: "'Devil,' I said, 'you better leave me alone.' Devil said, 'Look there, mama, that's a fine-looking dress. You owe yourself a try-on.' That's when he shoved me in the store, and he pushed me over to where the dress was, and he made me try it on. Then he pulled a *gun* and made me sign your name to a check."

The Rev asked, "How come the devil's always making you do something for yourself? When's he gonna do me a favor?"

"I asked him about that, and he said he did already. Devil said if it wasn't for him, you wouldn't have a job."

January 1, 1960, came in clear and cool, a white thumbnail moon over Miami Beach. Flip, still buzzed after a New Year's Eve gig, walked east from Overtown on the Venetian Causeway. The sun wasn't up yet, so he was defying the curfew as well as several other laws, including one against possessing marijuana, one against loitering, and one of his own. Before the show he'd pulled one of "Flip's Laws" from his notebook: *Bitches ain't worth it*. Now he took that page out of his pocket. He tore it up and tossed the pieces to the wind.

Blonell was no bitch.

A cocktail waitress at the Sir John, Blonell Pittman hailed from Florida's Gulf Coast, scrubland near Tampa where the pretty girls like her dreamed of moving to Miami. Flip had seen her on and off for a month, and they'd spoken often enough for him to hear her honeyed accent in his most private moments. She was twenty-nine, older than Flip. More angular than Peaches, with dark-mocha skin and long legs, Blonell had a smooth, unhurried walk that men liked to watch: crossing the lobby with a tray of drinks, slipping through the showroom doors with their diamond-shaped windows, bending at the knee beside a front-row table to distribute cocktails. Flip's heart shifted gears the night he saw her fend off a clumsy pass by Sonny Liston, deflecting the Big Bear's paws and clearing his table without missing a beat, leaving Liston with a kiss on the forehead that probably doubled her tip.

Flip sat a few tables over that night. He'd asked around and learned that her shift was almost over. When Blonell asked if he wanted another drink, he shook his head. "No, dinner. With you, *chérie*," he said, trying out a little of the French he'd picked up in his reading. She let him down easy, saying she never mixed work with pleasure.

Flip looked affronted. "Pleasure? Perhaps you haven't heard of my reputation," he said. "I can assure you that we'll have a *terrible* time." She smiled and touched his hand, a brush of skin that sparked his ardor more than a striptease could have. At twenty-six, Flip was still conflicted about sex. He saw women as a different species. He felt chivalry, disgust, and indifference for them as he tried to believe there was more to love and sex than what wild dogs do. Sure, he wanted to screw Blonell, but he wanted to buy her flowers and open doors for her, too, to hold an umbrella over her head when it rained, to rescue her from a life of waiting tables, to keep her safe from other men, to tell her how interesting she was, and to mean it. Still nervous about undressing, ashamed of the whip scars on his butt, he felt his healthy libido dueling with un-easy memories, his marriage to Peaches curdling quickly into bick-ering, bad sex, and divorce. Looking back from middle age he would guess he might have been "a little torn about bitches" all along.

Blonell was less than smitten with him at first. She already had a daughter with Lawrence Trice, an airport skycap who'd wooed and won her but never married her. After that, Blonell saw herself as a sadder but wiser girl. She paid no attention to Flip when he was onstage—she was working—and deflected the fast-talking lit-tle comic's flattery when he nursed a white port after his sets, al-ways sitting in her section of the club, flirting every chance he got. Then, on the day he called his V-B day, he found her paging through a fashion magazine in the Sir John's coffee shop. Blonell listened politely while he burbled about how the models in her magazine would tie for last in a beauty race with her. She thanked him for offering to pay for her coffee. "But you're too late," she said, nodding at the dollar bill she'd put beside her cup.

"No, I'm not." Flip pocketed Blonell's dollar and replaced it with one from his wallet. "I insist," he said. "And now we can call this our first date. Get it out of the way just like that." He snapped his fingers. "So let's talk about our second date."

She agreed to have dinner with him. A proper date, but nothing fancy—dinner right here at the coffee shop.

She arrived on the appointed night, but there was no sign of Flip. She waited half an hour, thinking he'd stood her up. At last he bustled out of the kitchen dressed as a French waiter, a white towel draped over his forearm. He bowed, begging m'amselle's pardon for his "tardy-tay." It was a long swim across the Atlantique, he said. Other diners laughed while he took her order. When he fell to one knee to propose "matrimonay," they applauded.

"Oui!" she said, going along with the gag. Flip and Blonell accepted congratulations through dinner, dessert, and coffee. But all he got at the end of their date was a kiss at the threshold of the room she shared with another waitress.

He proposed for real after New Year's. *"C'est vrai.* I mean it." Blonell almost believed him.

"So when is it?" she said, pouring him a cup of coffee. "Our wedding."

"What's the rush?" They were sharing a place of their own, half a duplex near the hotel. Blonell looked after her kindergarten-aged daughter, Michelle, by day and waited tables at night while Flip paced their narrow apartment in his bathrobe, chain-smoking Pall Malls and joints, plopping down at the kitchen table to speed-type a few lines when inspiration struck. Blonell paid the bills—rent, groceries, dry cleaning for her slinky work clothes, plus twenty or so dollars a week to his dope dealer—after Herbie Shul's checks stopped coming. Still a fixture on Miami's nightclub scene, Shul swore he loved "Flipster" as much as ever but said he wasn't crazy about some of his new material, what with the sex jokes and blue language. "You don't have to work blue. You're better than those guys," he said. Most of Flip's sex jokes were harmless enough. *This drunk in a bar, he's totally depressed. His buddy says, "Joe, what's the matter?" Joe says, "Blue balls. It's my wife—she's cut me down to one time a week." His buddy says, "Hey, it could be worse. I know three guys she cut out completely."* Others were edgier, like an old Chitlin' Circuit line that applied his Native American theme to female genitalia. *The first time you saw pussy, didn't you think, "Is that pussy, or a tomahawk wound?"* Shul thought Flip was losing touch with one of his own rules: *We are in fun.* Flip protested that he was just doing what worked. Self-taught Clerow Wilson was proud that he knew Shakespeare, Mark Twain, Eastman, and Du Bois as well as Bert Williams and Dewey "Pig-meat" Markham, but who cared? Every audience laughed at drug and dick jokes and went mute if he mentioned Othello. "Chumps don't want no Moor," he grumbled onstage one night. He was the only one who laughed. He told Shul he was determined to stick to another of "Flip's Laws": *I don't care if you laugh.* But as Shul said, "Who wants to like you if you don't like them?"

"Me, blue? Blow me," Flip said. "We don't need Herbie. I've been doing my own thing since I got out of Jersey City."

Blonell said, "So when is it?"

"Our wedding? Woman, why do you keep going on about that?"

She placed his hand on her belly. "Why do you think?"

Flip backed a forty-foot moving van over the curb, scattering pigeons and pedestrians. Piloting this whale helped pay bills while Blonell was pregnant. He hated it. It was one thing to be an open-road trucker like Eleanor's husband and his Jersey City friends, and something else to make a dollar an hour hunting around Colored Town for a place to double-park. Drivers of all creeds and colors leaned on their horns and flipped Flip off. He'd greet traffic cops with a lively "Hello there, ossi-fer!" and talk his way out of trouble, but his sidewalk stand-up didn't always work. One cop stuck a parking ticket in his mouth.

Blonell came home to find him stoned, talking to himself. One night he sat hunched over one of her fashion magazines, sniffing the cover. White dust on his upper lip. She complained that he spent more time getting high than working. "You're about to be a father, but you'd rather be a junkie." He said he was getting high *and* working. Anyway, he was sticking to weed from now on. "A little reefer's a long way from a junkie. Satchmo smokes twenty joints a day."

"Well, he's not trying to make it, is he? He's *there*."

Flip said he'd make it, too. Lots of artists used drugs to unlock their creativity. Charlie Parker. Edgar Allan Poe. Van Gogh. Samuel Fucking Coleridge. Those guys were artists, not junkies. "I know what a junkie is."

"Last I heard, Charlie Parker's dead." Blonell said she wouldn't be surprised if Poe and Samuel Fucking Van Gogh were, too. "And Billie Holiday, she's one I saw with my own eyes. Billie used to play the Sir John." She must have been in her late thirties the first time Blonell saw her, but looked fifty. She was on the plump side at first, and still alert enough to compliment Blonell on the gardenia in her hair. As the years passed Billie wasted away a little at a time into a slumpy old thing that couldn't walk a straight line to the stage microphone or sit in the coffee shop without putting her head on the table. "I wasn't surprised she died." Lady Day dead in New York the year before, nothing but narcotics police watching over her, arrested on her deathbed for the dope in her purse, seventy cents to her name. *There* was an artist, Blonell said, and here sits my man, so proud of himself with his comedy laws, calling himself one.

Flip nodded. She wasn't sure if he wanted to kiss her or shove her. With a sheepish smile he said, "Touché."

* * *

A month after the end of *I Love Lucy*, Desi Arnaz declared that he didn't. He and Lucille Ball were divorcing after twenty years of marriage. Flip heard the news on the radio. The next story was about U.S. Army sergeant Elvis Presley, who was leaving Fort Dix, New Jersey, with his honorary discharge, a mustering-out check for $109.54, and the thanks of a grateful nation. Not that Sergeant Presley did much during his two-year hitch, Flip thought, like entertain the other men or even learn to type. Screw Elvis.

"I quit today," Flip announced. "Not gonna drive a truck. If I can't make it with my act, I won't make it at all."

"You quit. Where does that leave me?" Blonell asked. Her belly was round as a basketball.

"Right here. I'll send money from the road."

There was no point in arguing with him. He'd just go silent. He could shut people out as easily as switching off the radio. There was no point asking what made him so different from all the performers she'd seen come through the Sir John, talented, cocky musicians and comics, some of them junkies, some straight as Count Basie's cuffs, all 100 percent sure they were *going places*. Out the swinging doors they went and she never heard their names again.

There was no point asking again for a wedding ring, either. He'd just want to know what the rush was.

Flip told her he was going to New York on the fourth of March. He liked the timing: it was the only day of the year that was also a command. "March forth!" he said, trooping around the kitchen. Blonell helped him pack his satchel with his suit, two ties, everyday clothes, shaving kit, a handful of books, his loose-leaf notebook, and, no surprise, a bag of reefer. As it turned out, she was the one with a surprise. Blonell went into labor before he got away. On March 5, 1960, she delivered a healthy baby boy. They considered calling him Clerow, or maybe Leroy after Flip's real father, but chose the name David. The way the child kicked his legs and clenched his fists reminded Flip of the giant-killer in the Bible. Little David had barely settled into the crib beside his mother's bed in the Overtown duplex when Flip left town.

6

Flip Flops

◈ The club towered over 125th Street in Harlem, its flame-colored name blazing over a marquee lined with marching lights: APOLLO. The marquee showed headliners' names in letters a yard high—the Basie and Ellington orchestras, Ella Fitzgerald, Lena Horne, Miles Davis, James Brown. Dance acts and comics were billed in smaller letters below. Inside the theater, crystal chandeliers hanging from a carved rococo ceiling sparkled over 1,475 seats that faced the center of the universe.

Like every other entertainment arena from the Cotton Club to Yankee Stadium, the Apollo was once for whites only. Not until 1934, after Harlem became the de facto capital of black America, did the club open its triple doors to anyone who could buy a ticket. That was the year Ella Fitzgerald, a seventeen-year-old siren with a three-octave range, won the twenty-five-dollar prize on one of the Apollo's first Wednesday-evening Amateur Nights. Later Amateur Night contenders included Sarah Vaughan, Gladys Knight, and Jimi Hendrix, who all won, and Flip Wilson, who didn't. On the night he arrived in New York, Flip stood on 125th Street with traffic streaming by, staring up at the marquee like a tourist. He felt his life was about to turn a corner.

Comedians never won Amateur Night and were lucky to escape the hook. A top-hatted "Executioner" portrayed by a soft-shoe dancer named Sandman Sims waited in the wings while the competing singers, dancers, and comics performed. If the Apollo's famously unruly audience booed, the Executioner hustled onstage to put the contestants out of their misery. Sometimes he wielded a six-foot hook, sometimes a broom or a toy gun. Flip, a professional of seven years' standing who qualified as an amateur because he was new here, avoided execution on his Amateur Night. Nobody remembered which singer won that particular contest, but Flip's funny stories and boyish energy impressed Apollo manager Bob Schiffman. "He was an accomplished comedian when he got to the Apollo, thanks to his years on the road," Schiffman recalled forty years later. "A storyteller. The difference between Flip and some of the others is that he told long stories that were funny all the way through. So I brought him back for four hundred dollars a week. That was a top rate at the time, four hundred dollars for thirty-one shows—four shows on weekdays, five on Saturday, six on Sunday." Flip's salary was half what Schiffman paid headliner Gladys Knight—but then she had to split her $800 with her backup singers, the Pips.

The Apollo's loud crowd would make sure Flip earned his $12.90 per show. Early in his first paid set he said, "This junkie I know—"

A woman's voice boomed from the balcony. "Not another goddamn junkie bit!"

A man downstairs yelled, "Bitch, shut up and let him talk."

The woman wasn't finished. "Every time I come in this damn place—"

Now Flip was the spectator, his head swiveling as he followed the shouts.

"—I've got to hear that junkie shit?!"

"Bitch, if you don't let the man talk, I'll come up there and pitch you off the balcony!"

Flip told a long story about a junkie in the Army. He was supposed to inform Private Jenkins that his mother was dead. It was an old joke that had the fellow barking, "All you men with mothers, take one step forward. Jenkins, not so fast." Flip updated the old joke by having his Army junkie say, "Jenkins, *be cool.*" It worked.

"We had a tough crowd," Schiffman recalls, "a discriminating crowd. Not racially, but discriminating between talent and no-talent. Come out shuckin' and jiving and trying to fake your way through and they'll kill you. They'll boo you all the way home. But they never booed Flip. Not once. And it wasn't because he was always so great. It was because he was always in there pitching. He gave his best all the time, and they loved him for it."

Flip suggested that "us Negroes" invite Indians to join the movement. "We should let them into the NAACP. Of course we'd have to change the name. Maybe we call it the N-double-A-C-P-double-I-G-B, the National Association for the Advancement of Colored People Immediately, and Indians on a Gradual Basis." The Apollo crowd liked that. He soaked up the cheers, more intoxicating than any drug.

He spent his free time listening to comics who got their names on the marquee. One was Jackie Mabley, the first female comic he ever liked. Frumpy as her torn gingham dress and house slippers, "Moms" Mabley was everybody's favorite horny old lady, a persona she'd been refining since she was a teenager trading barbs with Step-in Fetchit and Pigmeat Markham on the TOBA circuit. As brazenly ethnic as Fanny Brice, dirtier than Mae West, she leered at good-looking members of Basie's and Ellington's bands, musing aloud about the size of their instruments. Ribald as ever at sixty-three, she said, "A woman's a woman till the day she dies, but a man's a man only as long as he can." Flip would weave Mabley's proto-feminist sass into his own drag characters' DNA, but it was her racial material that impressed him the most. Moms's satiric needle was so sharp that even the harshest jibes came across in fun. Why did she turn down gigs in the South? "The Greyhound ain't going to take me down there so the bloodhounds run me back." One of her stories told of two bank robbers, one black and one white, who accidentally killed a policeman. Sentenced to death, the white crook panics. "Oh Lord, save me, I don't want to be hung!" The black one says, "They're gonna hang us, so why don't you face it like a man?" The white one replies, "That's easy for you to say, you're used to it."

Flip sat in the back row taking notes. If a local comic accused him of being a joke thief—Milton Berle and other white comedians were said to pay spies to stake out uptown clubs—Flip showed them his notebook. "I'm studying, not stealing, dig?" His notes read more like Eastman than Mobley, with reminders rather than jokes: *Pause for effect. Role reversal.* That got him some cross-eyed looks from comics who were sure the little newcomer was overthinking his funny. Flip figured that gave him a leg up on them. Everyone at this level had talent, but he had talent and a theory.

"When Flip got up there, he made the most of his sets," Schiffman recalls. "Fifteen to eighteen minutes, never the same way twice." He'd done enough emceeing at smaller clubs to master the craft of bantering with the crowd, sometimes taking questions. When a girl asked, "What do you do if a fifty-year-old man goes for you?" Flip took a beat. "You have to do it *all*, honey!" He'd never get rich at the Apollo, working thirty-one times for the twenty twenty-dollar bills Schiffman paid at the end of the week, but it was enough to buy a double-breasted suit from a Garment District tailor. The tailor chalked his cuffs while Flip marveled at the thought of being served hand and foot by a white man. "Money," he said, "is the cure for being black."

He wired a hundred dollars to Blonell and mailed a twenty to Pops, care of Eleanor, in Jersey City. The old neighborhood was only ten miles from the Apollo, a taxi and a ten-minute ferry ride away, but he wasn't going back there yet. He planned to see Pops when he had a car and driver to take him. He thought he might even look up his mother when that day came. She was sixty by now. He heard through friends of friends that she was living with her latest husband on Brinkerhoff Street, not half a mile from Pops. Flip imagined showing up on her stoop wearing a fine suit and tie, maybe a diamond stickpin and a watch that cost more than her man made in a year. Flip had pictured such a moment so many times that he knew what he'd say when it happened. When he got rich, he would reflect on all the other poor kids who made it big and bought cars and houses for their mothers, and then he'd say, "Fuck my momma, I'm buying me some drugs."

He walked the streets of Harlem, pleasantly buzzed on weed and wine, enjoying the lights, the honking traffic, the smoke of countless cigarettes, the music and voices, pedestrians flowing through crosswalks, in and out of shops, bars, and restaurants. The women's clothes and hats were as colorful as an Easter parade, the men in dark suits with shirts so white they almost glowed. He saw a few stern faces over the red bow ties of the Nation of Islam. Everyone was black, but not plain black. Some were so dark they reminded him of African onyx, others so pale they could have passed for white. To use a beatnik phrase Flip adopted, Harlem was where it was at, and an *X* marked its heart—but it should have been two *X*s. Circling back to the Apollo, he saw that Schiffman's workmen had misspelled the name of that night's comedian. Running short of *X*s, they billed him as REDD FOX.

Born John Elroy Sanford in St. Louis in 1922, Redd Foxx grew up in Chicago. His half-Seminole mother was a chambermaid. His father, an electrician, ran off when the boy was four. Young Sanford's first stage name was Red Fox. "Later on I doubled the letters to make the name unforgettable, like me," he liked to say. Making his way to New York in the early 1940s, Foxx ate in Harlem restaurants and skipped out without paying. He slept on rooftops, using news-papers as blankets. Arrested for armed robbery while still in his teens, he served ninety days with rapists and murderers in down-town Manhattan's infamous jail, the Tombs. Upon his release he found a straight job washing dishes at Jimmy's Chicken Shack in Harlem, a hub of Harlem nightlife where Charlie Parker had worked as a dishwasher a decade before. (Legend has it Parker took the nickname "Yardbird," southern slang for chicken, in those years.) Foxx soon befriended a gaunt, freckled Chicken Shack waiter from Detroit named Malcolm Little. To the glum Little, he was "the fun-niest dishwasher on this earth. He kept the kitchen crew in stitches." Friends called them Chicago Red and Detroit Red until Little took a name he liked better, Malcolm X.

A star student in Detroit until a teacher told him, "Being a lawyer is no realistic goal for a nigger," Little dropped out of school in the eighth grade. At Jimmy's Chicken Shack he waited on Parker and his mentor Art Tatum and others including Ralph Ellison, who sat near the kitchen working on the typescript of a book he was calling *Invisible Man*. Little and Foxx spent their off hours shoplifting, deal-ing pot, and robbing local merchants. One of their victims, a dry cleaner, came to work one morning to find his shop cleaned out. Keeping several zoot suits for themselves, they sold the rest of their haul out of what must have been New York's only rooftop haber-dashery.

"Malcolm and I joined the Communist Party together, too," Foxx recalled. "Maybe not joined, but signed something, because they had white broads and food. You'd dance with the chicks, smell their perfume, and eat sandwiches. There was cake and lemonade, even baloney you could put in your pocket. I'd have joined the Ku Klux Klan if they had some sandwiches." They drifted apart after a while, with Little turning to pimping and racketeering before he converted to Islam, while Foxx told off-color jokes on the Chitlin' Circuit and recorded a series of uncensored "party records" that made him an underground celebrity.

Like Flip, Foxx had honed his native wit by playing the dozens, one-upping other boys with funny insults. He liked to surprise and even shock audiences, which made him a useful foil for the Baltimore comic Melvin "Slappy" White, whose bumptious marriage to singer Pearl Bailey was falling apart. White told old-fashioned rimshot jokes: "The trouble with unemployment is, the minute you wake up in the morning, you on the job." As the comedy duo Redd and White, he and Foxx played Chitlin' dives up and down the East Coast, squabbling all the way. They were arguing about money one night when Foxx threw a .38-caliber bullet at his partner. "What's that for?" White asked.

"A reminder," Foxx said. "The next one will be a lot faster."

Finally the duo landed a $350-a-week gig at the Apollo.

"I'm Redd," Foxx said to open their show.

"I'm White," added Slappy.

"You're kidding!" Redd replied. That night, Apollo co-owner Frank Schiffman typed a capsule review on an index card: *Corny. Do not repeat*. Redd and White went on to tour off and on for years, returning for a handful of last-chance Apollo engagements that went better, but Foxx wasn't much of a partner. As his raunchy party records attested, he was a solo star who could make Moms Mabley sound dainty. "What's the difference between a pickpocket and a Peeping Tom?" he asked. "A pickpocket snatches watches." Even more hostile to audiences than his white contemporary Don Rickles, Foxx told one heckler, "I hope your dog dies." To another he snarled, "That's some big lips you got. If your lips were filled with quarters I could buy a farm with the lower lip and save the upper lip for Social Security." Flip preferred Redd's mainstream material, like his bit about the little boy in a candy store. "The kid asks, 'How much are those candy bars?' The man says, 'Two for a quarter.' Kid says, 'How much for one?' Fella says, 'It's fifteen cents for one.' Kid says, 'Well, give me the *other* one.'"

By the early sixties Foxx was salting his act with racial riffs. "They found a Mississippi Negro with six hundred pounds of chains around his body," he said. "Found him in the river. The sheriff says, 'Ain't that just like a nigger, steal more chains than he can carry.'" He and Flip crossed paths on the circuit. Flip introduced himself, but Foxx barely noticed the youngster pumping his hand. He was flying on professional-grade pot, which is tantamount to saying Redd Foxx was awake. Flip liked to get high, but Foxx was an astronaut by comparison. His pupils were black holes on the night Flip reintroduced himself at the Apollo.

"Redd, it's Flip, Flip Wilson."

Foxx blinked. "Flip Flip Wilson," he imitated in his cement-mixer growl.

"It's just 'Flip.' You don't remember?" Redd had seen his act at least half a dozen times.

Foxx gave him a shove. There was always a touch of aggression to Foxx. Moving past Flip as if he weren't there, he said, "'Course I do. You're funny as shit." For years Flip would joke about black people's blushing—"Yes, we do!"—pointing out that it's obvious in light-skinned blacks but invisible in darker ones like him, which made secret blushing one of three advantages to having dark skin, the others being nighttime hide-and-seek and never having to worry about being president. He blushed at Foxx's compliment. He couldn't wait to call Blonell with the news that Redd Foxx thought he was funny as shit. He wanted to ask Redd which parts of his act he liked best, which ones he'd cut, and which he'd edit or expand. They could discuss Eastman's theories of comedy, or just sit and smoke and laugh.

The next night, Foxx brushed past him again. "Redd, it's Flip." Foxx ignored him. Flip stalked out of the club to a phone booth.

Blonell sounded sleepy. "You're going to kill Redd Foxx?" she said. "Well, that should get you in the papers."

Flip showed up in Overtown with a gift for Blonell and little David, a portable TV. They twisted the rabbit ears, and the snowy screen flickered to a black-and-white image of President Kennedy announcing his plan to win the space race. Flip could do a little Kennedy. "Befoah this decade is out," he said, presiding over breakfast, "we shall land a man on the moo-oon and retahn him safely." Safely to where? "To the uth!" In the same speech, Kennedy called for $50 million to establish "space satellites for wuhld-wide communication." At the time a Boston comic named Vaughn Meader had the biggest comedy album in the country. His uncanny Kennedy impression, which the president himself loved, made Meader's 1962 album *The First Family* the number-one record in America, with sales of seven and a half million copies, more than any other record in any category. Then, in November of the following year, the TV in Flip and Blonell's split duplex showed CBS anchorman Walter Cronkite at his desk, choking back tears as he announced that the president had been shot. That night, Lenny Bruce took the stage in New York. After a long sigh, Bruce said, "Man, Vaughn Meader is fucked."

It was true. Meader vanished. Flip mourned Kennedy and added a note to his comedy laws. *Be topical, but not too topical.* Topical comics had to ride the rapids of current events without getting sunk. On his occasional visits to Miami he gigged at the Sir John, referring to "the movement" and "the struggle" without wading into the turbulent details. He had a hard time finding the funny in subjects like King's nonviolence, Malcolm X's talk of white devils, and Eldridge Cleaver's call for black men to rape white women. It was simpler to stick to sex and drugs, topics that most nightclub crowds thought were hipper.

"Your act's dirtier," Blonell said.

"The fuck it is." He packed his bags and left. By 1963 he was spending only a few weeks a year with her in Florida. He wired Blonell money from Atlanta, Baltimore, Philadelphia, and New York but seldom phoned, claiming long distance cost too much. She knew he was tired of hearing her ask about marriage. "One of these days," he'd say, but he never bought a ring or set a date, even after she got pregnant again. Their second son was born in March 1962. They named him Kevin.

"Stay," Blonell said.

"You see these other guys shootin' past me? Dick Gregory? Bill Cosby? I'm not saying I'm better than them, but I'm not worse." Flip said he needed to stick to his plan to work the New York clubs until TV scouts discovered him, too.

"Oh, I remember. Your fifteen-year plan," Blonell snapped.

At the Royal Peacock in Atlanta, he opened for Gladys Knight and the Pips. "Flip was a brilliant cat. I was in awe of his talent," recalls Bubba Knight, Gladys's brother and lead Pip. "He had a loneliness to him, but he took up with us, Gladys and me and our mom, the other two Pips, all our cousins, like we were a family he never had. My aunt had a house on Adele Avenue in Atlanta, and Flip would break bread with us there. He loved his southern home cooking. Then we'd all go bowling."

"Flip had his frustrations. He was getting older and he hadn't made it yet," says Gladys Knight. "But he loosened up, those times with us. He was a very good bowler, so he'd always win."

"Had his own ball," Bubba says. "We were bad bowlers, and sometimes he'd act annoyed at us. He'd get a lane of his own, go over there and roll strike after strike."

On the road, Flip added a few lines about home life to his stage patter. He spoke of how lonely he got on the road, and how he went home to Miami every chance he got, to take his lady out on the town and express his love to her in the most romantic way possible. "And nine months later I find out *how* romantic." Sometimes he called his lady "my wife" in those routines, but he never mentioned her by name.

Late in 1963 Flip scored a weeklong booking at the Village Gate, a downtown club where New York's hippest crowds went to hear Gregory, Cosby, Lenny Bruce, and Woody Allen. It was his biggest gig yet, at a racially mixed venue where there were sure to be talent scouts and TV bookers in the house. Flip believed comedy was color-blind, at least in its purest forms, but even in a hip setting like this his race was issue number one from the moment the spotlight hit him. At the California state convention that sent delegates to that summer's Republican National Convention in San Francisco, conservatives pushed a resolution to "send Negroes back to Africa."

Early in his first set, Flip tried a new bit. He complained that the club's manager had rigged the audience with people who were paid to laugh. Flip hated tricks like that, he said. "If at any time I feel the audience is rigged, I'll walk off." With that he scanned the crowd suspiciously. "Now, I happen to know there are riggers in the audience. Two riggers followed me in here." Nervous laughs flitted through the crowd. "Nigger" was still a risky enough term that even a close rhyme carried a charge. "The guy on the door said he saw a whole carload of riggers pull up out front!" The laughter rose as he mentioned the many riggers working in the club. Flip could point them out individually, he said, "but I won't. Because if you've seen one rigger, you've seen 'em all."

The hip audience roared. Moving downstage, nimble as a dancer, he shared an aside with a white couple. "I'm taking a hell of a liberty here—I might be banned from the movement." Here was another part of his plan. As he'd told Blonell, he wasn't going to be pigeonholed as a Negro comedian. Flip Wilson wasn't a joiner, as he proved with a dig at Redd Foxx's old wingman. "Malcolm X don't dig nobody." His act was evolving as he sought a distinctive take on his times. At the Village Gate he often sounded angry, shouting lines for emphasis. He scored with the long Foxxy tale of a man who took his woozy date to a motel only to find she had a wooden leg. When she passed out, he removed the wooden leg, which promptly fell apart in his hands. Running out for some tools, he told his story to a drunk he met in the hall. "You think you got trouble!" the drunk said. "I got a girl in my room with *both* her legs apart, and I forgot the room number." Flip referred to the reefer he'd rolled before the show, hoping for "a fantastic discovery—reefer is the cure for cancer." Not very funny and barely in fun, but his Greenwich Village listeners dug contraband, verbal or herbal. He closed with a story about a pot party.

The Village Gate crowd ate it up. After the show, he phoned Blonell: "Everybody's gonna want me now."

They didn't. There must have been a dozen talent bookers representing the TV networks and New York's leading nightclubs on hand during Flip's first week at the Village Gate, but nobody called. Rather than make his TV debut on *The Ed Sullivan Show* or Johnny Carson's *Tonight Show*, he spent the winter of 1964–65 on the club circuit, playing the same dives he'd been working for years. Why? Dick Gregory, a Village Gate regular, had seven records and a book out. The clean-cut, college-educated Cosby, three years younger than Flip, was a *Tonight Show* favorite with a best-selling album.

"Finally I saw what was wrong," Flip recalled. "Here I am saying, 'So Jack, like I'm busting down to see my man and like, dig, that's where it's at.' These Greenwich Village people tell me how great I am, but everybody else says, 'What the hell's he talking about?' Talent scouts considering me for a television show would say, 'He's too dirty.' I began to think it was better to lose four or five cool people and get across to fifty. I was worried at first. Will my hipness diminish? Then it dawned on me that the important thing wasn't being hip, it was being Flip."

Long ago an uncle had given young Clerow a joke book full of what Flip later called "old slave humor—*dis, dat, dem*. Terrible stuff." Thinking back to the book's tall tales of "darkies" and "tar babies" outsmarting tigers, white masters, lynch mobs, and "God Hisself," Flip now began seeing himself as part of a tradition that led from Reconstruction-era minstrel shows through vaudeville, the Chitlin' Circuit, and Amateur Night at the Apollo. He set out to retool his act, cutting anything too blue to play on TV, writing material that had less to do with what he thought was hip and more to do with what he thought was funny. In those weeks, he said, "I found my blackness."

The Village Gate booking he'd expected to lead to the promised land of TV guest spots led him to a comedy desert where he smoked less, wrote more, and got fewer laughs. When he opened at jazz clubs where the blue, pungent air got him buzzing, his Chris Columbus bit always drew applause, but it was only seven minutes long. Newer stories about black power and girls—not bitches—fell flat. One club manager handed him a few dollars off the bar and said he wouldn't be needed the rest of the week. Flip retreated to his hotel room. He knelt by the bed and prayed. "Jesus, you don't know me. I'm not one of the ones always asking you for shit. But I need a break. . . ."

In Baltimore he performed his best material, new and old, in a half-empty room. A drunk dozed at a corner table. "It was so quiet," he recalled, "you could hear my self-esteem drop." Later that night the headliner ambled onstage. Redd Foxx woke the place up with a XX-rated set about dope, pubic hair, anal sex, and a housewife who happened to own a lathered-up donkey: "I rode her sweaty ass all night!" With the crowd clamoring for more, Foxx headed for the door.

Flip got in his way. "Redd, got a minute?"

Foxx looked him over. "Listen, kid," he said, "I'm a little short tonight. Gimme five for cab fare."

"*You* need cab fare?"

"Be cool. I'm good for it. I'll hit you back tomorrow."

Flip handed over his last five. Foxx went out to hail a cab. He didn't show up the next day, leaving Flip to do two thankless sets in a row.

In his State of the Union address in January 1965, President Lyndon Baines Johnson vowed to support "Negro Americans through enforcement of the civil rights law." Johnson said he was determined to follow Kennedy's lead by making racial harmony a national priority, right up there with the space program. "Americans of all races stand side by side in Berlin and Vietnam. They died side by side in Korea. Surely they can work and eat and travel side by side in their own country." After a year during which racial unrest had roiled the nation's cities, he closed his speech with a line borrowed from the movement: "We are strong enough to keep the faith."

LBJ wasn't so politic in private. Chatting with cronies on *Air Force One*, the president bragged that with the epic Civil Rights Act of 1964 and his progressive Great Society programs, "I'll have those niggers voting Democratic for the next two hundred years."

Six weeks after Johnson's speech, Malcolm X spoke at the Audubon Ballroom in upper Manhattan, a dance hall where the King and Queen of Harlem were crowned each spring. Redd Foxx's old accomplice was there to address the Organization for Afro-American Unity. After splitting with the Nation of Islam and becoming the movement's most divisive figure, he was beginning to turn from the politics of schism to the more difficult work of fence mending. He stepped past a piano and drum set on a stage decorated with a mural of an alpine lake. Greeting an audience of about four hundred, he said, *"As-salaam alaikum."* Peace be with you. Then two men moved toward the stage. "There was a scuffle," an eyewitness reported. "I heard Malcolm X say his last words: 'Now, now, brothers, break it up. Be cool, be calm.'" A Nation of Islam member named Thomas Hagan charged from the crowd with a sawed-off shotgun and fired, blowing Malcolm off his feet. Two men who were never conclusively identified shot him sixteen more times. Dead at thirty-nine, Malcolm X was the first martyr of the second half of the sixties.

It was a time of convulsive change that left many Americans pining for old-fashioned distractions. Ten days after Malcolm X's murder, record-setting crowds lined up to see Julie Andrews play a singing nun. In an era that produced *Easy Rider, Bonnie and Clyde, The Graduate,* and *Dr. Strangelove, The Sound of Music* became the most popular film of all time. During the week the musical opened in Alabama, state troopers attacked peaceful black marchers in Selma with batons and tear gas.

Flip followed the news the modern way, watching white men in business suits narrate it on TV. Like most Americans, he noticed when a black face appeared on television. One mid-sixties study found that only three blacks appeared among the hundreds of white people seen on a typical night of American TV. And one of those three black faces—as dark as those of the marchers in Selma but still somehow as welcome in prime time as Gomer Pyle's—pissed Flip off. Switching channels in Blonell's Overtown kitchen or on one of the dented Philco sets he encountered in hotel rooms, touching the rabbit-ear antennae to a window screen to improve reception, twisting the vertical- and horizontal-hold knobs on the back of the set to keep the image in frame, he kept seeing the placid face of Bill Cosby.

Cosby, twenty-seven, debuted on *The Tonight Show* in 1963 and quickly became one of Johnny Carson's favorite guests. His first album, *Bill Cosby Is a Very Funny Fellow . . . Right*, recorded at the Bitter End in Greenwich Village, featured Cosby's clever sound effects and a no-nonsense shipbuilder, Noah. When God's voice boomed out of nowhere—"*Noah! I want you to build an ark*"—Noah said, "Ri-i-ght. Who is this really? Am I on *Candid Camera*?"

"I want you to build it three hundred cubits by eighty cubits by forty cubits."

"Ri-i-ght. What's a cubit?"

Three hit albums and stand-up spots on *Tonight* and *The Ed Sullivan Show* had made Cosby the country's top comic. He'd left Temple University in Philadelphia, where he played football and moonlighted as a glib bartender, for New York, where Greenwich Village audiences adored "Cool Cos." Cosby had killed on Carson's *Tonight Show* in 1963. Now he was America's favorite black comic. Flip resented him for it but couldn't hate him; hating Cosby would be like hating Mary Poppins, kittens, or sheer comic talent. With the three TV networks beginning a tentative civil-rights push of their own—to disprove claims that they were antiblack and to claim an untapped black public that accounted for 8 percent of the population—the squeaky-clean Cosby was the obvious choice to lead the march. In 1965 NBC made him Robert Culp's second banana on a lighthearted secret-agent series, *I Spy*. Cosby's arrival as TV's first crossover star gave hope to other black comics while irking a few like Flip and Redd Foxx, who saw themselves as his equal or better.

Still Foxx, forty-two, swore he'd never sell out by cleaning up his act. "My act is adult," he said. "If you don't have an adult mind, get the hell out." On one chat-show appearance he mocked the white host and all-white audience by coming onstage in golf knickers. Asked about black power, Foxx said he believed in green power:

"money." Asked why money was green, he said, "Jews pick it before it gets ripe!" Yet despite his touchy material and notorious party records, he got on *The Tonight Show*, thanks to Apollo manager Bobby Schiffman.

Foxx was griping to Schiffman one night, complaining that television was rigged. "You got thirty million suckers a week watching cracker shit. *Bonanza. Gomer Pyle. Andy Griffith.*" And TV comedy was no better. Bob Hope. Phyllis Diller. He didn't want to hear about *I Spy*, Cosby running around in tennis togs looking about as black as Billy Graham.

"You dumb motherfucker," Schiffman said, "you're jealous. But they'll never put you on TV. You're too dirty. They'll pass you by like you don't exist."

As Schiffman recalls that night, Foxx shrugged and said, "Nothin' I can do."

"There is," Schiffman said. "If you promise you won't embarrass me, I'll get you on TV."

Foxx was game. "Okay. I promise!"

Schiffman knew almost everybody in New York's nightclub demimonde but nobody in television. He phoned NBC and asked for *The Tonight Show*'s production office. Lucky for him Skitch Henderson, Carson's bandleader, picked up the phone. Henderson knew Schiffman's father, who'd founded the Apollo. "Skitch, I've got a great comic for your show," Schiffman said. "Redd Foxx."

Henderson said, "Redd Foxx? Love him. But I've gotta go; call me in an hour."

The phone went dead. "So now I had a dial tone in my ear," Schiffman recalls. "But I had to make my point. I'm sitting there telling the dial tone, 'Oh no, Skitch, don't worry, Redd gave me his word. He'll work clean. . . .'"

Schiffman hung up.

Foxx was hanging on every word. "What'd the man say?"

Schiffman aimed a finger at him. "Redd, don't screw this up." The next night, Foxx did eight clean-as-a-whistle minutes on *Tonight*. That same week his name jumped from the base of the Apollo's marquee into the yard-high letters on top, and Flip had another reason to change channels on his hotel TV. At thirty-one, he felt locked out of the moment as well as the movement. With Redd Foxx on *The Tonight Show*, Flip couldn't claim that only white comics or clean-cut or young comics could make it big. Blonell said thirty-one was old enough to know when to quit beating your head on a wall. "Come home," she said.

Flip said he *was* home. He said he belonged on the road, falling asleep with a legal pad on his chest. "I'll come back when I make it. I'll come back and buy you a house."

Following Dick Gregory into Playboy Clubs in the mid-sixties, Flip scored with a new bit on the lions eating Christians in the Roman Coliseum. "The Christians had a great coach, but their team was shaky." He joked about collecting garbage "for a dollar an hour and all you could eat." His take on race was evolving, often indirect, with the barb hidden under the punch line. And he surprised Playboy Club patrons by saying he thought slavery was a good idea. "Good for the economy." But to bring slavery back, "you've got to give it a new spin, dig?" He was for bringing slavery back if white folks agreed to take turns.

Baltimore. One in the morning. Flip jumped when somebody banged on the flimsy door of his hotel room. "This is the police. Open the motherfuck up!"

Redd Foxx clomped in, dressed in a sweat-stained seersucker suit. He'd just finished a set. He squinted at the room—peeling wallpaper, wheezing radiator, a mess of yellow legal pads on the unmade bed. "Flip Flip Wilson," he said. "Got any blow?"

Flip had enough blow to get him through an all-night writing session. Not enough to share with a fat and happy headliner who probably had a wad of twenties if not C-notes somewhere in his tacky suit, a moocher who still owed Flip five bucks for a cab ride Redd had forgotten.

"Come on, you know I'll hit you back."

Flip fished his stash from a dresser drawer and razored two white lines, one for Redd and one for himself. Foxx produced a fifty-dollar bill. He rolled and snorted both lines. "Mm-mm good." Unrolling the fifty, he licked off a trace of powder and put the bill back in his pocket.

They sat on the bed watching the end of an old cowboy movie. Foxx cheered for the Indians. When the credits rolled, he said, "Damn cavalry wins again." An American flag filled the screen, and a brass band played the national anthem, ending the programming day. Then the screen went blank, the only sound a low test tone. It was three A.M. Flip shook himself from a TV-watching stupor as Foxx left, kicking the door shut behind him.

Sonny Liston fell to a poetry-spouting Louisville fighter named Cassius Clay, who joined the Nation of Islam and changed his name to Muhammad Ali. Slums from Newark to Watts roiled with what newspapers called race war. For Flip, one road hotel blurred into another while Blonell stayed in Overtown with their sons. Before long his sons would be old enough to wonder where Daddy was. Who Daddy was.

One night that summer he was watching *The Tonight Show*, fuming as Johnny Carson introduced Redd Foxx for another stand-up segment. After his short set, Foxx got favored-guest treatment, a seat beside Carson's desk. They batted a few lines around, then Carson asked, "Redd, who's the funniest comedian out there right now?"

Foxx didn't hesitate.

"Flip Wilson."

RICHES

7

Surprises

◈ Foxx's endorsement led to a phone call that comics answered in their dreams: "Johnny wants you to be on the show." On the night he was scheduled, Flip reported to NBC headquarters at Rockefeller Center with more than an hour to spare. *The Tonight Show* began taping at 5:30 P.M. and ran for 105 minutes, airing from 11:15 until 1:00 A.M. Flip was slated for the show's final segment, after the last commercial break, when newcomers and no-names often appeared. Dressed in a slate-blue suit and thin tie, with a gold tie clasp and gleaming gold cuff links, he paced a sixth-floor hallway, chain-smoking and watching the clock as the taping began. A few minutes after seven, a girl with a clipboard popped out of Studio 6-B.

"Mr. Wilson? Sorry, we're running long." Johnny Carson was clicking with other, better-known guests and wasn't going to cut them short to introduce an unknown. "We'll reschedule," the girl promised. Flip rode a brass-trimmed NBC elevator to the lobby and passed through a revolving door to the street. He'd planned to celebrate his national TV debut that night. Instead he walked uptown to his hotel alone, the red sun sinking over the skyline to a fiery crash landing in New Jersey.

It happened again the next time. Booked for the final segment, he paced and smoked until Carson closed the show with a wave to the camera, saying, "We'll have Flip Wilson on another night." Flip told himself to keep the faith. Newcomers got bumped all the time.

Eventually they got their shot. Still, he'd heard about a few comics who kept getting bumped until *The Tonight Show* quit calling. He wondered what happened to them. All suicides, probably.

By the time of his third booking on the Carson show, Watts was in flames. The riots had begun on August 11, 1965, when a white highway patrolman stopped a black motorist named Marquette Frye in the poverty-stricken Los Angeles neighborhood. A crowd gathered, shouting and throwing rocks. Soon Frye, his mother, and dozens of others were battling the cops, triggering five days of fights, looting, and arson that left thirty-four dead and more than a thousand people hurt. Los Angeles police chief William Parker, a crusty import from Deadwood, South Dakota, compared the rioters to apes in a zoo. Flip watched news footage from Watts—shattered storefronts, whole blocks burning, angry black men shaking their fists or getting handcuffed—with mounting worry for the dead and injured. He worried about his career, too. A black guy probably wouldn't seem so amusing to Carson's audience that week.

Later in August, Flip made his third trip to Rockefeller Center expecting to be bumped. Sure enough, the clipboard girl emerged from Studio 6-B during the second-to-last segment, looking for Mr. Wilson.

"Present," he said.

"Two minutes," she told him.

Waiting offstage during the last commercial, he lit a cigarette. Like a lot of stand-ups in the sixties, Flip often smoked onstage. It looked hip and gave him a prop to gesture with. Some comics said it calmed them down. Flip never suffered from nerves before night-club sets, but he was glad for the nicotine now. Taking a drag as Carson introduced him—

". . . Flip Wilson!"

He stepped through applause to his mark on the soundstage, a masking-tape *X* ten yards to the left of Carson's desk. Flip smiled and launched his best story. When he got to the punch line—*"Chris gonna find Ray Charles!"*—the studio audience burst into the percussive laughter he'd hoped for. Carson's own voice was part of the sound. An expert monologuist and patron of the craft, Carson caught his breath and said, "Funny!"

Then it was over. After seven minutes of Chris Columbus and Queen Isabelle Johnson, Carson said his goodnights. Skitch Henderson and the band played through the closing credits, and Flip returned to the brass-trimmed elevator, nodding to the black elevator operator. He could still hear Carson's magic word, "Funny!" Leaving the building, lighting another smoke, he passed under the blue and red Radio City Music Hall sign and joined the flow of foot traffic crossing Sixth Avenue, hundreds of people hurrying to their hundreds of destinations. They didn't know it, but in a few hours some of them would be watching Clerow Wilson from Jersey City kill on *The Tonight Show.*

Carson brought him back a month later. That night Flip told the story of a woman who took her newborn on a train. Another passenger whistled and said, "That's an *ugly* baby!" The mother wept, but the rude rider persisted. "I mean, *u-u-gly!*" When the mother told the conductor what had happened, he swore that such things would not be tolerated on the Pennsylvania Railroad. To make amends, the conductor offered her "a free meal in our dining car . . . and maybe we'll find a banana for your monkey." Flip delivered the punch line with such exquisite timing that Carson laughed for almost half a minute, pounding his desk. He stepped out from behind it to interrupt Flip's bows, pumping his hand and saying, "That is one of the funniest things I've ever heard in my life!"

Eleven years into his fifteen-year plan, Flip was suddenly the hottest "new" comic in the country. Over the next two years he would make twenty-six more *Tonight Show* appearances. Carson liked him so much that he would eventually appoint Flip a guest host, one of the favored few who subbed for Johnny when he took a night off. Talk shows like *Tonight* didn't pay much—industry scale of a few hundred dollars—but the exposure boosted Flip's club fees. Apollo manager Schiffman gave him a raise from $400 to $1,000 a week, or almost $33 a show. "We paid top dollar for top talent," recalls Schiffman, who economized on newcomers. (Two years later, when the Jackson Five won Amateur Night, he signed them for the same $1,000—$6.45 per Jackson per show.) As Flip approached top-talent status, filling the prime fifteen to eighteen minutes before musical headliners took the stage, his Apollo rate doubled again to $2,000 a week, worth about $13,000 in 2012 dollars.

Some out-of-town club owners paid even more. "Customers wanted acts they'd seen on TV," says Bill Bateman, who ran Baltimore's Club Venus. "I paid Flip fifteen hundred a week, and then twenty-five hundred as he got better known. Serious money, but he was worth it. Flip never gave less than his best. Night after night, they stood up and cheered." Between shows he and Bateman played cards with Bateman's drinking buddies. Flip always purchased a jumbo stack of chips at the buy-in. Bored by ordinary five-card poker, he insisted on playing bouncy variants like baseball, a seven-card game with threes and nines wild and any four, representing a base on balls, worth a free card. "He was crazy about wild cards. Flip would rather go bust chasing five aces than win with a pair."

In 1966 Flip returned to Las Vegas. No bus ride this time; he flew into town. The neon city was growing fast, Glitter Gulch casinos with sawdust on the floors losing business to mammoth resorts on the Strip, where gala floor shows drew tourists like moths to searchlights. Modernization included integration, thanks in part to Frank Sinatra, who refused to appear at any venue that barred his friend Sammy Davis Jr. Hotel managers who would have drained their pools had Davis gone for a dip there a decade before now welcomed him as a star, though Sammy was still advised, like Nat Cole before him, to avoid eye contact with white women when he sang love songs.

Flip had never played any of the Strip showrooms when he agreed to open for Bobby Darin at the Sahara in 1966. The showroom manager balked at the last minute, as much for Flip's inexperience as for his skin tone. Then Darin, a finger-snapping hepcat from the Bronx who'd topped the singles charts with "Dream Lover" and "Mack the Knife," made like Frank by threatening to tear up his contract unless Flip got the job. He and Flip had gigged together in East Coast nightclubs. They shared a taste for cool jazz and potent pot. After the Sahara caved in to Darin's demand, Flip would stick around after his own performance, waiting for Bobby to close their sold-out show with "Mack the Knife." Then they'd go out for postmidnight meals or long, bleary bull sessions in Bobby's penthouse suite. Sometimes they teamed up with the Rat Pack, the five stars of the Vegas-based 1960 caper film *Ocean's 11*: imperious Sinatra; wisecracking scat cat Davis; Dean Martin, the tipsy Romeo; deadpan comic Joey Bishop; and Peter Lawford, the Brit with his aquiline nose in the air. While Davis claimed to remember Flip's sets at the Sir John Hotel ("You were crazy, man"), Flip doubted Sammy had any recollection of him.

Sinatra was only about an inch taller than Flip, but his presence made him appear bigger. Even as it softened with age, that famous face loomed over any gathering like a parade float. Frank seemed to like hearing that Flip was from Jersey City, next door to his own hometown of Hoboken. At least he gave a positive-sounding mumble to that effect. Flip never felt he had the man's full attention. Sinatra's icy eyes didn't rest for long before flitting to Dean or Sammy or some luckless maître d' he was giving a hard time. Flip wasn't awed or cowed by Frank, but felt his magnetism and admired

him as a true liberal, a friend to black men in general and particular. When Davis lost his left eye in a 1954 car crash, it was Sinatra
who had taken him into his Palm Springs mansion while Sammy
recovered, joking that he'd call him "Old Brown Eye" from then on.

Bobby Darin emulated Sinatra in every way he could, from song
stylings to a fondness for grand gestures. One night he dragged Flip
outside to watch a man on a double-length ladder change letters on
the Sahara's blazing marquee. The sign featured Darin's name in giant letters on top, with Flip's name smaller below. "Watch this,"
Darin said. The workman reached up and removed the *F* in Flip's
name. For a moment the Sahara offered a bill of BOBBY DARIN
and LIP WILSON. Then the man replaced Flip's *F* with a larger *F*. He
switched letters one by one, each new letter larger than the one it
replaced, until Flip's name was nearly as big as Darin's, the way
Bobby wanted it. Flip was moving up in the world, making friends
who could help him rise higher.

On another night Flip and Darin were splitting a joint backstage
when the Sahara's night manager tapped at the door. He whispered
to Bobby, who suppressed a laugh. "Sure, send him in!" The next
thing Flip knew he was hugging Elvis Presley. Presley, a strapping
six-footer with jet-black hair and muttonchop sideburns, smiled
down at Flip and said, "You're right about the devil." Apparently he
took Reverend Leroy's shopping-spree temptation as a moral lesson.
Falling to his knees, he clasped hands with Flip and Darin and led
them in prayer. "Get thee away, Satan," Presley intoned as they
tried not to laugh. After the prayer, they all hugged. Elvis thanked
them and invited them to his show.

That was the year Elvis married Priscilla Beaulieu at the Aladdin.
Later that year Priscilla discovered that Elvis was having an affair
with Ann-Margret, his Swedish-American costar in *Viva Las Vegas*.
As Priscilla recalled in her memoir *Elvis and Me*, she confronted
him. "I picked up a flower vase and hurled it across the room, shat-

tering it against the wall. 'I hate her!' I shouted. 'Why doesn't she keep her ass in Sweden where she belongs?'" Presley swore he was sorry. "The silence between the two of us continued until Elvis said, 'Forgive me, please.' Then, with that little-boy look that always seemed to capture my heart, he said, using Flip Wilson's favorite line, 'I guess the devil made me do it!'"

Flip hired a manager named Monte Kay, a New York jazz impresario with bushy eyebrows and a smile as quick as his handshake. Kay was freckled and deeply perma-tanned, dark enough that some people thought he was black, which he took as a compliment. He'd started out at age seventeen, organizing jam sessions for Billie Holiday, Dizzy Gillespie, and Charlie Parker. In 1949 he and Parker launched Birdland, the legendary club on Broadway. Five years later, moonlighting as casting director for the Harold Arlen–Truman Capote musical *House of Flowers*, he met and married the show's co-star, Diahann Carroll. Kay went on to manage Herbie Mann, Stan Getz, Sonny Rollins, and the Modern Jazz Quartet while serving as a vice president of United Artists Records. Carroll went on to star in the groundbreaking sitcom *Julia* and to cheat on Monte with Sidney Poitier. Kay forgave her; they stayed friends after their 1963 divorce.

Monte Kay was Jewish—a plus for Flip, who liked to say he believed in Irishmen running the country, Jews running his business affairs, and black guys running the hundred-yard dash. Kay assured him they'd make a great team. "Flip, you can rise above color," he said. "With the right management you can be bigger than Redd Foxx, bigger than Red Skelton."

"How about Bill Cosby?"

"Bill who?"

Flip liked the sound of that. "Let's shake on it." Kay offered to draw up a management contract on the spot, but Flip said a handshake would do. "Because I trust you, Monte. And because if you ever screw me, I'll come after you." He was joking, but Kay would remember that tone of voice years later, when they fought.

Kay wanted to move fast while Flip was hot. His first comedy album, *Funny & Live at the Village Gate*, a tinny, cheaply made recording of his 1964 show, had gone nowhere. His second would be a different story. Flip churned out material, honing new riffs at top-tier clubs like the Bitter End in New York and San Francisco's hungry i, where Kay got him $3,000 a week. After taking years to pare down his Chris Columbus routine to an airtight seven minutes, he needed to find a more efficient gear. He told Kay that he wanted to present "an uninhibited celebration of black life." But how free could he afford to be? In hip clubs on the coasts and in Vegas he salted his sets with drug talk and four-letter words. On the Carson and Ed Sullivan shows as well as bland variety hours hosted by Pat Boone and Andy Williams, he shifted to a TV-safe vocabulary. He was creating what would later be thought of as a brand: Flip Wilson, the black comic who was safer than Redd Foxx, hipper (and cheaper) than Cosby. Accordingly his favorite twelve-letter word vanished from his act, even in Vegas. He could make it sound funny— "Motherfucker wants to ride a tin can to the moon!"—but onstage he now said nothing bluer than "hell," "damn," and "ass," all of which he claimed could be found in the Bible. (He was fudging on "ass," making Jesus' donkey the butt of a joke.) While claiming to be uninhibited he was hedging his bets, becoming more like Cosby and less like Foxx. And that didn't bother him. He saw it as strategy, not a sellout. Flip was never driven to reveal his inner self to the audience; he was out to entertain. His message, if he had one, was that race is only skin deep. His mission was now a three-year plan he and Kay concocted in 1966: get his own network TV show before the decade was out.

That summer he signed on as a regular on the *Kraft Summer Music Hall*, a rerun-season replacement for Andy Williams's prime-time variety hour. Flip promptly fell in with a pair of young stand-up comics working on the show. With their short hair and nervous smiles, George Carlin and Richard Pryor could have passed for management trainees. Onstage they wore jackets and ties and told jokes that wouldn't offend Captain Kangaroo. Carlin, twenty-eight, a New Yorker whose abusive father stalked him and his mother when George was young, escaped to the Air Force, like Flip, and apprenticed as a disc jockey before trying stand-up. Pryor, twenty-five, the son of a Peoria, Illinois, prostitute, grew up in his grand-mother's whorehouse and escaped to the smoky dives of the Chitlin' Circuit. A shy Cosby imitator stricken by stage fright, he made his television debut on a 1964 show hosted by ancient crooner Rudy Vallée, whose career dated back to the age of silent movies. Now Carlin and Pryor goofed around backstage, making fun of the crap they wrote for the *Kraft Summer Music Hall* while they mourned Lenny Bruce, who had passed away that summer of a morphine overdose, naked on his bathroom floor with his arm tied off. Apparently he died after falling off the toilet.

"To Lenny," Pryor said, sniffing a line of coke.

"Amen," Carlin said.

"Let me give you a word of advice, young motherfuckers," Flip said. "You're too good for this Kraft—"

"Cheesy shit?"

"I mean it." Flip had seen Pryor, newly arrived in New York, tip-toeing onstage at the Village Gate with a secondhand sport coat hanging on his spindly shoulders, trembling. Singer Nina Simone, the headliner that night, comforted the kid. "He shook like he had malaria," she said. "I couldn't bear to watch Richard shiver, so I put my arms around him and rocked him like a baby till he calmed down." Pryor worked squeaky-clean in those days, joking about Right Guard deodorant. "You ever read the deodorant can?" he asked. "It says, *Caution: Highly flammable. May explode.* I don't know about you people, but I don't want something under my arm gonna *explode*." He was what black comics called an Oreo comedian: black on the outside, white inside. And if Pryor was an Oreo, Carlin was a Rice Krispies treat, pale and square. Irish Catholic, a former altar boy, he wrote innocuous jokes for the animatronic *Summer Music Hall* host John Davidson, a pop star with a Pepsodent smile.

"You guys suck," Flip told Carlin and Pryor. "Why not do your own thing?"

"Right on, Mr. Featured Regular," they answered. "Easy for you to say. You got it made."

"Took me eleven years, Mr. Sitting Here Pulling John Davidson's Dick," Flip said, passing a plump joint to Carlin.

"Oh yeah? What if people knew you're a bigger doper than—"

"Than us!"

The joint came back around to Flip. "Who's going to tell 'em?"

Timothy Leary stood behind a microphone in San Francisco's Golden Gate Park, urging the assembled crowd, *"Turn on."* A shaggy-haired Harvard professor fired for skipping classes to do personal research on psychedelic drugs, Leary was a featured speaker at a gathering called the Human Be-In. He considered LSD a sacrament, and on this chilly January Saturday in 1967 he was instructing more than twenty-five thousand swaying, flower-bedecked celebrants to drop acid. Many complied, touching drug-laced sugar cubes or bits of blotter paper to their tongues. *"Tune in,"* Leary implored, encouraging his followers to share a wavelength with everyone else at the Be-In, one of the first late-sixties sit-ins, love-ins, and other -ins that would soon give NBC's *Laugh-In* its name. *"Drop out,"* Leary added.

Thanks mostly to television, trends and slogans that would once have taken years to grow from local to national could now spread so quickly that Leary's *"Turn on, tune in, drop out,"* introduced that afternoon in Golden Gate Park, would go from battle cry to cliché in record time.

Leary's flower children dropped out of middle-class, middlebrow society and into something new: a counterculture. Six months after the Be-In they welcomed a season they called the Summer of Love. But the hippies' optimism clashed with the war plans of Lyndon Johnson and Huey Newton. President Johnson had poured almost 500,000 U.S. troops, most of them draftees, into South Vietnam, a nation the size of Missouri. Fifty-eight thousand American soldiers would die there. Newton's Black Panther Party, meanwhile, spread east from its birthplace in Oakland, across the Bay from the Be-In, its ten thousand members dead serious about armed revolution. The Panthers' H. Rap Brown declared "guerrilla war on the honky white man." Eldridge Cleaver called for raping white women as "an insurrectionary act." More than a hundred race riots torched U.S. cities that summer, the worst in Newark and Detroit. Newark's July riots left twenty-three dead and more than a thousand people injured. The following weekend rioters set fire to hundreds of buildings in downtown Detroit, hurling trash cans through storefront windows, making off with everything from shoes, socks, and swimming suits to toys, TVs, and burglar alarms. Michigan governor George Romney dispatched troops from the state's National Guard to keep order. (Romney's son Mitt, twenty, who would run for president forty-four years later, led conservative students counterdemonstrating against a sit-in at Stanford.) President Johnson sent U.S. Army units to reinforce Romney's National Guardsmen. Detroit's street battles resulted in people dead, more than seven thousand arrested, and more than two thousand buildings in ruins. Johnson, turning his hound-dog eyes to a TV camera in the Oval Office, announced a National Day of Prayer for July 30, 1967. His aim was not to suppress black protest, the president said, but to curb "disorder in our cities. Innocent people, Negro and white, have been killed.

Damage to property owned by Negroes and whites is calamitous. Worst of all, the fear and bitterness which have been loosed will take long months to erase." On the Day of Prayer, another riot left parts of Milwaukee in flames. A government panel called the Kerner Commission, charged with finding the causes of the '67 riots, blamed white racism most of all. The commission declared that TV networks "must hire Negroes, must show Negroes on the air, must schedule programs relevant to the black ghetto."

Panthers and peaceniks alike declared their support for Muhammad Ali. After beating Sonny Liston for the heavyweight title in 1964, then felling Liston with a "phantom punch" in their rematch, Ali succeeded the Big Bear in the celebrity crowd at the Sir John in Overtown. Like Liston before him the twenty-three-year-old champ pawed the pretty waitresses in the Knight Beat lounge. Blonell fended him off, but like millions of others she hoped Ali would win his fight with the U.S. Army. "I got no quarrel with them Viet Cong. No Viet Cong ever called me nigger," Ali said after the Army drafted him. Stripped of his title, banned from the ring, he would lose the prime years of his career and millions of dollars in a three-year legal fight with the U.S. government while winning the hearts of Americans, black and white, including George Carlin.

Clean-shaven Carlin, still sporting the jacket and tie of a vice principal, had mocked the counterculture with characters like stoned Al Sleet, the Hippy-Dippy Weatherman. ("Tonight's forecast . . . *dark*.") With encouragement from Pryor and Flip, he turned his gimlet eye to Ali's troubles.

"Muhammad Ali has an unusual job," Carlin said. "Beating people up. Now, the government drafted him. The government wanted him to kill people. He said, 'No, that's where I draw the line. I'll beat 'em up, but I don't want to kill 'em.' And the government said, 'Well, if you won't kill 'em, we won't let you beat 'em up.'"

Flip touched on hot-button issues in his own way. Facing a mixed crowd after the race riots of 1967, he called his snazzy suit "my riot outfit. Got it in Detroit, right out of the window." He said he did all his shopping in the summer, when the prices went down, way down, to zero.

It was quite a suit: an orange satin shirt, paisley tie, double-breasted whipcord jacket, corduroy slacks, and alligator cowboy boots. Flip could afford to indulge his taste in threads. By now a semi-regular on *The Tonight Show*, he also signed a lucrative deal to make regular appearances on the prime-time *Ed Sullivan Show*. The time was ripe for a black comedian who was hip but just inhibited enough to reassure TV viewers that blacks and whites could get along. Reviewers called Flip hip, but they also called him nice. Calm. Friendly. Unthreatening.

"Mr. Wilson is a Negro," *The New York Times* reported, "and his material touches on matters that the average nightclub patron could not be expected to find amusing—race riots, looting, police brutality. But, hold, it is all in fun."

Flip opened his '67 sets with a trope he'd used before, a race riff with a twist. "I asked myself, 'Should I do racial material tonight?' I decided, 'Why not?' Why be hesitant about expressing my opinion? Why shouldn't I say to you, 'Ladies and gentlemen, we've got to do something about the Indians.'" This became the first cut of his 1967 album, *Cowboys and Colored People*. "The Indians are not ready for equality," Flip said. "I mean, do you want to build a fifty-thousand-dollar house and have some guy put a wigwam next door?" He went on to make fun of greedy preachers and tell a revisionist Bible story about his favorite underdog, Little David, who strummed a sweet harp. "Play that harp, honey!" cried a groupie, Bathsheba, after David slew Goliath, leader of a biker gang called the Philistines.

The album was a hit, and though it lost the Grammy to Cosby's

Revenge, Atlantic Records cashed in. Monte Kay, fielding new, better offers from TV and nightclub bookers, was delighted.

Flip wasn't. "What's our split with Atlantic?" he asked.

"Industry standard," Kay said. "We earn back our advance and get more after that."

Flip said that wasn't enough. "I've been living out of a suitcase for thirteen years. I might be on a roll now, but for how long?" He said they should start their own record label. "Grab it while we can, while we're hot."

"Grab what?"

"More."

With Kay's help he created a label of his own, Little David Records, an Atlantic subsidiary that started out with two comedians, Flip Wilson and George Carlin.

Herbie Shul picked an envelope off his coffee table in Miami Beach. "What's this?"

"Open it," Flip said, watching his old benefactor's eyes while Herbie read the amount on the check.

"I gave you six hundred. This is—"

"More."

"I knew it," Shul said, his eyes welling. "I knew you'd make it."

"Not yet. I ain't done yet." Flip hugged him. "In fact I gotta run."

Miami Shores, fifteen minutes from all-black Overtown, could have been another country. Palm trees thin as fashion models leaned west, caressed by inland breezes off Biscayne Bay. Boulevards lined with date and squat windmill palms curled past Bermuda-grass lawns fronting stucco ranch homes with tile roofs and two-car garages. Flip and Blonell arrived in a taxi, stopping in front of the biggest house on the block. He kept his hands over her eyes as he walked her up the driveway, past the carport to the porch.

"Okay," he said. "Open your eyes."

The sun blinded her at first. As her eyes adjusted, Flip led Blonell through her new white-carpeted living room and sparkling kitchen, through glass patio doors to a backyard that opened out onto a small, shimmering lake. "House is air conditioned," Flip said. It had four bedrooms, two and a half baths, a two-car garage. "But there's one little problem with the neighbors," he whispered. *"They're all white."*

8

One Giant Leap

◆ Flip and Blonell settled into their lakeside house with twelve-year-old Michelle, Blonell's daughter with Lawrence Trice, and their sons, eight-year-old David and six-year-old Kevin. The three kids spent long afternoons in the backyard, climbing a rope ladder to a tree house in a sprawling ficus that shaded the patio. "It was like a party just for us," Michelle remembers. "As the only people of color in the neighborhood, we felt special." Blonell quit waitressing and stayed home, keeping house, cooking the fried chicken and waffles Flip loved, and meting out punishment when the kids misbehaved. "She was the disciplinarian," recalls Kevin, who looked so much like his father that Flip called him Junior. "Pops gave us a few whippings with his belt, but his heart wasn't really in it. Mom was the tough one. If we really screwed up, she used an extension cord that left welts." Flip took them all to the bowling alley, where he rolled scores in the 170s and 180s, sometimes topping 200 and doing a victory dance in his two-tone bowling shoes. He liked to watch his kids swim, too. Flip couldn't swim a lick, so he hired a private lifeguard to watch over the children while they splashed in the lake behind the house. A black lifeguard, for extra safety.

In the evenings they'd make Jiffy Pop and watch TV, with Flip giving the boys a master class in comedy. "I was the little guy, just trying to keep up," Kevin recalls. "I'd hear a line and say, 'Joke! That's a joke. The man on TV made a funny face.'"

"He's mugging," Flip said. "You can be funny with facial expressions or movements. Or even just waiting." He pointed out how comics paused for an instant before delivering a joke—that was timing. "Or you can be funny with words. You two haven't gone far enough in school to understand a lot of verbal humor, but you'll dig it as you learn more words."

Looking back forty years later, David says, "Those were the times we loved, just hanging out with Pops." Seeing Flip with one of his legal pads, "We'd ask what he was doing. 'Working on a joke,' he said. And he'd try it out on us." The boys didn't always laugh. Flip called them a tough crowd and said he liked that about them. As he put it, "Who wants bullshitters for kids?" Not that David and Kevin thought he was anything less than the funniest man alive. They heard the people laugh and cheer when Flip was the man on TV. It was just that sometimes his sons felt too gloomy to laugh because Pops was getting ready to leave again.

After a monthlong family honeymoon in the new house, Flip left and never stayed there for more than a few days. He split his time between three residences: a bachelor pad in the Hollywood Hills with a pool and a sauna; a Greenwich Village brownstone he shared with Monte Kay, where he crashed during club gigs and stints guest-hosting the Carson show; and the Miami house, where he quickly got antsy. Blonell suspected he was eager to reconnect with "road girls" like Sylvia Davis, a Jamaican beauty who sometimes traveled with him. Flip countered by accusing Blonell of cheating on him. Sometimes he said he couldn't wait to get out of Florida, out of her "clutches." Despite their Jiffy Pop nights and comedy lessons, the boys' prime memory of Flip in those days was his departures. Flip told them to think of him as a traveling salesman. His job was on the road, selling fun. David and Kevin would stand at the picture window watching him drive off in a rental car, then cry themselves to sleep.

Hating those moments as much as his sons did, Flip reacted with his usual pragmatism. He started leaving later at night, after they went to bed.

He wasn't lying about his job. He *was* selling fun, and the price was going up. Flip was now at the top of his powers, winning raves for his guest shots on the *Ed Sullivan Show, Carol Burnett Show, Dean Martin Comedy Hour, Merv Griffin Show, Hollywood Squares, Jerry Lewis Show, Andy Williams Show, Joey Bishop Show,* and *Laugh-In,* where he and Sammy Davis Jr. turned Pigmeat Markham's "Here come the judge!" into the country's favorite catchphrase. A *New York Times* profile, "It Pays to Be Flip," reported that he was "scheduled for his own special on NBC, and that network has signed him to a fat five-year development contract which will lead to his own series." The deal included $40,000 for a one-hour pilot.

Then as now, an Angeleno needed wheels, so Flip spent $18,000 (equal to about $120,000 today) on a silver-blue Rolls-Royce Corniche convertible. It was the first car he'd ever owned. Tooling around paradise behind its mahogany steering wheel, he rolled from meeting to meeting, filling the car's ashtray with pungent-smelling roaches. At one powwow with manager Monte Kay and a handful of "financial advisers," he listened restlessly while the money men pitched investment opportunities. Kay couldn't imagine how a grade-school dropout, however sharp, could choose among the stock, bond, and real-estate offers the advisers described. One was for a cattle ranch, prompting Flip to shout, *"Yee-ha."* Yet Kay knew better than to patronize his client by volunteering too much advice. Or to underestimate him. When the men finished their presentations, Flip thanked them and delighted them by saying, "Okay, I'm in." Turning to Kay, he added, "Monte, you're in, too. But I'm not sifting this shit. I want you and these guys to pick the best investments. And every dollar I invest, you and them are going to match. If I go broke, you motherfuckers going with me." It was a policy he would stick to for twenty years, earning him more than $10 million.

NBC still needed the right vehicle for its Rolls-driving pop phenomenon. At first the network hoped to team him in a sitcom with Lincoln Perry, better known as Stepin Fetchit. That pairing fizzled after a 1968 CBS documentary, *Of Black America*, portrayed the sixty-six-year-old Perry as a discredited throwback to the days of vaudeville and silent-film darkies. In the documentary Bill Cosby, then thirty, described Perry's work as that of a "lazy, stupid crapshooter, a chicken-stealing idiot." Perry objected, saying, "They're making me a villain. If it wasn't for me there wouldn't be no Bill Cosby." But his career was effectively over. With Stepin Fetchit on the sidelines, Flip wrote and shot a pilot in the *Laugh-In* mode. While less overtly topical than the slyly political *Smothers Brothers Comedy Hour* on CBS, his pilot was full of nods to current events. That was Monte Kay's idea, and his timing couldn't have been worse. With Martin Luther King assassinated on a Memphis balcony that April, and Robert Kennedy killed in a Los Angeles hotel kitchen in June, viewers wanted escape, not confrontation. NBC never aired Flip's pilot, but the network still believed in him.

"When Flip grins, he lights up the stage," NBC executive Herb Schlosser told writer James Hudson. Audience research showed Flip Wilson topping the charts in a factor called likability. As Richard Pryor told Flip, "You're the only performer who goes onstage and the audience wants *you* to like *them*." According to Schlosser, president of the network's West Coast operations at the time, "We kept building him up with guest appearances on other shows, and filling in for Johnny Carson." As Carson's most popular substitute, Flip proved he could please middle America as well as the Nebraskan king of late night. In fact *The Tonight Show*'s ratings went up when he hosted. One memorable evening Jimi Hendrix, backed by

Tonight's tight band, tore into "Lover Man" and promptly blew an amp in a shower of sparks. Guest host Flip improvised, joking and soft-shoeing for several minutes while technicians found and connected a new amp, then Hendrix ran through a performance that his fans still YouTube today.

Schlosser and his NBC colleagues saw Flip as a TV pioneer who could draw millions of black viewers as well as the great white majority, but couldn't decide how to use him. Should he star in a sitcom, a sketch-comedy show, or a variety hour? Or an all-black talk show for the "urban" demographic? One compromise would have cast him in a sitcom about a talk-show host. With time running short, Schlosser and company decided not to decide just yet. Rather than put Flip on the fall 1969 schedule, they'd give him another shot at a special and make a final decision when the ratings came in.

The network sent Bob Henry to discuss the special with Flip at the Chateau Marmont in the foothills of Hollywood, just off Sunset Boulevard. Henry, a veteran producer-director, was an amiable fellow who claimed he could get along with anyone. He'd steered Dean Martin and Jerry Lewis through a *Colgate Comedy Hour* in the last angry days before their mid-fifties breakup, when Dean greeted Jerry by saying, "You're nothing to me but a fucking dollar sign." Henry had called the shots on song-and-dance hours starring Roy Rogers, Dinah Shore, and Andy Williams, and he'd produced Nat Cole's ill-fated series back in 1956, which gave him what some insiders called a "black track record." "Color didn't matter to me," Henry said. "I wanted to work with Flip because he had a rare magic. Bob Hope, for instance, could walk onstage and say 'Hi,' and the audience laughed. Flip had that, too."

Henry was not quite five and a half feet tall, his large head topped with shaggy auburn hair. Sporting a tan blazer over an open-collared shirt that showed a thatch of chest hair, he found his quarry getting a rubdown by the hotel's swimming pool, facedown on a padded table and wearing nothing but a towel around his waist. Flip made no move to interrupt the session, but gave a little wave when Henry introduced himself.

Henry began by saying how much he admired Flip's work, particularly his intimacy with the audience. He quickly regretted the word. "Intimacy" had sounded just right when he was rehearsing these remarks in the car on the way over, but now it registered as somehow almost dirty, as if Flip were stripping or screwing the audience. "I mean, um . . ."

Flip grunted. He wasn't going to make this easy for the network's hired hand. The cat wasn't even Jewish like the white advisers he trusted.

"Look, Flip, if I could stand here and ad-lib a show for you, I would. I'm not that smart, but I've got some ideas." Henry had been thinking about the camera's eye. A typical TV screen was twenty-one inches across, he said—barely enough to get a clear view of two faces. Yet producers tried to mimic the movies and Broadway with panoramic views of the action, reducing TV performers to mouse size. "We need to get closer. Clutter up the screen and you lose the most interesting thing in the world, the human face." Henry had Flip's own rubbery face in mind. If he got the chance to direct Flip's special, he'd shoot tight enough for viewers to see every raised eyebrow and devilish grin. He'd strip everything down—no elaborate scenery, no more than two or three faces in the foreground. And he'd shoot most of the show in the round, so that viewers felt like part of the racially mixed studio audience, sharing that . . . intimacy.

Flip had shut his eyes. Was he asleep? After a moment, he said, "I hear you." That was it; the meeting appeared to be over. Henry retraced his steps through the lobby, wondering if he'd blown his chance. Several days later he heard from the network. Flip liked him. He wanted Henry to produce his special.

David and Kevin raced to answer the phone. Flip was due home any minute. "It's Pops. Hi, Pops! Where are you?"

But Flip wasn't coming. He had to stay in L.A. and work. It was a make-or-break time in his career, he explained. He couldn't afford to waste his time with some snot-nose kids who'd probably give him the mumps. Maybe he'd get to Florida next month or the month after that.

Kevin burst into tears. David moped to the kitchen to give his mother the news. "Typical," Blonell said, pulling a dinner plate off the table. She made no move to answer the doorbell when it rang.

Michelle and the boys ran to the door. "Who's there?"

"It's God," said a rumbling voice. "Dominus Nabisco. Want a cookie?" Flip barreled in with his arms full of gifts. He'd called from a pay phone around the corner. He had candy, stuffed animals, and Archie comic books for Michelle and toddler Tamara, born in 1966, as well as footballs and miniature boxing gloves and G.I. Joes for the boys. Blonell settled for a peck on the cheek.

One night that summer they all piled onto the couch to watch grainy pictures from the moon. At 10:56 P.M. Miami Shores time on July 20, 1969, astronaut Neil Armstrong stepped off the last rung of a stainless-steel ladder attached to Apollo 11's lunar excursion module. He was fulfilling President Kennedy's vow—*before this decade is out*—with five months to spare. With the Wilsons and 600 million others watching worldwide, Armstrong planted a rubber boot on the lunar surface, saying, "That's one small step for a man, one giant leap for mankind." But during the radio transmission to Mission Control in Houston, a quarter-million-mile trip that took 1.3 seconds even at the speed of light, a word got lost in transit. Armstrong's slightly nasal voice reached earth as "one small step for man," a glitch that NASA wouldn't acknowledge for another decade. The difference mattered only to those who parsed syllables for a living. Flip, for one, couldn't help thinking that "for *a* man" would have been better. Armstrong's original quote was tautological, since "man" and "mankind" meant the same thing. Saying "for *a* man," on the other hand, would contrast Armstrong's short stride off the ladder with the monumental achievement it represented. Not that NASA was consulting Flip Wilson on its astronauts' scripts. But Mission Control could have done worse than to call the lakeside house in Miami Shores. Sitting up late with his kids, watching Armstrong and Edwin "Buzz" Aldrin tromp through moon dust that had sat undisturbed for ten million years, Flip was thinking about syllables.

What you're lookin' at is what you're gonna get.

What you're seein' is what you could get.

What you see is . . .

Six weeks to the day after the Apollo astronauts began their long voyage home, NBC aired *The Flip Wilson Special.* For a month beforehand rumors spread that the network regarded the Labor Day special as an on-air pilot for a weekly Flip Wilson show. Flip had written and rewritten material and worked on sets and blocking with producer Henry, who as planned would shoot much of the show as TV theater in the round.

Flip's opening monologue featured the Reverend Leroy and his shopaholic wife. Standing on a carpeted island ringed by a multiracial studio audience, he channeled the Rev's wife as she battled temptation before reaching the line that always brought down the house: "The *devil* made me buy this dress!" A day later school yards, construction sites, college campuses, and office bullpens from coast to coast rang with the line: *The devil made me buy this dress!*

Less quoted but no less important was a sketch that came later in the Labor Day special. Jonathan Winters, cross-dressing as gray-haired, matronly Maude Frickert, boarded a plane ruled by a stewardess decked out in high heels, a hip-hugging minidress, and a wig with a flip. "Anything I can get for you, little old broad?" the stewardess asked.

"Yes," said Winters-as-Maude. "Get me a little old man, Miss . . . ?"

"Geraldine," Flip said. *"Geraldine Jones, honey. That's J-O-N-E-S . . . honey!"*

Here was the coming-out of a character that would dominate Flip's act and much of the rest of his life. He named her after the real Geraldine, the prettiest girl in The Hill neighborhood of Depression-era Jersey City, who'd duped little Clerow into shoplifting fake fingernails for her. Her voice recalled the squeaky screech of Butterfly McQueen as Prissy, the *Gone with the Wind* maid who "don't know nothin' 'bout birthin' babies," as well as Ernestine Wade as Sapphire, the nagging wife on *Amos 'n' Andy*. While Geraldine's hip-rolling walk might have come straight from burlesque, her attitude—*"Don't you touch me!"*—suggested women's lib. Her catchphrase was a deeply ironic assertion of self that owed much of its punch to the fact that it came from a man in a skirt:

"What you see is what you get!"

This brassy, sexy, liberated "woman" was the apotheosis of Flip's drag characters. Geraldine was the right girl at the right moment, and Flip knew it. That's why he saved her for his make-or-break special.

"With Geraldine, I had several things going for me," he said years later. "I had the element of surprise, with people seeing her for the first time. I had the generation gap between Maude Frickert, a grandmother, and Geraldine, a women's libber. And then there was the black and white." Some white viewers didn't like seeing stewardess Geraldine boss little old Maude around, but by the end of the flight they were girlfriends. Flip had found a way to sashay through some of the most divisive issues of the era and make a safe landing.

Flip's 1969 special mixed the sweet (Jackie DeShannon singing "Put a Little Love in Your Heart") with the strange (Andy Williams singing Johnny Cash's "A Boy Named Sue," Flip and *Laugh-In*'s Arte Johnson spoofing *Midnight Cowboy*), but it was Geraldine and the devil who made the show a smash. Flip's showcase grabbed 42 percent of the viewers in its time slot. It ranked eighth among all shows that aired that week. *What you see is what you get* went viral the old-fashioned way, by word of mouth. Monte Kay was ecstatic. "They'll give you your own show for sure," he said.

The program Flip had in mind would steer clear of politics. It was true that nobody in his inner circle would dream of voting for Richard Nixon. Flip hated thinking of 400,000 American boys in Vietnam, many no older than Airman Wilson had been. He grieved for the martyred Martin Luther King and Malcolm X, and seethed when fourteen Chicago cops sneaked into a Black Panthers hideout and shot two Panthers dead while they slept. Still, Flip believed that politics and comedy were matter and antimatter. He wasn't surprised when CBS canceled the satirical Smothers Brothers, who ridiculed people who voted for Nixon. Why piss off half your potential audience? A slicker approach might keep everybody tuning in.

Monte Kay scheduled a series of meetings with NBC's West Coast executives in the balmy Burbank winter of 1969–70. Again there was talk of a Flip Wilson sitcom. "We were afraid of tackling all the variety-hour competition," Herb Schlosser recalled. *Laugh-In* was TV's number-one program. The 1969–70 ratings also featured *The Red Skelton Hour* at number seven and *The Doris Day Show* in tenth place. Among the top twenty were six other variety shows, starring Bill Cosby, Jim Nabors, Carol Burnett, Dean Martin, Johnny Cash, and Glen Campbell. As Schlosser told Flip and his manager, "We're afraid of tackling all that variety-hour competition. We see Flip in a half-hour situation comedy."

"I'm not up for that," Flip responded. "I've got a great deal of experience emceeing and performing in nightclubs. I *know* I can carry a variety show."

According to Schlosser, "We looked at Flip, then we looked at each other and said, 'The heck with it. Let's go for broke.'"

They offered him a Thursday-night variety hour on the fall 1970 schedule. Flip felt a lump in his throat. His fifteen-year plan was paying off right on time. Fifteen years had passed since he mustered out of the Air Force and now here he was, sitting in a conference room while half a dozen powerful white TV executives told him how brilliant and likable he was. They proposed the standard TV-star deal: Flip would headline a show owned by NBC. He would earn up to a million dollars a year. Residuals would add more if the show ran in syndication. It was Clerow's dream come true, the last thing a Jersey City dropout who'd ridden Greyhounds on the Chitlin' Circuit had any business imagining. Except that Flip *had* imagined it. Every night that he had passed the hat and come up short, he pictured this moment. Typing up invoices at the Manor Plaza, bumping his hip on Charles Calloway's piano in Stockton, dozing under a Joshua tree by a California highway, soaking up applause at the Apollo, shaking Johnny Carson's hand on the best night of his life—Flip had dreamed of the day when one of the networks offered him the most precious commodity in the entertainment world, a weekly hour of prime time.

Flip said no. "Not good enough." He knew NBC had made a handsome profit off his Labor Day special. Knowing how much the network wanted him on its 1970 schedule, he was about to give everyone in the room a lesson in going for broke. "I'll do it, but it's my show," he said. "I want to own it."

It was a ballsy demand. By "own it" he meant he wanted syndication rights. Not the usual residuals that contract players received, which might amount to $50 or $100 per rerun when a show went into syndication, but more—the much greater share that producers got in the same situation. Owning syndication rights to *I Love Lucy* was what made millionaires of Lucille Ball and Desi Arnaz. It's the arrangement that brought coproducer Jerry Seinfeld hundreds of millions of dollars while his *Seinfeld* supporting cast collected tens of thousands in residuals. Still, Flip's demand would be an issue only if his show became a multiyear hit. Schlosser and the others knew as well as he did that four out of five new shows died within a year. As a producer, Flip would have to take less money up front in exchange for his ownership stake, so the immediate risk was at his end of the table. If he happened to be right his stake might cost the network a few million, but it would mean they had a hit show on their hands. They could live with a bargain like that. So why not give the rookie what he wanted?

Schlosser said, "It would be very unusual. We'd like you to reconsider."

"I won't."

"In that case . . ." Schlosser offered a handshake. Unlike Dean Martin, Carol Burnett, and the vast majority of other TV personalities, Flip would be both producer and star when *The Flip Wilson Show* opened that fall.

On their way to the parking lot, Monte Kay turned to his bullheaded client. "I sure hope you know what we're doing," he said.

9

Thursday Night Lights

◆ He bounded through a cheering crowd onto a six-sided stage. Behind him, 644 lightbulbs spelled *FLIP* in giant arrow-shaped letters, the glittering logo for his show. Brassy theme music played as he bowed, bobbing on the balls of his feet, to the ecstatic fans seated around the stage. On TV screens across America, he was framed in a wide shot that showed his whole body. Dressed in a groovy suit, pink shirt, and orange silk tie, Flip grinned like a cat who had just eaten the world's tastiest canary.

"For quite a while now, everyone's been asking me what *The Flip Wilson Show*'s gonna be like," he began. "Yesterday a guy ran into the side of my car and said, 'I stopped you because I want to know what *The Flip Wilson Show*'s gonna be like.'" He laughed, and the mostly white audience joined in. "I decided the best way to put it would be to say . . . *Watch out!*"

Dancing sideways, he let the line hang for a second, milking the moment.

"We think you're gonna dig it," he told the world.

It hadn't been easy. By premiere night, running on fumes and adrenaline, he looked relieved to have the show under way. He'd spent months writing jokes, scenes, guest lists, and reminders to himself on his legal pads for five or six hours at a stretch. The great multitasker of 1970 honed his dance moves by watching himself on videotape and improved his squeaky singing voice by working with a voice coach. Then, after producer Henry hired a writing team, Flip found himself cooped up for weeks with five graying industry hands. Herbie Baker, an old friend of Henry's, led a team that included Hal Goodman and Larry Klein, who'd written for the old *Jack Benny Show*, as well as Bob Weiskopf and Bob Schiller, a pair of *I Love Lucy* veterans who'd worked together since the early days of sitcoms. The youngest of the five writers was fifty-six. And then there was Winston Moss, twenty-five, sitting on a couch in the corner. "Flip and I were the black guys in the room," recalls Moss. "The others were older and Jewish, extremely liberal but not what you'd call 'street.' It was funny to watch them acting out jokes, trying to sound black. The Panthers were saying 'Right on' in those days, so these guys jumped around saying 'Left on' and 'Right off' and 'Right Guard' to see if it sounded funny."

As the junior member of the writing team, Moss earned $450 a week, less than half what the others got. "And I was thrilled to be working with these old pros on a network show. Flip still thought of himself as a nightclub comic, not yet a TV guy. He'd change stuff around, make it sound more like him—Bob Henry called it 'putting a layer of Flip on top'—but he got along with the writers, gave them respect even when he changed their lines."

Flip wanted to make the show as hip as he could without losing the middle of the country, a place he passed through during his Chitlin' Circuit days but could hardly claim to know. Yet he had a sense of what Omaha and Evansville would accept from a black man. Goodman and Klein never quite caught on, though they contributed some of the early shows' memorable lines, and Henry eventually fired them. The two old jokemeisters wept when he gave them the bad news. Flip wanted progress, not stasis. He wanted his buddies Carlin and Pryor on his staff, but they were both on the road, remaking their own acts with no TV cameras around. Carlin the clever conservative had started hanging with hippies and folk-ies, smoking pot and dropping acid ("value-changing drugs," he called them), rejecting his past work, including fake-news bits he'd performed with Flip on *The Tonight Show*. "I thought, 'I'm doing su-perficial things about the media and disk jockeys, and I'm doing them for the enemy,'" Carlin said. Trading his blazer for jeans and a sweater, he grew out his Republican haircut and joked about being a "tokin'" comedian. "Buddy Hackett says 'shit' in his act," Carlin told a starchy Vegas crowd. "Redd Foxx, too. I don't say 'shit,' but I'll smoke a little of it." He insulted his audience at the Frontier Ho-tel, calling them "golfing assholes." His riffs on the Vietnam War at a Playboy Club in Wisconsin got him booed off the stage. Banned from Playboy Clubs as well as *The Tonight Show*, Carlin was soon collecting unemployment.

Richard Pryor was having an even worse time than his former writing partner. Stoned and coke-addled, stricken by stage fright, Pryor struck back at one heckler by stabbing the man with a fork. He silenced a gray-haired matron at a front table by unzipping his fly and peeing on the stage, saying, "Think *this* is funny?" Finally, in 1970, he froze onstage one night at the Aladdin Hotel in Las Vegas. As he recalled years later, the twenty-nine-year-old Pryor suddenly "realized what a sellout I was." He stood in the spotlight for an end-less minute, looking lost, and then asked, "What the fuck am I do-ing here?" and walked off. Stalking through the casino, he yanked off his jacket and dropped it. Next came his shirt and tie, pants, shoes, socks, and finally his underwear. He hopped onto a green-felt card table, stretched out naked, and said, "Blackjack!" In one ver-sion of the story, a bystander points at Pryor's penis, saying, "There goes *that* myth!" Whatever his shortcomings, Pryor was in no con-dition to join a TV writing team in 1970. Flip would have to make do with the writing staff Henry had assembled.

The worst headache in the tense hours leading up to the first *Flip*

Wilson Show had nothing to do with the writing. It was James Brown. "James made everybody nervous," Moss remembers. "Everybody but Flip." Flip wanted to make a statement with his guest list, to prove that his sort of comedy could transcend color or ethnicity. What better way to do that than by starting with a roster that included the stiffly British David Frost, the Muppets of *Sesame Street,* and the Godfather of Soul? The only trouble was that Brown wanted to make jokes about Afro Sheen, a product head writer Baker had never heard of. Baker nixed that idea. Then, hours before dress rehearsal, producer Henry pulled Flip aside. Brown was throwing a fit, he said. "He wants his own band backing him, not our musicians." Brown threatened to walk unless Henry hired his men at Vegas-showroom rates.

"I'll handle it," Flip said. He found Brown stewing backstage and offered him a hug. "My brother James, the second-hardest-working man in show business!" But Brown wasn't buying Flip's brother act. He shook his big pompadoured head, complaining until Flip finally cut him off. Flip walked Brown to the wall behind the stage. The wall was covered top to bottom with Flip's name, right-side-up and upside-down. "James, look at that. That's equal opportunity right there," he said. Flip told Brown that he wasn't a hired hand around here. He was the boss, which meant he paid the bills, and the house band was already in the budget. "If your cats want to play for free, bring 'em on. Otherwise it's my show and my band." Brown gave that a moment's thought. Then he smiled, a blaze of pearly whites, and went to rehearse with Flip's band.

Finally it was time for lights, camera, Clerow. The first sketch on the September 17, 1970, debut of *The Flip Wilson Show* exemplified the host's amiable, self-referential approach. After his opening *"Watch out!"* he shifted into a discussion of what the first sketch should be. "Since this is our first program, everybody thought we'd open with a big production number—great scenery, beautiful costumes, dancing girls, the works. We found out that would cost a hundred and four thousand dollars." This was a meta-version of the budget discussions he'd been having with everyone from Henry and NBC executives to James Brown. "I said, 'Gentlemen, that's ridiculous. The show's gonna start out in the hole if you do that. Everybody's seen those production numbers on other shows. What they *haven't* seen is a hundred and four thousand dollars.'" An actor dressed as a policeman brought him an overstuffed envelope. Flip announced, "So I decided we'd open by showing you what a hundred and four thousand looks like." It was actually a puny sheaf of fake bills, a fact Flip explained by saying that his $104,000 included "five hundred in *cash*." The point wasn't the money anyway. The point was his byplay with the cop. The tall, stern, white cop kept a close eye on the nattily dressed host, who reached for the cash and mimed running away—Flip's old Stockton "dash." The cop kept a hand on his gun as if warning him. Five minutes into its existence, the show had nodded to Watts and Newark, updating Flip's "riot suit" riff while alluding to the crucial behind-the-scenes matter of who owned and paid for the show. Flip pointed at the cop's twitchy gun hand—a *gotcha* moment—and grinned before dismissing the cop with a wave of his hand. "With remarkable narrative economy," wrote pop-culture critic Meghan Sutherland of Oklahoma State University, "Wilson has raised the specter of real racial violence, laughed in its face and roused the audience with the prospect of a new kind of variety show. All without a single dancing girl. It is hard to imagine a more fitting debut."

Next, Reverend Leroy presided over his Church of What's Happening Now. Decked out in a ready-for-prime-time tailcoat, string tie, and spats, the covetous preacher paced around his pulpit with a seraphic smile on his face. Here as in the first skit, Flip could have been commenting on his own changing fortunes when the Rev cried, "We're in a new era now. Movin' up!" Turning to his favorite theological topic, the collection, he adds, "But before this church can run, it's gotta crawl."

"Let it crawl," his deacons chime in.

"And before this church can run, it's gotta stand up and walk."

"Let it walk, Rev, let it walk."

"And to make it run, it's gonna take *money*."

"Let it crawl, Rev, let it crawl!"

After James Brown sang with Flip's musicians, Flip danced with Big Bird from *Sesame Street*, spinning faster and faster until he fell flat on his back, exhausted. As the camera zoomed in, Flip said, "This equal opportunity is killing me."

Next came David Frost in a sky-blue Carnaby Street suit, his hair hanging over his ears. Playing himself, the urbane host of a syndicated chat show, Frost introduced "an unusual young woman. The, um, 'average' woman . . . Geraldine Jones!" The house band played her onstage with a bump-and-grind stripper tune. Flip wore a purple Pucci miniskirt with matching hose, pumps, and purse. He was no hairy old drag queen like Jonathan Winters's Maude or Milton Berle's galumphing goon—Geraldine was *sexy*. She had Flip's shapely legs and a bust that attracted the attention of NBC censors. Though he was known for keeping a close eye on production costs, Flip hired costumer Bill Belew, who made Elvis Presley's capes and leather jumpsuits, to design Geraldine's eye-catching bra. A year after the Smothers Brothers' war with CBS censors led to their cancellation, NBC's standards-and-practices department objected to Geraldine's falsies. Once Flip took an inch out of the bra, the censors left him alone.

Frost kissed Flip's hand and got scolded for it. "You don't know me that well," Geraldine chided him in her trademark yowl. Anyway, she said, she already had a fella. "His name's Killer." As viewers would learn, Killer was never seen with Geraldine in her appearances because he was "currently incarcerated."

"Are you engaged?"

"Not exactly. He gave me a ring, but I couldn't keep up the payments."

Frost offered a cigarette. No thanks, Geraldine said. "I don't drink, I don't smoke, and I don't do windows." Lounging in a swivel chair, she showed a little leg, telling him, "What you see is what you get!" Writers Goodman and Klein had helped Flip pare the line down from earlier versions. Delivered with such sass that the audience whistled and applauded, it was twice as funny coming from a man in a dress. That may help explain why it became TV's most popular catchphrase, topping *Laugh-In*'s "Here come the judge" and "Sock it to me!" as well as Flip's own "The devil made me do it." Soon "What you see is what you get" inspired a thousand imitations, a pop song, and a software graphics acronym, WYSIWYG, that would carry the term into the twenty-first century. The line would chase Flip through the rest of his life, delighting and eventually annoying him. Now, though, waiting for the applause to ebb, he gave Frost a lascivious wink. They were rolling. When Frost complimented Geraldine on her outfit, she said she'd made it herself.

"You're quite a couturier," Frost observed.

"You better watch your mouth, honey!"

After Flip sang a gender-bending "All of Me," flexing meaty biceps on "Take my arms, I'll never lose them," he traded jolly fist- and hip-bumps with Frost. As the credits rolled—wobbling in the way of shaky seventies TV graphics—Henry's lens closed on Flip's round, glowing face as he straightened up to his full five-foot-six, beaming at the camera and uncounted millions of viewers. Uncounted till the Nielsens came in.

A flustered assistant brought Herb Schlosser a sheaf of pages fresh from the Xerox machine. "You need to see this." The NBC vice president scanned rows of numbers copied from the new season's first ratings book. He'd expected solid ratings from *The Flip Wilson Show*. Schlosser thought Flip might win his Thursday-evening time slot against the twee CBS sitcom *Family Affair* and a new medical drama on ABC, *Matt Lincoln*, starring Vince Edwards of *Ben Casey* fame. He thought Flip might even have a chance to crack the Nielsens' top twenty for the week. Instead he saw *The Flip Wilson Show* dominating its time slot. Flip had done more than crush his Thursday competition; he had won the night and even the week. Flip's show was the number-one new program of 1970. And the reviews were as strong as the numbers. According to *The New York Times'* influential Jack Gould,

> Flip Wilson scored last night as the television season's first new hit. The burgeoning talents of Mr. Wilson, whose energies are matched by a felicitous sense of timing, had been increasingly obvious in his many guest appearances.
>
> But for the debut of his own show he and his producer, Bob Henry, were truly astute showmen. There is probably no routine more hazardous than a female impersonation, but Mr. Wilson pulled it off hilariously as the swinging Geraldine.
>
> If his luck holds, the comedian could be proof of the theatrical adage—where there is personality and ability, matters of race are sublimely irrelevant.

Ten days later, Gould summed up the new season: "The energetic and personable Wilson easily walked off with the first week's honors, frolicking through monologues, sketches and choreographic nonsense with a contagious relish. Wilson will have his hands full doing what amounts to a special a week, but he and his producer, Bob Henry, are on the right track."

Henry, Schlosser, and Monte Kay popped corks and lit cigars.

NBC's new number-one program had drawn almost forty million viewers. (That year's Super Bowl had attracted only six million more.) As the weeks passed, Flip consistently beat perennial ratings leaders like *Gunsmoke* and hot properties like *The Mod Squad*. His ratings surpassed even those of *Laugh-In* and *Bonanza* to make *The Flip Wilson Show* not only NBC's number-one program but the top variety show on television. Throughout the fall Flip would duel ABC's doctor drama *Marcus Welby, M.D.* for the ratings lead among all shows. For the moment, at least, America was gripped by what newspapers were calling "Flip Fever."

Whoopi Goldberg, who was then a fourteen-year-old growing up in the New York City projects, never missed Flip's show. "Everybody watched. It was appointment TV," she recalls. "I'd go to my Catholic school the next day and kids were all doing Geraldine, saying 'What you see is what you get, honey!' Even the nuns! You'd hear the nuns say, 'The devil made me do it,' and they'd giggle."

The star was thrilled by his ratings, but not surprised. "I worked hard for this," he told Henry. "It took me fifteen years to be an overnight success." In October *Time* magazine hailed the "sly black face" of what it called "America's fastest-rising comedian, black or white. Not so long ago, Flip was scratching something like $15 a night out of low-rent nightclubs. Then he made a one-night stand on Johnny Carson's *Tonight* show. He has mastered the deceptive ease of the first-class TV host. Even with all of the mugging, eye rolling and Negro dialect, Wilson's routines are inoffensive and totally devoid of racial rancor." Flip owed some of his success to the country's five million or so black TV households, where each week's show was a special event, his success celebrated as a turning point comparable to Jackie Robinson's breaking baseball's color barrier. Yet Flip's vast audience was at least 80 percent white, a factor that vindicated his booking instincts. That fall he shared his hexagonal stage with Perry Como, Lola Falana, Louis Armstrong, Bing Crosby, Stevie

Wonder, Tony Randall, Lena Horne, Robert Goulet, Loretta Lynn, and the Supremes. Only on *The Flip Wilson Show* would you find B.B. King paired with Sid Caesar, or Andy Griffith with Curtis "Superfly" Mayfield.

"Making fruit salad," Flip called it. "There's something for everybody."

NBC boosted the show's ad rate from $44,000 a minute to $53,000. Soon it was up to $65,000 a minute, a sum Flip called "a hell of a price for a goddamn dropout." Due to his ownership stake in what the wobbly credits labeled "Clerow Productions," much of the money Gillette, Ford, Campbell's Soup, and other sponsors paid for commercials wound up in his pocket.

Flip's momentum was contagious. His second show featured his old friend Bobby Darin, who hadn't had a hit song in years. The network didn't want Darin on its top-rated new program any more than the Sahara had wanted Flip to open for Darin in '66, but Flip wasn't asking. He instructed Henry to book Bobby, and a string of guest shots on *The Flip Wilson Show* helped revive Darin's career. In one of Flip's favorite sketches they played expectant fathers in a baby-care class run by Tim Conway. When Conway, calling the roll, cried, "Booker T. Washington Jones," Darin said, "Here!" while Flip answered to "Pat Muldoon." He grabbed a Caucasian doll from a box for diapering practice only to be stopped by Conway, who said, "Yours is in the back of the box." Flip settled for a black doll, saying, "They all look alike to me." In the end Flip and Darin role-played a trip to the hospital, with Darin as doting husband to contractions-timing "wife" Flip, surely one of the weirder moments of 1970s TV. Despite his shiny toupee and deteriorating health—he said he'd soon need surgery for his "bum ticker"—Darin came across as such a winning presence that NBC gave him a variety hour of his own in 1972.

Moms Mabley was another trouper who got a late-career boost

from Flip's show. In a November 1970 skit, beauty-shop worker Geraldine takes a look at toothless Moms and cries, "I'm a beautician, honey, not a magician!" Budget-conscious Flip might cut corners on music and costumes but he paid guests $7,500, equivalent to more than $40,000 today, a windfall for seventy-six-year-old Mabley. Another appreciative guest was thirty-three-year-old George Carlin, who joined Flip's writing staff during that year, recorded a comeback album for Little David Records, and scored a lucrative stand-up segment in February 1971.

The ratings held up no matter who the featured guests were—Carol Channing, Sugar Ray Robinson, Pat Boone, Marcel Marceau, Sha Na Na—which could only mean that viewers were tuning in for Flip. "All of a sudden he's a monster star," writer Moss recalls. "The guests—even Cosby at that time—could only dream of having a number-one show. They treated him like royalty. But the network guys thought they could manipulate him. That was the treatment they gave successful blacks. 'Don't let him know how much power he has.' Flip was in a tricky position. He'd never run a TV show. What should he push for? How hard should he push?" When the network resisted booking Redd Foxx as a guest, Flip pushed. "He wanted to help black acts in general, but he *really* wanted to help Redd," Moss recalls. "So Redd gets on. He keeps it clean, and the ratings go up." Later that season Flip brought his old Chris Columbus routine full circle: Geraldine, strutting onstage, discovers Ray Charles sitting at a piano. "I never thought I'd see the day I'd be sittin' next to the greatest blues singer of all time," she marvels, and they duet on "I Can't Stop Lovin' You" and "Hey Good Lookin'."

Flip made fruit salad while pushing the prime-time envelope further than *I Spy, The Mod Squad,* or even *Laugh-In* did. In his show's third week, he and *Laugh-In*'s Lily Tomlin played lonely singles trying a new service, computer dating. At the top of the sketch Tomlin sighed and said, "If a computer can put a man on the moon, surely it can put one in my living room."

A Compu-Date technician looking over Flip's data asked, "You're six-foot-two?" Flip, twenty years before the dawn of Internet lying, said, "If I have to be."

The two characters he and Tomlin played discovered they were a perfect match, except for skin color. She told him he reminded her of O. J. Simpson (a compliment in 1970), and while flirting they learned that they both loved the Temptations, that night's musical act, and Jimi Hendrix. (The latter reference turned out to be Flip's farewell to Hendrix, who died of an overdose between the taping and the night the show aired.)

"Flip was a transitional figure. He was so lovable and cute he charmed middle America into accepting a black TV star," says Tomlin today, recalling how her relatives drove from Kentucky to Burbank to attend that night's taping. "My aunt and uncle were *not* enlightened, but when I took them to meet Flip, they almost knocked me down going into his dressing room. 'Oh, Flip, you're our favorite comedian—after Lily, of course!'"

In the Compu-Date sketch a computer wound up matching Flip with someone "square" and presumably black, as he looked longingly at Lily. This was only two years after white singer Petula Clark caused a furor by touching Harry Belafonte's sweaty arm on national TV, and *Star Trek* drew death threats for a 1968 kiss between white Captain Kirk and black Lieutenant Uhura. The skit's unstated premise was that while Flip and Lily might be made for each other, race would keep them apart. The scene ended with Flip wandering off, clearly wishing the machine had done the right thing. Would he meet Lily again? Alone onstage as the lights came down, she lifted one hand into a spotlight, fingers crossed.

Flip said the scene gave him goose bumps. Tomlin recalls a

"culture changing so fast as the sixties turned into the seventies. Nobody knew where the limits were. It helped that Flip wasn't a 'threatening' black man. That was part of his appeal, so we didn't push it too hard. We certainly knew better than to kiss or hold hands." Three years later, when Tomlin hosted her own NBC special with Pryor as a guest, the network made the limit explicit: *Do not kiss him.*

Race entered every discussion of Flip's popularity. Flip was "funky," *Life* magazine's John Leonard wrote. "Week after week, Wilson breezes into the attic of the white American mind, where all those fantasies of sex and rhythm sit around, and he plays there." To Leonard the "jive-talking" newcomer was more authentically black than Bill Cosby. "He has not sanitized his blackness for home consumption." But was Flip black enough? Leonard wasn't sure. "He has taken the *threat* out of blackness. He wouldn't hurt you any more than Glen Campbell or Carol Burnett or Ed Sullivan would hurt you. Or Captain Kangaroo," he wrote, closing his column with a Fosbury Flop into white-liberal guilt: "I like him, but maybe liking him is part of the problem instead of part of the solution. He wouldn't hurt me, but maybe, just maybe, he should."

Flip wanted his work to speak for itself. "Why does it have to be a question of black and white?" he asked. "The funny has no color." Quizzed about race, he insisted that some of his best friends were colored people. Asked about the Panthers, Muhammad Ali, and the war, he said, "Look, I have feelings about these things, but I'm selling entertainment. Politics is for politicians. My show is my statement." His politics were evident to anyone who was paying attention. After Flip told Henry to book Ali as a guest, Geraldine hugged the champ and asked him not to hurt Joe Frazier, "'cause he's one of us." Flip shared his spotlight with dozens of black performers and occasionally, talking with an interviewer he trusted, admitted that he wasn't colorblind. "I cannot tell you how much I've wanted to have a successful variety show hosted by a Negro," he told *Ebony*. In a talk with jazz pianist and writer Leonard Feather for *Penthouse*, Flip came as close as he ever got to explaining his view of his place in the world: "A show hosted by a black had never been accepted, so the first time that knob's turned on, people are judging against all they have ever been taught. I may have been the first black in that home. And when a young kid sees the rapport between the guests on my show, maybe that will ring a little bell. He says, 'I like that cat.' Then somebody tells him, 'Niggers ain't no good.' He'll say, 'Now hold it. I like that nigger.' This is meaningful, more important than money or anything else." Later in his talk with Feather he mentioned another rule he relied on: "It's very hard not to like somebody who is smiling at you."

Determined to stay on top, Flip worked eighteen-hour days and expected his guests and staff to keep up. Most variety shows stuck to a three-day rehearsal schedule. *The Carol Burnett Show*, with a large cast of improv comics including Harvey Korman, Tim Conway, and Vicki Lawrence, had a four-day schedule, while loose-limbed Dean Martin might not meet his guests until the cameras were rolling. Flip's show used the whole workweek. He joined his staff and guests each Monday to read through that week's script in Rehearsal Room 4, a room the size of a small gym at NBC Studios in Burbank. On Tuesdays they moved to the soundstage, blocking out their movements. Wednesdays were for run-throughs and rewrites, with camera angles added on Thursdays. Flip oversaw everything from director Tim Kiley's camera placements to blocking, props, and sound effects. Once, when a doorbell on the set rang with what Flip called a "boring" tone, he went out and bought a better-sounding doorbell. He often changed the shooting script during dress rehearsal, which began at five on Friday afternoon, only to change it again for the official taping at eight. Per standard variety-hour practice, producer Henry and director Kiley filmed both the dress rehearsal and the "real" show. That way Henry and Flip could splice a dress-rehearsal bit into the tape if it was funnier than the later version, then deliver a final forty-eight-minute show to the network on a fat film cassette for airing the following Thursday.

Cosby appeared in an early episode, playing himself as a hospital patient ogling nurse Gina Lollobrigida. When Nurse Gina told him she was about to be replaced by the night nurse, the audience buzzed. Flip's fans knew what was coming. Night nurse Geraldine got an ovation as she sashayed to Cosby's bedside in her heels and $500 Pucci minidress. Asking pointedly if Mr. Famous Celebrity Bill Cosby was in the hospital to have his "great big ego" removed, she popped a thermometer into his mouth before he could answer. There's subtext here: Flip, riding high, needling the younger star he'd envied for years. But in the spirit of Eastman's rule *We are in fun*, it was a good-natured needle. Cosby got a kiss on the cheek and a toy hypodermic in the butt before Geraldine booted him out of bed and phoned Killer.

Flip's album *The Devil Made Me Buy This Dress* won the 1971 Grammy for comedy record of the year, ending Cosby's record run of six Grammys in a row. Comic Nipsey Russell was capitalizing on Flip's moves with a dance called "Doing the Flip, Baby." *TV Mirror* magazine put Geraldine and Dean Martin on its cover, billing them as "The Sexiest Couple on TV." Shindana Toys put out a foot-tall talking Geraldine doll—pull her string and she said, "What you see is what you get, honey" and "Help, y'all, I'm trapped inside this doll," thanks to a miniature vinyl record inside. Soon the price for commercials on *The Flip Wilson Show* rose to $80,000 a minute, almost double the premiere's rate, at a time when thirty-second spots on the Super Bowl telecast sold for $72,000. Flip was getting rich as fast as any comic ever had. Mobbed at Roscoe's House of Chicken 'n Waffles, his Hollywood soul-food hangout, he signed autographs, hugged fans, and bought lunch for everybody in the place. His generosity didn't stop at the cash register: anyone celebrating a birthday got a hundred-dollar bill from Flip, as did anyone named Geraldine. One schoolgirl named Geraldine who went to Roscoe's on her birthday hit the daily double: she got a free lunch and $200.

Later that year Flip flew to Chicago to make his only live stand-up appearance of 1971. The occasion was the first annual Black Expo, a trade fair for black businesspeople at the sprawling International Amphitheater, site of riots at the 1968 Democratic National Convention. More than half a million attendees vied for tickets to main-stage concerts featuring the Jackson Five (fronted by twelve-year-old Michael), Aretha Franklin, Isaac Hayes, the Temptations, Roberta Flack, and Donny Hathaway—and Flip, who turned out to be the main attraction. During opening ceremonies the Reverend Jesse Jackson called for "green power, not black power." Hard work could overcome inequality. Ambition was "the first step out of the ghetto," said Jackson, who swore that black Americans were about to take that giant leap. "We do not want a welfare state. We have potential. We can produce. We can feed ourselves."

Backstage, Dick Gregory put his arm around Flip. "I want to say something," the first modern black comic told the most modern one. "I want to thank you personally for what you've done for black people." A minute later Flip took the stage to what *Ebony* called "a tumultuous ovation." There were ten thousand people in a hall that seated nine thousand. Everyone stood for Flip, calling his name, calling for Geraldine, and for once Flip couldn't stay in character. He couldn't even move. According to Jackson, "There was such a massive outpouring of love and affection that it overwhelmed the cat and broke him down." Flip stood on the stage looking out at the crowd, too choked up to speak, tears rolling down his cheeks as the cheers went on and on.

10

Top of the World

◈ In 1971 America's favorite comedian added a pair of Emmy awards to his Grammy for *The Devil Made Me Buy This Dress*. Johnny Carson hosted the ceremonies at the Hollywood Palladium that spring. First Flip and his staff won an Emmy for comedy writing over Carol Burnett's team, then *The Flip Wilson Show* beat out *Laugh-In* and *The Carol Burnett Show* for Outstanding Variety Series. "Flip's done a lot for the black man," Carson quipped. "He put him in a dress."

Flip tossed his Emmy into the passenger seat of his new Rolls-Royce Corniche convertible, a car that cost twice as much as the entry-level Rolls he traded in. The $40,000 he paid for it was more than the L.A. Rams were paying quarterback Roman Gabriel, more than Richard Roundtree got for starring in *Shaft,* and not much less than California governor Ronald Reagan's $49,000 salary. The sky-blue Rolls wore one of the old vehicle's KILLER license plates, which Flip claimed federal inmate Killer had made himself. The car weighed more than a small yacht and went from zero to sixty, he said, "just as fast as it wants." Flip customized it with one of the country's first mobile phones. The device got service on only a few scattered blocks, but he was willing to wait for more and better satellites to improve reception. For now he had his bullhorn. Motoring from the NBC lot to Roscoe's House of Chicken 'n Waffles at Sunset and Gower, Flip would roll down his window and use the bullhorn to direct traffic. Startled motorists heard a familiar voice say, "Attention! Where you going, Jack?" One day he used it to stop a CHP officer. "Pull over, ossifer, park it right there!" He gave the cop a ticket . . . to *The Flip Wilson Show*. Later he improved on the bullhorn by installing a loudspeaker like the ones on police cars. When fans recognized him and called "Do Geraldine" as he drove by, Flip hit a dashboard button and blared through the speaker, "The devil made me run that light!"

He parked at a Laurel Canyon mansion and lay low during the hiatus between his first and second network seasons, "resting and writing, building up a greater fund of material." When *Life* commissioned a feature on him, Flip ignored the magazine's reporter. "This guy from *Life* would say, 'Hello, Flip. What did you do last night?'" an insider recalled. "Flip would say, 'That's a personal question.' It went on like that for three days. Finally they dropped plans for the article."

He escaped distractions by going on road trips. "I head for the desert, put the top down and get burnt blacker than a piece of toast," he said, quoting the line his pops had used against him, the blackest of the brood. Flip and his assistant George Whittington, whom he liked to call his valet, drove back and forth across the country three times that summer, putting more than eleven thousand miles on the Rolls's odometer. Flip did most of the driving. He enjoyed the wide, quiet spaces between cities, the sun spinning heat mirages off the road during the day, the Milky Way brightening the sky at night, reminding him of his nights as a hitchhiker, when he'd curl up under a Joshua tree if he didn't get a ride. Whittington manned the tape deck, playing pop and R&B. He rolled joints on the dashboard, handing them over while Flip drove with one hand and smoked with the other, pleasantly buzzed, the open road ahead.

Girls flocked around him at a Holiday Inn in Texas. "Five or six soul sisters, all asking for kisses and autographs, but I was tired," he remembered. "'Maybe tomorrow,' I said. So they camped outside my room." The girls parked their dusty beater beside the only Corniche in the parking lot. They played the radio and danced between cars, jumping and waving when he peeked through his curtained window. He dozed off, and when he woke at dawn they were still out there, not dancing anymore but crowded into their car, sound asleep. Flip tiptoed out with a stack of glossy eight-by-tens, woke the girls, and took them to breakfast. He autographed the pictures for them, making sure to spell their names right. "This is the best day of my life," one of them said, and it might have been true, her one brush with celebrity, that photo of Flip in a black jacket and bow tie hanging on a wall overlooking her TV for years to come.

After breakfast, Flip kissed the girls and hit the road. Twelve hundred miles later he and Whittington were heading east on Alabama Route 80, a fifty-mile stretch of blacktop between Selma and Montgomery. "It was Sunday morning. The sun was shining and we saw a little church," Flip remembered. When KILLER pulled up outside, churchgoers came out to see who was behind the wheel. Kids pointed and quibbled—"It's Flip!" "No, it ain't." "Is!" "Why'd he be here?" "Ask him." "*You* ask him!" At last a brave girl asked Flip if he was Flip and if so, what he was doing in Lowndes County.

"Driving," he said. "And God told me to stop and say hello." The little girl ran into the church, and soon more congregants came out to shake his hand. Some thanked him for what he was doing on television. Whittington could see that Flip was near tears as he drove off again, with happy kids chasing the Rolls as it pulled onto the road to Montgomery.

Two days later KILLER sped through Pennsylvania's humpbacked Blue Mountains into the wooded shadows of the Delaware Water Gap, a tall, crumpled pile of 400-million-year-old rock. From here it was a straight shot east to Jersey City.

"What an event it was when Flip came home," says his nephew Rashon Khan. "We all watched his show—his brothers and sisters, cousins, aunts and uncles. We'd get on the phone on Thursdays before it came on and say, 'You watching?' Nobody said, 'Watching what?' Everybody knew. Everybody was talking about him. Not just Jersey City, the whole country. John Wayne, Bob Hope, Muhammad Ali, Johnny Carson. Shoot, *Richard Nixon* knew my uncle Flip. So you can imagine the sensation it made when he came home."

He hadn't gone back the year before, when his mother got her name in a newspaper for the first time. On May 1, 1970, *The New York Times* ran an item headed FLIP WILSON'S MOTHER DIES. Datelined Jersey City, it read, "Mrs. Cornelia Wilson Carter, the mother of Flip Wilson, the comedian, died yesterday at her home after a long illness. Her age was 68. She was the mother of 12 children." Flip had stayed in touch with a few relatives and had heard about Cornelia's illness. He had also heard what she said about him. According to the family grapevine, when someone asked about her prodigal son, she said, "I forgive him." He couldn't believe it. The woman who ditched him when he was a defenseless child forgave *him*? "I am so glad I wasn't raised by that selfish woman," he said. As for her funeral, forgiveness was beside the point. Flip hated funerals. "I don't do death."

His relatives were amazed to see him in Jersey City again. "Here's this giant Rolls-Royce, the first one anybody around there ever saw," Khan recalls. "I'm thinking, *Nobody died, and here's a big limo.* Then he gets out in his tailored suit, gold watch, and cuff links. Flip in the flesh. He looked like a million dollars."

Neighbors gathered outside a crumbling brownstone. The street wasn't Jackson Avenue anymore: changing times and a killing in Memphis had turned it into Martin Luther King Drive. Kids ran their hands over the big car's fenders and climbed onto its wide, warm hood. Whittington led his boss up the front steps, Flip waving like a visiting diplomat. Inside he climbed a half-lit stair-case. Whittington and a row of relatives followed him to an apart-ment where Clerow Wilson Sr. waited, sitting in the rocking chair he slept in every night. After sixty years of steady drink and inter-mittent work, Clerow Senior had reached his biblical lifespan of threescore years and ten. His yellowing eyes were half shut. His nose wrinkled at the scent of Flip's aftershave. He smiled and gripped his son's hand as they talked. Working a plug of chaw be-tween his cheek and his remaining teeth, he leaned over to hock into a brass spittoon. After a half hour or so, Clerow Senior said he was tired. It was time for his nap. Flip kissed his pops's cheek and nodded to Whittington. He and his assistant were close enough by now that Whittington understood all that nod implied. He should keep the rent checks coming to this address, make sure relatives got hundred-dollar bills and the others waiting downstairs got auto-graphed photos, ease Flip through the crowd after a few minutes of hugs and handshakes, and make sure they got back on the road in time for the event Flip came home for.

Flip pulled the rings off his fingers and handed them to Whit-tington for safekeeping. It was a tactic he'd learned from Elvis, he said. You had to be careful shaking hands in a crowd, lest your hand come back minus a ring.

Time magazine reported the reason for Flip's return to Jersey City without grasping its meaning. According to *Time*, many of his rela-tives had "succumbed to the ghetto syndrome" of welfare and crime. "They sometimes reflect a mood of bitterness and envy. Per-haps inevitably, that mood can focus on Flip, producing a complaint that he is not doing all that a rich and successful brother should do. But the evidence is not all against Flip. An electrician named Leroy Taylor, who had served as a father figure for Flip and several other kids in the neighborhood, learned that he had terminal cancer and committed suicide. Flip made a special trip to attend the funeral and paid all the expenses."

Leroy Taylor—the first black electrical foreman in Jersey City. The man who took young Clerow for his first drive in an automobile, his first visits to the circus and the zoo, and his life-changing trip to a music-and-comedy show at the old Mosque Theater in Newark. Flip might not "do death," as he put it, but he went to Taylor's funeral. He paid for the funeral as well as for Taylor's burial and gravestone. Sitting in the front row at the service, Flip asked himself why he had never reconnected with Leroy Taylor, who must have watched *The Flip Wilson Show* with button-busting pride but never embarrassed Clerow Senior by claiming to be Flip's biological father, and never asked Jersey City's favorite son for a cent. Bowing his head in a front pew, Flip had time to ponder the lonely misery that led his real father to take his own life.

He wanted his second season to top his first. Other variety shows had faded after fast starts. The Smothers Brothers had racked up top-twenty ratings in 1966–67, bridging the so-called generation gap by pairing guests like the ancient Jack Benny and George Burns with hipper acts like the Doors and Jefferson Airplane. During one Smothers show, guests Bette Davis and Mickey Rooney stood offstage watching the Who, who'd packed Keith Moon's drum with gunpowder before the band played "My Generation." The drum exploded, damaging the hearing in one of Pete Townshend's ears and setting his hair on fire. Davis fainted, Rooney cheered. Yet for all the noise the controversial Smothers Brothers made, their show seldom won its time slot. *The Smothers Brothers Comedy Hour* topped out at number 16 in the Nielsens and fell from there as the show's clever young writers skirmished with CBS censors and eventually alienated much of middle America. In 1968 *Rowan & Martin's Laugh-In* made the Smotherses look like last year's fad with quick cuts and goofy catchphrases: "Here come the judge," "You bet your sweet bippy," and "Sock it to me." The last got boosts from frequent guest Flip and 1968 presidential candidate Nixon, who appeared just long enough to ask, "Sock it to me?" (It took Nixon six takes to nail the line.) *Laugh-In* dominated the ratings in 1969–70, the season before Flip stepped onto his hexagonal stage. Once he got there, he intended to prove he had more staying power than the Smothers Brothers, *Laugh-In,* or the latest ratings phenomenon, the fearless CBS sitcom *All in the Family.*

With guests Lucille Ball, Ed Sullivan, and the Osmond Brothers, Flip's second-season debut was his whitest hour so far. Playing the tail end of a horse in a vaudeville sketch, he backed up the sixty-year-old Ball, who doffed her plastic horse-head to reveal a wig that was a brighter shade of orange than Pete Townshend's flaming hair. "I thought we was gonna be an equal-opportunity horse," Flip griped. "The schoolteacher asked all the kids what their fathers did, and when my kid told her they suspended him for two weeks."

Pointedly, Ball replied, "Look, you cannot become a front end overnight." They teamed up for a soft-hoof rendition of "There's No Business Like Show Business" as corny and heartfelt as Flip's regard for his comedy elders. Later, dressed in hot pants that showed off two pairs of shapely legs, Lucy and Geraldine played carhops at a drive-in restaurant. "Killer calls me Switchboard," Geraldine boasted, "'cause when I walk, all my lines are busy!" The women flirted with an ancient "hippie" played by Ed Sullivan. "Cool it, girls!" said Sullivan, age seventy. His appearance was Flip's thank-you for his twenty-six sets on *The Ed Sullivan Show* through the years. Sullivan's costume—a fringed vest and purple bell-bottoms—was almost as campy as the pastel scarves and glittery jumpsuits of Flip's somewhat musical guests, the Osmond Brothers.

"I thought the Osmonds were as cool as the Jackson Five," remembers Kevin Wilson, who sat in the audience that night. Flip had flown Kevin and his big brother, David, from Florida to see the season-two opener. During a break in the taping he asked the studio audience for "a round of applause for a couple of very special guests, my sons." The boys, dressed in their Sunday best, took a bow. Backstage later, nine-year-old Kevin was starstruck. "Donny was thirteen. Marie was eleven. She wasn't singing with them yet, but she was there," Kevin recalls. "And *very* cute."

David Wilson calls that Hollywood visit "unforgettable." His little sister Tamara and another recent addition to the family—Stacey, born in 1970—had stayed in Miami with their mother. One of Tamara's first memories of her father was seeing him on television. ("That's your dad," Blonell said, pointing to the TV.) David and Kevin had seen almost as much of Flip on TV as in person, "but now we were really part of his life, running around backstage, meeting famous people, going home with him." For two weeks the boys bunked at Flip's place in Laurel Canyon, near Lookout Mountain. The house had the biggest backyard swimming pool they'd ever seen. It took them half a day of coaxing to get their father, who still couldn't swim, into the pool.

"C'mon, I'll teach you," yelled David, the daring one.

Flip dipped a toe into the water. "If I drown, NBC's coming after your ass."

Bobby Darin dropped by in the evenings, always sharply dressed in a jacket and tie. He and Flip were as close as the cowboys they played on the show, Butch Cassidy and the Suntan Kid. Darin had suffered from rheumatic fever as a boy. The disease had left scar tissue on his heart, and sometimes he needed oxygen from a tank after he sang. Several weeks after a *Flip Wilson Show* taping in 1971, Darin had open-heart surgery and had two plastic valves installed. Still he went on toking with Flip, joking that he was ahead of the game. "I expected to kick off by the time I was thirty," he said after the operation, "so I bought a few extra years." They liked to fire up a joint, eat homemade apple pie, and rap—it still meant talking then—for hours. They'd strip down to towels and get rubdowns from Flip's pie-baking masseur. Flip told Joe the masseur to give the boys a rubdown, too, but David and Kevin were ticklish. They wiggled free and ran for their lives.

One morning Flip gave the boys some money and asked his girlfriend Sylvia Davis to take them to Disneyland. David remembers his pops's paramour as "nice enough, but a little distant. . . . He told us to treat her like we'd treat our own mother." On the way to Disneyland, Kevin spotted a Tower Records and asked Sylvia to stop the car. He ran in to buy a copy of *The Devil Made Me Buy This Dress*. When he showed it to his father that evening, Flip was annoyed. "You spent my money on my own album?" Kevin explained that he wanted to keep hearing Flip's voice after he went home to Florida.

Blonell was raising the boys in the Miami Shores house with the tree house and the little lake out back. Compared with the Laurel Canyon mansion, it seemed as small and plain as Blonell must have felt seeing pictures of the younger, prettier Sylvia with her man. Blonell knew Flip had other girlfriends, too, plus the groupies who slipped into his dressing room for ten or fifteen minutes at a time, girls whose names he probably remembered for less time than that. But Blonell was the only one he called his wife, the one David, Kevin, and their younger sisters, Tamara and Stacey, called Moms.

Flip told *Penthouse* he was raising "all-American boys. They belong to Little League and the Boy Scouts. They go camping, fishing, boating, play cards, pool, ping-pong. They fix breakfast for me." But not often. As his sons got older they realized that they weren't the only reason for his occasional trips to Miami, and maybe not even the main reason. Pot was cheaper and better in Florida. "Flip was reupping his shit," says a former supplier. "Three hundred dollars a pound in Overtown. It was nowhere near as strong as today's weed, but not bad, and he trusted the people he got it from." After buying in bulk, he gave the pot to Lawrence Trice, Blonell's first baby daddy, the father of Flip's stepdaughter, Michelle. Trice worked as a skycap at Miami International Airport. He would slip Flip's stash onto a flight to L.A., where Flip's man Whittington would pick it up. By then it took up less space than when he'd bought it, having passed through a kitchen-table assembly line Flip set up in Blonell's kitchen.

"We cleaned Pops's dope for him," Kevin recalls. Flip and the kids spread newspapers on the floor. Kevin, David, and one of the girls sat at the kitchen table with a couple of one-pound bags, listening to the radio, sifting through Flip's stash. "We used colanders to strain the dope. One kid picked out the seeds and stems, shook the shit around, passed it over to the next kid. The next kid had a colander with smaller holes. The last kid rolled joints. That was the tricky part. You had to crimp and tuck in the ends so they didn't leak." Blonell disapproved but didn't complain. Hardly anyone quibbled with Flip Wilson in those days. "It was boring, and your fingers got tired, but it was fun, too," Kevin says. "We were helping Pops. And he made it clear that we were never to smoke it ourselves. He said reefer and blow helped him work. Work tools, he called them. 'They're no good for you,' he said. 'They're only good for me.'"

Flip's ratings rose in his second season, averaging more than forty million viewers in the fall and winter of 1971–72. While dueling *All in the Family* for the top spot overall, Flip attracted four million more viewers than any other NBC show, five million more than *The Mary Tyler Moore Show*, six million more than former ratings champs *Laugh-In* and *Bonanza*. *Monday Night Football* was another ratings leader that year—a surprise hit that made celebrities of announcers Howard Cosell, Frank Gifford, and "Dandy" Don Meredith—but Flip had 75 percent more viewers.

He and George Carlin got through late-night writing sessions with plenty of help from Flip's "work tools." Sometimes Redd Foxx joined them. Foxx had a sitcom in the works, *Sanford and Son*, which NBC green-lighted in hopes of doubling down on Flip's success. At a time when many movie and TV stars flaunted their drug habits, Foxx was a standout, wearing a silver coke spoon on a chain around his neck. He and Flip and Carlin kicked ideas around, with Flip and the gleefully profane Foxx spooning coke and spouting words they couldn't say on the air. Carlin thought it was absurd that network censors banned certain "obscene" words without saying what they were. Performers had to deduce which words were taboo, as Carlin did in a classic routine on *Class Clown*, his 1972 album for Flip's Little David Records:

> *Shit, piss, fuck, cunt, cocksucker, motherfucker, and tits.* Those are the heavy seven, the ones that will curve your spine and keep the country from winning the war. *Tits* doesn't belong on the list, you know? It's a friendly sounding word, like a nickname. 'Hey, Tits, c'mere. Tits, meet Toots. Tits, Toots. Toots, Tits.' It sounds like a snack, doesn't it? But I don't mean a sexist snack. I mean 'New Nabisco Tits.' The new Cheese Tits, Corn Tits, and Pizza Tits. Sesame Tits, Onion Tits, Tater Tits. Yeah, betcha can't eat just one. . . .

With Carlin making more on-screen appearances while developing what he later called "a really nice cocaine habit," Flip drubbed *Marcus Welby*, the previous season's number-one show, while battling *All in the Family* at the top of the Nielsens. Viewers ate up Flip's brand of fruit salad: second-season pairings included Stevie Wonder and Raymond Burr, Slappy White and Jim Nabors, Jack Benny and Pearl Bailey. In November 1971 he welcomed the Jackson Five, featuring roughly an acre of Afro as well as thirteen-year-old Michael, seemingly comfortable in his coffee-colored skin as he teased Flip's character Herbie the Ice-Cream Man. Herbie offered the Jacksons "every flavor from chocolate to vanilla" out of a cart emblazoned *What You See Is What You Get*. He was paying them the usual $7,500 guest fee, or $6,500 more than they'd earned for a week at the Apollo four years before. (The money went to their father, Joe, who signed his sons' contract with Clerow Productions.) Michael and his brothers got an ovation for "Never Can Say Goodbye." Another big-haired star, Geraldine Jones—fresh off a victory over Carol Burnett and Mary Tyler Moore in a poll that named her "America's favorite comedienne"—came next. Flouncing past sexologist Dr. David "Everything You Always Wanted to Know About Sex" Reuben, Geraldine said she knew all about his new book, *Any Woman Can!*.

"Any woman *can*, but most don't," she said, "'cause they use too many four-letter words. Like *Stop, Don't,* and *No no!*"

For all her popularity, Geraldine now encountered a backlash. Or "blacklash," as he called it. To Flip's consternation, many black men who liked and supported him recoiled from Geraldine. "We all watched the show," one recalls, "but I shut it off when he did that part. I had sons eight and ten years old, and I wasn't letting them see him dress up as a woman. That wasn't the way to represent a black man." Other critics saw Geraldine as an insult to black womanhood, a throwback to Sapphire and *Amos 'n' Andy*, loud and none too smart, with a boyfriend in prison. One pundit opined that she threatened conservative whites as well as homophobic black-power activists, making her "a loaded figure." (Fully loaded, given her custom-made bra.) Flip stuck to his guns, refusing to apologize for being *funny*, but the controversy irked him.

He called Geraldine a modern role model. Recalling how white men in mixed clubs used to ask him to "Get me a girl," he told Mel Watkins, "I took offense! Black guys wouldn't go to a white club and say that. I wanted Geraldine to show pride in herself and dedication to her man. She'd say, 'Watch out! You can look if you want to, but don't touch nothin', sucker.'" To Flip, Geraldine's swoony voice had nothing to do with *Amos 'n' Andy*. It evoked the howls of front-row girls in Chitlin' Circuit clubs where black people got to be themselves. "When they saw something they really liked, they'd let themselves go. They'd say, 'Whooee!' And for a second they'd be free." He listed Geraldine's virtues: "She is constantly in the company of glamorous male celebrities. Most women would say, 'Boy! Joe Namath! Perry Como!' But Geraldine says, 'I got Killer!' Geraldine may not project the image of a refined, sophisticated lady, but she's honest, she's frank, she's affectionate, she's independent. I think every woman should be like that." As he saw it, "Geraldine is liberated, that's where *that's* at."

"I liked Geraldine," Lily Tomlin says. Tomlin returned for the second-season episode featuring the Jackson Five and Dr. Reuben, playing her telephone-operator character, Ernestine ("One ringie-dingie, two ringie-dingie"), who arched an eyebrow as temp worker Geraldine proclaimed, "If you're having trouble with your circuit, I'll show you how to work it!" Initially leery of each other, the two women chatted, disconnecting hapless callers, until Ernestine turned to her new friend to say, "It's a pleasure to plug in beside you. We have so much in common."

"Flip made Geraldine a tough woman, strong and assertive," Tomlin says today. "He got some flak for not being, quote-unquote, militant enough, but you have to be who you are, or it won't work. The audience can tell."

That week *The New York Times* sent Josh Greenfield to profile Flip. Greenfield had a double-edged view of *The Flip Wilson Show*: "Even though Wilson has been heavily criticized for defusing his blackness, he is a consummate practitioner of ethnic black humor, perhaps the first Negro comic to celebrate on television the total down-home, street-smart black experience."

Flip sounded wary as they sat down for lunch. "I don't want to sit here and talk jive politics," he told the mop-topped reporter. Greenfield thought he sounded unfriendly, even "uppity," to use Greenfield's word. He tried to draw him out by asking about his family.

"Mention my family and I'll walk away. Touch my personal life and I'm gone," Flip warned him. "I know this is part of having a TV show, this interview jazz, but I will not let it intrude."

This wasn't the charmer Greenfield had expected to meet. The reporter knew that Flip didn't need publicity, didn't need *The New York Times*, didn't need money. Greenfield had done his homework before their talk and realized that Flip made more than the whole staff of *Monday Night Football*. He figured Flip would earn $10 million over the next five years. What Greenfield couldn't figure was why the man would sit for an interview if he didn't want to talk. "How come you come over so nice on the screen, so ingratiating and warm and likable," he asked, "but off-camera you seem to be totally lacking in those qualities?"

"Whoa! That isn't called for." Flip laughed and apologized. "Look, I didn't mean to come on uptight, but my personal life is irrelevant," he said. "Not because I'm trying to hide anything, but because it's so dull."

Of course he was hiding things: his dressing-room liaisons, his joint-rolling assembly line in Miami. Druggy days and nights with celebrity friends didn't make him a rarity in seventies Hollywood, nor did bowdlerizing his biography. He must have enjoyed telling Greenfield his plans for the evening. "I'll have a manicure, a pedicure, a massage, and I'll get my rest." The next morning, as usual, he'd be the first one on the set before rehearsal.

"Flip was loose. He was fun," says Tim Conway, whose twelve *Flip Wilson Show* appearances made him Flip's favorite guest. "He ran a tight ship, though." Ever conscious of the show's network-mandated budget of around $1 million a week, Flip and Bob Henry produced a typical episode for $50,000 less. They kept part of the difference and gave the rest to grateful cameramen and other crew members as bonuses. According to writer James Hudson, "Efficiency is the watchword in taping *The Flip Wilson Show*." Working with Henry and director Kiley, Flip often taped the show without a single retake, because retakes cost money. "After delivering a monologue or doing a scene, Flip bows a couple of times and—*ffftt!*—disappears, no matter how loud the applause is. After all, if he took any more bows, they would just end up on the cutting-room floor." Comedy veterans like Sid Caesar, Don Rickles, and Joan Rivers might entertain the studio audience between takes; not Flip. "Flip's face is animated when one of the little red lights on the cameras is turned on. But as soon as the red lights go out, Flip turns off his face," Hudson wrote. "Instead of looking like the comedian we're used to seeing, he looks like a preoccupied businessman."

"As funny and fun as he was, he gave you the sense that work came first," Conway says. "You wanted to be very professional out of respect for this tight ship of his. There were performers who screwed around on other shows, but not Flip's show. Dean Martin, for one. Dean would horse around on his own program, but on Flip's show he hit his marks."

Flip completed one taping in seventy-five minutes, an unofficial record for an hour-long program. He was so efficient he pre-planned his bloopers. A close observer of the competition, he noted that Carol Burnett and her supporting cast got big laughs when they blew lines and broke each other up. So he blew lines on purpose. As *Life* magazine reported when he finally let one of its writers visit the set, "Nothing, not even the errors, is left to chance: three skits per show, a monolog with at least five laughs a minute, a laugh every 12 seconds, a laugh every third line, some from words, some laughs from body movements and some, at

Flip patterned one of his best-loved characters—Reverend Leroy, pastor of the Church of What's Happening Now—on one of his foster fathers. (Everett Collection)

In 1965, after bumming money and drugs from his friend, Redd Foxx (right) told Johnny Carson, "Flip Wilson's the funniest comedian out there." (Everett Collection)

"Here come the judge!"—an old Pigmeat Markham line—became the rising star's first famous catchphrase on *Laugh-In* in the late 1960s. (Everett Collection)

Geraldine cracked up David Frost on the September 17, 1970, debut of *The Flip Wilson Show.*
(Everett Collection)

The star's secret weapon was a writing team featuring his volatile friend Richard Pryor (right) and George Carlin. (Everett Collection)

George Carlin recorded six comedy albums for Flip's label,
Little David Records. (Courtesy of Kevin Wilson)

Frequent guest Lily Tomlin calls Flip "a transitional figure . . . he charmed middle America
into accepting a black TV star." (Photofest)

The Flip Wilson Show's second season found thirteen-year-old Michael Jackson singing and joking on TV's top variety show. (Everett Collection)

By 1971 Flip was one of the country's favorite celebrities, joining Elton John, Cher, and Bette Midler on a sparkly holiday special. (Everett Collection)

Tim Conway (center, with Pryor and Flip) says the host ran a tight ship that rocked when Pryor came aboard. (Everett Collection)

Offstage, the married funnyman hit the town with women, including longtime girlfriend Sylvia Davis. (Photofest)

While gushing over Muhammad Ali (right), Geraldine swore she was faithful to a never-seen boyfriend, Killer, "currently incarcerated." (Everett Collection)

Years after his buddy Bobby Darin stood up for him in Vegas, Flip helped resuscitate Darin's career. (Photofest)

Rookie comic Franklyn Ajaye found himself among "the giants" when he debuted on Flip's show.
(Courtesy of Kevin Wilson)

When *The Flip Wilson Show* closed in 1974, viewers finally met the mysterious Killer, played by none other than O. J. Simpson.
(Everett Collection)

On the day of Geraldine's TV wedding, Flip smooched longtime manager Monte Kay. (Courtesy of Roberta Kay)

The Rev's cameo stole the show in Sidney Poitier's and Bill Cosby's surprise 1974 hit, *Uptown Saturday Night*. (Everett Collection)

In the mid-1970s, Flip befriended President Gerald Ford and Ford's secretary of state, Henry Kissinger (center, with Nancy Maginnes Kissinger). (Photofest)

As a Las Vegas headliner, the dropout from Jersey City rubbed elbows with Elvis Presley and Frank Sinatra. (Courtesy of Kevin Wilson)

In 1979, Flip married Thailand-born Cookie Davis at his friend Rocky Aoki's Benihana restaurant at the Las Vegas Hilton. (Courtesy of Cookie Mackenzie)

Flip loathed starring in the 1985–86 sitcom *Charlie & Co.* despite his affection for Gladys Knight and nine-year-old Jaleel White—the future Urkel. (Photofest)

Semiretired after *Charlie & Co*'s cancellation, Flip lounged in the sunken living room of his Malibu mansion with sons Kevin (left) and David (center). (Family photo)

After years of Las Vegas gigs and TV guest shots, Flip bought a Harley-Davidson and began biking through the California desert. (Family photo)

Son David reluctantly followed his father's lead, taking Flip's Harley for a spin and then riding a motorcycle of his own, until tragedy struck. (Family photo)

The guest of honor got emotional during a 1993 tribute to Flip Wilson at the Museum of Radio and Television. (Family photo)

On December 8, 1993, a happy Clerow Wilson Jr. celebrated his sixtieth birthday with his family and a cake reading "You devil you!" (Family photo)

After a troubling diagnosis in 1998, Flip sought peace in the verses of Kahlil Gibran and the sea breezes that came into his living room. (Family photo)

least one per show, from intentional flubs, 'just to show you're not God up there.'"

The January 31, 1972, cover of *Time* magazine showed Flip under a halo of stage lights and a banner that dubbed him "TV's First Black Superstar." Roland Flamini's cover story hailed a comedy idol whose show was "regular Thursday night fare for an estimated 40 million Americans." Flip had five million more viewers than any president had ever gotten votes. In a precable three-network universe his ratings share of 44 gave him a million more viewers than *American Idol* racked up in the best week it ever had. Flamini thought he knew Flip's secret: "He has the talent to make blacks laugh without anger and whites laugh without guilt." Bill Cosby had a more practical view of Flip's appeal in an era when most homes had one TV set: "You have to have an all-appeal to survive in the top ten in television. It's no use reaching the teenager if the father wants to watch a western and the mother wants to watch some doctor thing. Flip takes in everybody."

Flip's cultural juice was so juicy that *All in the Family* creator Norman Lear—his CBS rival at the top of the Nielsen ratings—contributed a riff to the *Time* feature in which Archie Bunker, America's favorite bigot (played by Carroll O'Connor), talked about Flip.

> *Archie*: He's funny, I'm the foist to admit it. But I didn't split no gut. I do that maybe for Bob Hope. *He* didn't have what you call your natural endowerments. His people wasn't all singers and dancers.
> *Mike "Meathead" Stivic* (played by Rob Reiner): You mean he wasn't black.
> *Archie*: You're takin' what I said out of contest, Mr. Big Liberal. All I mean was, bein' colored, Flip had a natural advantage.

Mike: How the hell did we get from one hour of your solid laughter at Flip Wilson to another of your broadsides against all blacks?

Archie: When they're intraduced, one steps out in his black skin, and the other's in his white. I got eyes, don't I?

And yet at the very moment *Time* confirmed that he was bigger than Cosby, Foxx, Carol Burnett, or *Laugh-In*—even bigger in this moment than Sinatra—Flip began to feel less at home in his skin.

Joking with Flamini, he said he'd grown up "so poor that even the poor looked down on me." But when the writer asked for details, Flip bristled. "I have never met a better man than me," he boasted. "I may not be better than you, but I'm goddamn equal." An odd thing to tell someone who's about to put you on the cover of *Time*. He sounded less like a driven comedy pro and more like a diva with a drug habit that was eroding his talent. He was doing more coke, enough to call for a new preshow routine: before stepping in front of the cameras he had Whittington check his collar and cuffs for traces of white powder.

Time's Flamini had his suspicions. "In an interview, he turns off the moment that questions get around to offstage life—to the pretty girls who are special guests in his dressing room on taping days, often a different one each week," wrote Flamini, who tracked down Blonell and phoned her a dozen times but never spoke to her. "Flip is known to fly to Miami several times a year to visit Blondell [sic] and the children," he wrote. "They live in an expensive house in a predominantly white neighborhood."

Flip might have been a tough interview, but Blonell was impossible. She was well aware that the checks Flip's accountant mailed to 9160 Northwest Twelfth Avenue might stop coming if she spoke to reporters. "Don't talk about me. Not to TV, not to the papers, not even your friends," he'd warned her. "Our private lives belong to us." When Flamini phoned Blonell for his *Time* story, she hung up on him. When he flew to Florida and knocked on the door of the Miami Shores house, she called the police.

It was 1972, the year Nixon won reelection in the biggest landslide ever. The year Atari introduced Pong, the first successful video game, the year of *The Godfather, Dirty Harry, Cabaret, and Deliverance,* and the year the Supreme Court heard arguments in *Roe v. Wade.* Flip was thirty-eight years old, facing a question he never planned for.

After your dreams come true, what do you do for an encore?

11

Crossroads

◈ A third-season episode saw Flip welcoming Howard Cosell. "The heavyweight champion of rapping," he called Cosell, who at six-foot-two towered over the host. Cosell played along, honking in his goose voice that he, not handsome Frank Gifford or "Dandy Don" Meredith, was "the sex symbol of *Monn-day Night Football*." Still, there was no doubt who was the bigger star on Flip's red-carpeted stage. *Monday Night Football* might have been the biggest sports program in TV history, the one that paved the way for football's ratings dominance in the eighties and beyond, but its numbers never approached Flip's. When Flip snapped his fingers, Cosell bowed to him.

During a question-and-answer session with the audience, a boy asked how old Flip was. "Today's my birthday. Today I've been black for exactly thirty-eight years," he replied. In fact Flip turned thirty-nine that day. Did he fudge the number out of vanity, or some darker showbiz anxiety about aging and obsolescence? For the first time since his show was in the planning stages, change was in the air. Producer Bob Henry wondered how long Flip could work such fierce hours, writing much of each week's show from scratch and rewriting the rest. And the 1972–73 season brought stiffer competition: CBS went after Thursday-night viewers with *The Waltons*, a Depression-era melodrama in which a wholesome family doused bedside lights to close each episode with "Goodnight, Pa," "Goodnight, Ma," and "Goodnight John-Boy." It was clever programming, putting a corny heart-warmer up against TV's first black superstar. That fall *The Waltons* ran a close second to Flip on Thursday nights, sometimes capturing enough viewers to pull him out of the week's top ten while John-Boy and family inched into the top twenty.

During the same Q&A bit in which Flip trimmed a year from his age, another audience member asked if the rumors were true: Was Flip going to make a movie? The crowd cheered, but Flip said no. "I've devoted my attention to television. There's no picture that gets me to as many people as I get to here in one hour, and I'm not trading it," he explained. It was a good line, but Sidney Poitier and Bill Cosby soon convinced Flip that he didn't have to give up television to appear in a film. The two black superstars offered Flip a bully pulpit, a lucrative cameo in a caper film called *Uptown Saturday Night*.

In Poitier's box-office hit, Reverend Leroy rails against moral decay in his flock. Reciting the World War II bromide about loose lips' sinking ships, he claims that gossip can sink souls as well as aircraft carriers, "and loose lips won't help your buoyancy. If we were as fast with our hips as our lips, we'd have a bigger church here." The Rev prescribed "more romance and less hot pants. More midnight sleepin' and less midnight creepin'!" Film critic Vincent Canby gave thanks for his performance, calling him "marvelously funny . . . Wilson, a rousing orator, almost stops the film."

He'd taken his sons to the *Uptown Saturday Night* set, where David and Kevin watched their pops work with Poitier, Cosby, and Harry Belafonte. Then the boys piled into yet another, still-more-expensive Corniche with the same vanity plates—one of Flip's serial KILLERs—for the ride home. They were zipping along Pacific Coast Highway when eleven-year-old Kevin pointed at Catalina Island, twenty-two miles off the coast, and asked, "Is that Hawaii?" Flip laughed. "You little motherfuckers haven't been to Hawaii, have you?" He did a U-turn and headed for the airport. By dinnertime the boys were on Oahu, squinting up at a tropical sun. They had no luggage, so Flip bought what they needed at the Honolulu airport: shorts, flip-flops, floral shirts, straw hats, and big shiny nautilus shells they could hold to their ears to listen for the ocean. Flip pretended to phone Hawaiian singer Don Ho on one of the shells, inviting them to a luau at Don's place. He rented a car and drove straight from the airport to a volcanic plateau blanketed with sword-sharp, lime-green leaves that hid the biggest pine cones David and Kevin had ever seen. "Not pine cones," Flip corrected. "Pineapples." As usual, people came out of nowhere to fuss over him. Fieldworkers sliced the fruit and shared it with the comedian and his little boys. One of the workers got a laugh with a heavily accented "What you see is what you get." The Wilsons ate till their bellies were full. From there they drove to a gated estate near the beach.

A security man stopped the car. "Name, please?"

Flip said, "C'mon, brother. It's the Flipster. Just tell the man I'm here."

Mumbling into a walkie-talkie, the man waved them through. A driveway curled through bowers of multicolored blooms to a curb where, sure enough, Don Ho jogged up to greet them with hugs. Later, on the sand near his beachfront house, the kids played while the grown-ups smoked and drank. It was the Fourth of July, 1973. Flip must have flashed back to his first stop in Hawaii, when he was a teenage airman marooned onboard his ship because blacks weren't welcome in Honolulu's bars and brothels. Twenty-three years later, here he was with Hawaii's leading celebrity, a glass of fine wine in his hand, his sons dancing the hula with a girl in a grass skirt. Later they all watched fireworks popping over the water while a ukulele player strummed "The Star-Spangled Banner."

That was the year Richard Pryor joined the show, announcing, "Super Nigger is here!" After his 1970 Vegas freak-out and subsequent sojourn in Berkeley, the jumpy, brilliant character comic returned as a truth teller. His stand-up dredged laughs from his boyhood in his grandmother's whorehouse: "I had white dudes comin' down to my neighborhood to help the economy, saying, 'Hello, little boy, is your mother home? I'd like a blow job.'" As an actor he'd won raves for a tragicomic turn opposite Diana Ross in the 1972 film *Lady Sings the Blues,* only to lose the lead role in Mel Brooks's 1974 *Blazing Saddles.* Pryor cowrote the western spoof with Brooks and was shocked to hear he wouldn't be starring as Black Bart. Brooks had to tell him that no studio would bankroll a picture starring a comic with a "nervous breakdown" in his background and a well-known taste for blow. Cleavon Little got the part instead. Pryor gulped down his pride and went to work for Flip.

In addition to his writing chores, he did stand-up on the show and acted in sketches. "Flip's tight ship got loose when Richard was on," Tim Conway remembers. "*Extremely* loose. Richard would barely look at the script. Flip went along and we improvised. That was one of Flip's strengths, making use of everybody's ammunition."

Though Flip and Pryor called each other "brother," in comedy terms they were closer to father and son. Flip was only seven years older, but at age thirty-nine he had one foot in the psychedelic sixties and the other in vaudeville. Pryor, thirty-two, was a different sort of pioneer, redefining the role of a black man in comedy, blazing a trail for Eddie Murphy, Chris Rock, Jamie Foxx, and others who never had to perform for dimes 'n' drinks on the Chitlin' Circuit. As a result, the personal warmth between them coexisted with constant professional friction. Pryor didn't hide his scorn for what he considered Flip's accommodations to the network and its mostly white audience. He mocked the fruit-salad formula, calling Flip "NBC's house Negro."

Naturally Flip took the high road. "Fuck you, you late-on-the-scene motherfucker. This is prime-time TV," he said. "I'm selling

Rice Krispies. If we get some Cocoa Krispies in the mix, fine. But if you think this is going to be the H. Rap Brown show or the Richard Pryor show, you can turn in your jacket." Flip had given the cast and crew matching bomber jackets, partly to help them keep warm on his soundstage, which he kept below sixty degrees to save money, and partly to remind them who was HNIC around here. Those were the letters embossed on Flip's jacket, for Head Nigger In Charge.

According to Flip's nephew Rashon Khan, who later served as bodyguard to both men, Pryor deferred to Flip as much as he did to anyone. "It was Flip who taught Richard how to play a junkie. Richard wasn't doing junk yet. He looked up to Flip. That's not to say Flip could control him. Nobody could." Khan recalls a night when Pryor barged into the studio during a taping, shoving an usher who got in his way. The audience booed him. Pryor stopped in his tracks. He looked around—a performer's moment, waiting to make sure every eye was on him. "And then he reaches down, unzips his fly, and pulls his dick out. Tells the crowd, 'Suck it.' Now Flip runs over and he's hot. You could almost see the *energy* coming off him. I thought they might come to blows. But Flip took control. He got Richard out of there, and the show went on."

Pryor inherited a role Cosby had played before him, a jobless layabout philosophizing with Flip on the stoop of a crumbling tenement. Flip claimed these "Marvin and Howard" scenes allowed his audience to see how black men behaved when there were no whites around: "A few years ago, if they saw someone with a big natural and raggedy clothes, they'd think he's a hoodlum. With these characters they can see love between the guys, and beautiful funny thoughts said in a different way, even if it's not grammatically correct." He recognized that pop culture was accelerating. By the time he described what he and Pryor were doing in 1973, "a few years ago" meant 1970 or '71. He was slower to see how the same acceleration might threaten his own show. Two-plus years into its run, his brand of fruit salad didn't seem as fresh as it had in the heady 1970–71 season. *All in the Family* was more daring. *Sanford and Son* was newer. (So was *The Waltons*.) Challenged by the competition as well as by Pryor, who berated the boss as "passé as in pass-fucking *say*," Flip stepped up his efforts. He reread Max Eastman's *Enjoyment of Laughter* for the twentieth time. He spurned interviews and movie offers. Working harder than ever, he sat up late toking and typing after twelve-hour workdays, then took his Flair pens and legal pads to bed. But he couldn't—or wouldn't—change his version of the funny.

In one new bit Reverend Leroy announced a soul-saving mission to Nevada. "Sin runs *rampant* in Las Vegas! But I don't care how fast it runs, I am going to keep up. There are many fallen women in Las Vegas, and I am going to pick them up!"

An old-school punch line like that might not impress Pryor, but it hit a nerve with the Rev's real-world colleagues. Pastor Amos Jackson, a spokesman for the Tennessee Baptist Missionary and Education Organization, pronounced Reverend Leroy "an insult to God," despite the fact that Flip was careful never to mention God or cite Bible verses in his Church of What's Happening Now skits. "We are not trying to rip off Flip as a brother," Jackson said, "but few black preachers are buffoons. Few black choirs do the 'boog-a-loo' dressed in miniskirts. We feel that Flip is being used by some of his sponsors to emasculate the black church." The word "emasculate" really got to Flip, who was already smarting from the flak he'd caught from the black community over Geraldine. *Emasculate my ass*, he thought. "I have no regrets and no apologies," he told reporters, vowing that he would "absolutely in no way" alter the Rev's act. "I am a very spiritual person with a God-given talent to make people laugh."

Later that year, Franklyn Ajaye made his TV debut on Flip's show. "I was a neurotic, insecure kid thrown in with giants," he recalls. "Flip, of course, was the veteran pro. All those years on the circuit helped him master his timing and storytelling so that when his prime-time shot came around, he had his tricks *down*. Sammy Davis Jr. was like that, too, but if you were young and black with any militance in you at all, you looked askew at Sammy. That famous picture of him with Nixon, *hugging* Nixon, worked against him. A lot of us had trouble with Sidney Poitier, too. He couldn't act in black-militant films, so he became a director out of necessity. But Flip? He might be a little old-fashioned, but he was cool. Flip had a formula that worked." But the other giants Ajaye met on Flip's set were developing a more personal formula. While Flip was still shooting his cuffs like Sinatra, Pryor and Carlin ditched their suits for jeans and sweatshirts. Pryor grew a caterpillar mustache. Carlin recited a stoner poem about his scraggly beard and lengthening hair: "Fred Astaire got no hair, nor does a chair, nor a chocolate éclair, and where is the hair on a pear? Nowhere, *mon frère*."

"Flip saw how smart those guys were—give him credit as a talent scout," Ajaye says. "Richard, of course, was also nuts. A very tortured man. If you were a young comic on the show, you just held your breath and hoped Richard Pryor was having a good day. 'Hello there, Richard!' He might say hello back, or give you the evil eye and say, 'What the fuck you lookin' at?'"

The homophobic Pryor was almost theatrically leery of men who struck him as swishy. Before one taping a hairstylist gave him what Pryor considered a lascivious look. Pryor lashed out, poking the stylist in both eyes. "Richard practically blinded him," Kevin Wilson recalls. "They thought the guy was going to lose an eye." Network officials banned Pryor from the lot, but the ban ended when Flip intervened with his friends in the executive suites. NBC's lawyers made Pryor's attack go away with a settlement and a confidentiality agreement. After a couple weeks' penance, Pryor was back as if nothing had happened, without a word of thanks, still thumbing his nose at the "house Negro" who kept him on the payroll.

The writing staff now offered the backstage spectacle of Bob Henry's golden-age veterans writing quips for Jim Brown and Curtis Mayfield while the young dope smokers chipped in lines for Carol Channing and the Amazing Kreskin. Rustic Mayberry, North Carolina, was represented on Flip's hexagonal stage by cornpone actor Andy Griffith on one Thursday night and his stuttering TV deputy, Don Knotts, on another. Bigger cities sent Paul McCartney, basketball star Bill Russell, and husband-and-wife jokesters Jerry Stiller and Anne Meara, who left six-year-old son Ben at home that night. Other nights tossed together Taj Mahal and Sandy Duncan; Slappy White and Kris Kristofferson; male centerfold Burt Reynolds—one of the few guests Flip detested ("all ego," he called Reynolds)—and ethereal singer Roberta Flack. Few programs ever exemplified their cultural moment the way Flip's did. Still, there were signs that his moment might be starting to slip toward the rearview mirror. Flip's third-season ratings pleased Herb Schlosser and his friends in the executive suite but no longer gave them happy feet. From a peak of 28.2 early in his second season—not a 28.2 percent *share* of television households watching at the time, but a *rating*, which meant that more than 28 percent of all the TV sets in America were tuning him in—his average rating slid to 23.1 in his third season. It was still a strong number, good for twelfth place overall, but for the first time the trend was down.

"They still love you," manager Monte Kay assured him. *The Flip Wilson Show* was NBC's sixth-rated program, one of the top dozen among sixty-six prime-time network shows. Flip's business savvy had made it a model of economic efficiency that minted millions for the network and Clerow Productions as it racked up episodes on its way to many more millions in syndication. "Second place or twelfth, you're ahead of the game," Kay said.

Flip wasn't so sure. On days when he wasn't bleary from overwork and the previous night's weed, he was as jazzed as ever to be hosting his own show, performing for tens of millions of fans. Other days he couldn't wait to leave the studio lot. "I get tired," he admitted. "But in this business you've got to get it when you can."

"Every fiber of his being was going full speed," Henry recalled. "How long can any man keep that up?" The host was in every scene of every show except for musical numbers and sometimes he was in those, too, duetting with guests. He joked about his singing voice while taking lessons to improve it. "He used to say, 'I wish there could be a little less of me on the show.' We'd tape on Fridays, and there would be all this love and adulation coming from the audience, but all he wanted was to get in his Rolls and drive someplace far away."

Henry called Flip "a very private man." If so he was one with a limited tolerance for privacy. When he flew, it was always first-class, the star sitting in front-row splendor with a stack of scripts, working, thinking, or brooding, sometimes for hours. But at some point he'd get antsy. He would wander down the aisle looking for someone whose clothes suggested that he or she might never have flown first-class. "Hey, friend, let's trade seats," he would say. The coach passenger got an instant upgrade, while Flip spent the rest of the flight chatting and playing cards with the people in the back of the plane. His long drives to the desert were similar. He usually started out solo, but after a while he'd pick up a hitchhiker. "I go on vibes," he told an interviewer who wondered how he avoided getting robbed. It was easy, Flip said. For one thing, many of the hitchers he encountered were Flip Wilson fans. For another, he foiled potential thieves with what Flip called his robber-stopper policy: After picking someone up, he always pulled into the next filling station and asked his passenger for an ID card. If the hitcher couldn't produce a driver's license, green card, or school ID, the ride was over. But most had one. Flip gave the filling-station manager an autograph and a generous tip in exchange for writing down his passenger's name and ID number. "Now if anything happens to me," he told the hitcher, "you're Public Enemy Number One."

Bobby Darin was never healthy after cardiac surgery in 1971. A year later, his career revived by crowd-pleasing bits on Flip's show, Darin was hosting his own summer-replacement hour on NBC, *The Bobby Darin Amusement Company*, crooning and clowning between hits off an oxygen tank. "Butch and Suntan" were sitting around Flip's pool one evening when Bobby said he had a dental appointment coming up. Flip said he hated dentists. Darin shrugged. A little dentistry wasn't much compared with the open-heart surgery that had left him with two plastic valves in his ticker.

Most heart patients require antibiotics before dental work, but Darin apparently didn't mention his heart condition to his dentist. Some friends would later claim Bobby was depressed, skipping medication as a way of committing slow suicide. Others called him a born gambler who got a charge out of cheating the odds. Whatever his reason for not taking the antibiotics he needed, his choice led to an infection that moved through his gums to his heart. After months of fading health and six desperate hours in surgery at Cedars-Sinai Hospital, Darin died on December 20, 1973. He was thirty-seven, two and a half years younger than Flip.

His death hit his friend like a punch in the gut. Flip agreed to deliver a eulogy at a tribute to Darin arranged by Dick Clark, but as the service dragged on he became so distraught he couldn't speak. "He was panicked, totally out of control," says David Gershenson, Darin's publicist. It must have hit home to think of fun-loving Bobby's leaving his show behind as well as his music, friends, fans, and most of all his son. Dodd Darin was a chubby, curly-headed, brown-eyed boy of twelve, right between the ages of Flip's sons. Bobby had divorced Dodd's mother, the troubled singer Sandra Dee; his last words were said to be, "Save Dodd from the wolves." Flip must have wondered how his own children would remember him if he keeled over tomorrow.

After Darin's funeral, he sent for Kevin and David. Meeting their plane at the airport, he tried to lift both sons at once, but they were getting too big for that. He settled for hugs, and off they went to Pea Soup Andersen's, a glorified truck stop near Santa Barbara where Flip treated a couple dozen motorists and truckers to soup and barbecue. This was Flip at his most energetic, introducing David and Kevin around, signing autographs and doing Geraldine for fans, choking up when the boys asked why they couldn't stay with him all the time. Instead of answering he drove them to Vegas. He wanted the boys to see the sights, he said, so he rented a helicopter. They circled the city with its swimming pools, golf courses, mammoth hotels, and marquees with stars' names on them, then banked southeast for panoramic views of Lake Mead and Hoover Dam. When the pilot let Flip take the controls for a minute, he whooped and gave the boys a thumbs-up. By the time he was ready to call it a day they were driving into Flagstaff, Arizona. David and Kevin were spent. Flip booked them into a lodge where there were no TVs in the rooms, a feature he appreciated. "No TV, not tonight." He sat up late watching his sons sleep.

In the morning they drove north on a road framed by hundred-foot pines. "I've got something to show you little motherfuckers," Flip said.

Five miles out of Flagstaff the boys from Miami were already gaping at a spectacle that was new to them. "It's snowing!"

"Cool!"

Grand Canyon National Park is in high country, more than a mile above sea level. The farther north they went, the harder it snowed. The winding road glistened like glass. Flip was keeping time with the music on the radio when they crested a hill and KILLER's heavy back end began sliding sideways. Kevin remembers "a cliff at the bottom of the hill. Not the Grand Canyon, but pretty big." The two-ton car slid toward it. "Pops is wrestling the steering wheel. The Rolls starts doing doughnuts. It all seemed like slow motion. Finally we hit a guardrail. If not for that rail, we were going over the edge."

The Corniche lurched to a stop in a patch of gravel, one wheel tangled with the railing. Its radio was still playing. Flip took a long breath. "Oh . . . God." His sons had never seen his eyes so wide and white.

KILLER was a beached whale, harpooned by the guardrail. They climbed out and started walking. There was hardly any traffic on the snowy road. Flip would turn and stick out his thumb when a car approached. They hadn't gone more than a quarter mile when the boys started complaining about the cold. Eleven-year-old Kevin was about to cry, but Flip hushed him. He had a big smile on his face. "It's good. We're good," he told the boys. "It's good to be alive."

Before long a rusted-out van pulled over. A van full of hippies. Hop in, the driver said. He wore love beads and a George Carlin beard. He said, "We flip for Flip," and gave father and sons a lift back to the TV-free lodge.

The 1973–74 season brought heightened tensions at work and at home. Pryor dismissed his boss as a token, hooting with derision when Flip played celebrity golf tournaments, a choice that baffled Carlin, too. What could be more passé, ofay, and outré than golfing with Bob Hope? At the same time Blonell ripped Flip as a lying, cheating husband and fair-weather father while pleading with him to come home to Florida—or to bring her and the kids to live with him in California. Then his Nielsen numbers dipped again.

"Wilson is slowly sinking in the ratings after a couple of seasons of top-10 prominence," wrote *The New York Times*'s John O'Connor. "The descent is, of course, inevitable. The straitjacket of a weekly

TV format promises only depletion." Geraldine was still sizzling, but Reverend Leroy and some of Flip's other characters—Herbie the Ice-Cream Man, Freddy the Playboy, and Sonny the White House Janitor—had hit their expiration dates. Flip tried coining new catchphrases—"Red light!" was one—but cultural lightning isn't so easily bottled. Three years after he broke prime time's color barrier, nobody was surprised to see a black man anchoring a top-rated show. Redd Foxx's *Sanford and Son* finished the '73–'74 season in third place overall, behind *All in the Family* and *The Waltons*, while *The Flip Wilson Show* slipped out of the top twenty. "The life span of variety entertainment on television has been shrinking," TV critic O'Connor wrote in a prescient column, pointing to "the contemporary phenomenon of the 'generation gap,'" which had splintered the typical Nielsen family of a generation before. In the 1950s, O'Connor explained, American families gathered around black-and-white screens to laugh and sing along with hosts like Milton Berle, Ed Sullivan, and Mitch Miller, tolerating one another's favorite acts while waiting for their own. That was fruit salad fifties-style. "Over the past few years, however, the 'demographics' have become more compartmentalized as younger audiences drift toward counterculture talent and material. Increasingly, the established variety formats were left with older audiences. And many advertisers are pointedly more interested in the 'young adult' market." In short, fruit salad was going out of style.

Clerow Wilson Jr. turned forty in December 1973. *The Flip Wilson Show* was a month short of its ninety-fifth episode, close enough to a hundred to assure its long-term value in syndication.

"I was on the show that week," Franklyn Ajaye recalls. "Flip put his heart and soul into it, but he was running out of steam."

Bob Henry suggested reducing the Flip content in *Flip*. They could add a musical number. They could let guests do longer bits without him. Or maybe they could go to a four-day production schedule like normal workaholics. Flip said no. He said his fans expected to see him in every sketch. And working *less* wasn't his idea of a way to boost ratings. He told Monte Kay he was a victim of his own success. "I did what I set out to do." He'd made TV safe for black faces. He not only hosted a prime-time variety show, outdoing Nat Cole and Sammy Davis Jr. in that department, but vaulted his show to the top of the ratings at a time when three networks divided an audience of more than 100 million every night of the week. Maybe the top variety show was bound to lose ground in the twilight of the genre, but along the way he introduced America to his own upbeat version of the black experience. He'd helped dozens of artists, black and white, who no longer needed help. He'd given jobs to Carlin and Pryor, who would go on to be the most important comics of their time, and now the same suits who fretted about Flip's ratings were talking about giving Pryor—haunted, hair-trigger, cokehead Richard Pryor—a show of his own.

NBC sent word to Monte Kay that the network would not pick up *The Flip Wilson Show* for a fifth season. In fact it would end the show in the middle of the fourth season unless ratings improved.

"Wilson didn't like ultimatums," recalls Stanley Nathanson, a close friend who called Flip by his surname. "He told me he wanted to work his butt off and retire early. Wilson wasn't interested in playing out the string. He wanted to make a bunch of money and be free."

Flip took his bows at the end of a Friday-night taping, looking like the happiest man alive. The red light died, his eyes dimmed. *Ffftt*—he was gone.

"Bob, good work," he told Henry on his way out.

"See you Monday, motherfucker," he told Pryor.

"Yassuh, massa."

Flip backed KILLER out of his parking space behind the sound-stage, rolling past Johnny Carson's space toward the guard hut and barricade that separated the NBC lot from the real world. Two minutes later he was aiming the Rolls east on the Ventura Freeway. He still believed one of his cardinal rules—*In this business, get it while you can*—but now he found himself taking a longer view of life. Some would call it mystical or superstitious. Flip believed in things unseen. Hadn't the stripper in Stockton predicted his success? Hadn't his one down-on-his-knees prayer in a lonely hotel room ("Jesus, you don't know me . . .") been followed by Redd's telling Johnny Carson about him? Now, bombing east into the Mojave, he flashed on a more recent prediction. A fan had talked her way through security, "a very elegant woman, not flashily dressed but . . . special," Flip recalled. She found him backstage and clasped his hands in hers. "I have a message for you," she said. The message was that Flip would have thirteen years in the spotlight, but not necessarily thirteen consecutive years. He could stop if he wanted, the elegant psychic said, and resume his rise anytime he chose.

It was nine years since his *Tonight Show* breakthrough. *Get it now* might be the best policy, he thought, but every passing day made him more certain that there was something missing from his life. Something spiritual. He had enough money. He was worth between $12 million and $15 million, not counting the value of future syndication rights. His investments spun off enough interest to support three or four families in style. It was tempting to think of taking a break: Stepping off the treadmill for a year or two, doing an occasional TV special or a weekend at Caesars Palace. Becoming a real father to his children. And if this woman was right, he could always step back on that treadmill for what she called "the rest of your success."

"Thank you," he told her.

"Bless you," she said.

KILLER barreled through the desert. Flip upped the volume on the tape deck. Herb Alpert and the Tijuana Brass. He sped up and slowed down with the music. He plucked a vial of coke from the glove box, sniffed a boost that woke him up. Kingman, Ash Fork, Flagstaff—Arizona towns flew by like the credits at the end of the show. There was no snow tonight, just cold high-country air streaming over the windshield. Just north of Bitter Springs, near the Utah border, a side road led to a high-desert gorge, Marble Canyon. This was his spot, a mile off the highway, two thousand feet over the Colorado River.

He parked where the road dead-ended. Worn out by the drive, the coke, the smoke, and the beers he'd enjoyed on the way, Flip stretched out in the front seat with his feet on the dash, looking up at a star-strewn sky.

An hour later the first light of Saturday morning hit the canyon's far wall. Flip stretched and yawned. He got out of the car. He took a few steps toward the rim of Marble Canyon. The marbled rock that gave the gorge its name glinted red and pink and purple, brown and gold. *Like a painting,* he thought, *a living, moving painting.* He wanted to weep. Or jump. Instead he did what he was here to do. Watching the sun fill the canyon with color, he made his decision.

LIBERTY

12

Looking for the Why

◈ "I don't believe what I'm hearing."

Monte Kay ran a hand through his thinning hair. He and Flip stood in a conference room in Kay's offices at the corner of Sunset and Doheny in West Hollywood. A long glass table between them held glasses of ice water and small mounds of cocaine. Both men ignored the blow.

"You're pissed. I understand," Kay said. "But you'll cool off."

"They can't drop me, Monte. I'm out."

Flip wasn't inclined to slide down the shitter with President Nixon in the spring of 1974, not after nine years of nonstop success. "Tell them I'll do a few specials, but this is it for *The Flip Wilson Show*. I worked my ass off for seventeen years, and I won. I got the cookie. Now I want to be a dad to my kids."

Kay mimicked Butterfly McQueen. "You don't know *nothin'* 'bout raisin' babies!"

Flip laughed. "They're not babies. And I've got Sylvia. They love her like a mother."

"Sylvia *wants* this?"

"She will when she finds out. I'm telling you first. I'm going to be a father full-time!" Flip said it like a man whose wife was going into labor.

He had plenty of room for his kids in the house he'd bought the year before on Carbon Beach, a mile-long stretch of Malibu between Carbon Canyon Road and Malibu Pier. Some locals called it Billionaires' Beach. Flip paid $300,000 for the property, equivalent to about $1.4 million in 2013 dollars. Kay, who brokered the deal, called it a bargain. Modern, rectilinear, with dark wooden beams and smoked-glass windows, the main house dominated grounds that also featured outbuildings for guests and staff and a garage the size of a school gym. The deck overlooked a stretch of beach where Johnny Carson power-walked every morning.

Back home after breaking the news to his stunned manager, Flip got to work prepping the place for his sons' arrival. His daughters could come later—they were younger and probably still needed their mother. But the boys already knew Sylvia. Who had a question.

"Where do I fit in?" she wanted to know. Hadn't she been with him off and on for seventeen years, more on than off? Cooking for him, dressing up to look good for him at parties and premieres, sleeping with his scarred behind without ever asking for a ring? Hadn't she babysat his sons when they visited? Wasn't that enough?

"That's just it," Flip said. "I told them to think of you as their mother." He was missing the point.

"They've got a mother," Sylvia reminded him.

"Blonell's staying in Miami." Flip didn't mention that he'd asked Blonell to live with him and the children in California, but she'd turned him down. Too late, she said—her life was in Florida. Now he told Sylvia, "It's just the kids coming. Just the boys at first."

She shook her head. "I am not raising that bitch's kids."

"I'm not asking," Flip said. She was his lady, she lived in his house, and pretty soon his kids would, too. "You'll learn to love them."

Instead she packed up and left, then served him with legal papers demanding $4 million for "services rendered." Flip knew his attorneys could fend off the lawsuit, but being rejected was something new and different. He'd had sex with countless women since

the mid-sixties, when he started getting famous, from Blonell and
Sylvia to his so-called occasionals, who made time for him when he
came through their cities, as well as one-night groupies and giggly
backstage visitors whose names he forgot while their perfume still
scented his dressing room. Sylvia was the first in a decade to turn
her back on him.

He flew to Florida, rented a Cadillac, and drove to Miami Shores.
He wasn't bearing gifts this time, just his rich, happy, single-minded
self. He paused at the front door, gathering himself for a moment
the way he did before going onstage. Then he tried the door. Un-
locked.

"I'm here!"

The living room was still. Shoes, toys, and schoolbooks lying
around, paper plates on a TV tray, crumbs on the floor. Somewhere
a radio played bubblegum pop.

"Where is everybody?" he called.

This time the kids heard him. They came running, fourteen-
year-old David, twelve-year-old Kevin, seven-year-old Tamara, and
toddler Stacey, who was three. "Pops!" "Daddy!" He lifted Stacey.
He hugged and kissed them all.

"Where's your mother?" he asked, scanning the unkempt living
room and kitchen.

Out, they said.

Had she made dinner for them? No. So what where they eating
on the TV tray? Cereal.

"Does Mommy go out a lot?"

Yes.

"Mostly in the daytime? Or at night?" he asked, badgering the
witnesses. He was sure Blonell was sleeping around. Of course the
kids had no way of knowing how she spent weekdays when they
were at school or nights after they went to bed, so he was asking

about the hours between homework and bedtime. Prime time. They followed him to the kitchen, where he pulled cereal boxes and Twinkies from cabinets, asking, "Where's the *food*?" Next he tromped to their mother's bedroom.

"Oh, was he hot," Kevin recalls, his eyes wide thirty-five years later. "Pops goes into her walk-in closet and tosses her blouses and dresses around, cussing her out. Then he goes back to the kitchen. Comes back with a butcher knife and a jug of bleach. You'd think we'd be scared, but he wasn't mad at us. It was a hell of a show! He cut up Mom's clothes, put them in her bathtub, and dumped bleach on them. He took one of her lipsticks and wrote *Bitch* on her mirror. Then he looked at David and me. He said, 'Take a good look at this house because you're done living here.' We got a few minutes to get our clothes and some toys before he took us out to the car."

Flip's lawyers worked out an agreement with Blonell. As David remembers it, "Our mother got one point five million, and he got us." Budget-conscious Flip recorded the figure as $1 million in one of his notebooks. Either way, giving up custody of her children made Blonell a millionaire. Flip eventually took in Tamara and Stacey while Blonell kept Michelle in Florida.

"Check it out," Flip said the day he brought his boys home to Malibu. The beach house reflected the afternoon sun to the ocean. Flip's sunken living room held a mammoth coffee table hewn from a church door. The ashtrays were crystal. A spiral staircase led upstairs, where a pile of brand-new sports gear waited for Kevin and David. Two bulldogs bounded through the house, chasing a three-legged Siberian husky and a pair of Abyssinian cats sniffing at a birdcage that held a pair of snow-white doves. The birds were a gift from Richard Pryor, a peace offering after he and Flip patched up one of their feuds. Flip liked to get them high by blowing pot smoke into their cages until one of them—the one named Cheech, maybe, or was it Chong?—keeled over and hung upside-down from its perch. The three-legged husky, named Reno for one of Flip's favorite towns, was his "motherfucker-huntin' tripod." Everyone needed a motherfucker-hunting dog, he said, "because there's motherfuckers everywhere."

A garage near the Jacuzzi held two Rolls-Royces. One was the latest KILLER Corniche, the other a Silver Shadow with license plates that read ASANTE, Swahili for "thank you," Flip's grateful nod to God. The Rollses shared the garage with a turbocharged Porsche Carrera. Still there was enough room for a mirrored rehearsal space where he worked on dance moves—thus the cane, dancing shoes, and vaudeville-style straw boaters hanging on hooks by the mirror. One of the hats was Flip's. The other, which never left its hook, was Bobby Darin's.

Upstairs the master bedroom adjoined a bathroom the boys would swear was bigger than a car wash. Flip figured the shower was the last place thieves would look for valuables, so he put a wall safe in there that held documents, jewelry, coke, pot, a few stacks of fresh hundred-dollar bills, and a pistol, a Walther nine-millimeter.

"*That* scared us," Kevin says. "But Pops said he needed the gun. Some nights he took it out of the safe and stuck it under his pillow. 'You can't be too careful,' he said, 'not when you're the only nigger in Malibu.'"

As if to prove him right, a thief broke into the garage that summer. The culprit stole the Porsche, stripped it for parts, and left it on a side street, but it was an imperfect crime. Police tracked a suspect to his garage, where they found incriminating souvenirs: tennis rackets, tennis balls, a set of golf clubs—and six dozen golf balls with Flip's name stamped on them.

School was a culture shock for Kevin and David Wilson. Kevin transferred from a mostly black school in Florida to Webster Elementary near the emerald lawns of Pepperdine University. He was one of a handful of blacks among more than two hundred white students so tuned to the Southern California zeitgeist that they were already using Valleyspeak with ironic interior quotes: "'Grody to the max,' yeah right." Some taunted Kevin. "Your dad's a homo, dresses like a girl," they said. "The *devil* made him a homo!" The new kid knew he was in wonderland the day he came home from school, flipped on the TV, and saw one of his new classmates, twelve-year-old Kristy McNichol, starring in an *ABC Afterschool Special*.

David attended Malibu Park Junior High overlooking Zuma Beach. Flip liked to drive him to school. John Travolta, twenty, on the cusp of stardom after signing to costar in *Welcome Back, Kotter*, was renting the house next door; sometimes Travolta waved goodbye to Flip and David as they pulled onto PCH. One morning Flip stopped to help a driver whose Ferrari had a flat. David thought the stranded motorist looked like an alien, but Flip said not to worry: "Say hello to Miles Davis."

"It was exciting, being a black child in a Rolls-Royce, seeing people point at us," David says. "But it made me uncomfortable. I'd ask Pops to drop me off a couple blocks from school. I'd walk the rest of the way. I don't know if he was hurt by that. I was just a kid, thinking of myself. We never talked about feelings. He'd wave goodbye and say, 'Have a great day, son. Knock 'em dead.'"

David's schoolmates were a memorable bunch. "Rob Lowe was in some of my classes. Tatum O'Neal was there, and Steve McQueen's son Chad, Martin Sheen's sons Emilio and Charlie, Bob Dylan's daughter Maria, and Sean Penn. Sean was our class president. He was kind of a teacher's pet, but that didn't keep him from mooning cars from the school bus." The Wilsons hosted sleepovers for a youngster Flip knew from the show, Michael Jackson, who was David's age. Michael brought his sisters Janet and La Toya to play on the trampoline Flip bought for the kids, but was too scared to bounce too high. Kevin was the bold one. "Kevin, be careful!"

Michael cried, which only made Kevin jump higher until he bounced clear off the trampoline. Hearing Michael's high-pitched "Oh no!" he landed face-first in the sand. For a moment he lay still, taking inventory, the way his pops had done after jumping off a barracks roof to win a bet. Then Kevin stood up, dusted himself off, and took a bow. Michael hugged him.

With Sylvia out of the picture, Flip spent evenings with a former "occasional" named Rosylin Taylor. A onetime Playboy Bunny with long hair and a hundred-watt smile, Roz was twenty-eight. Blonell had introduced her to Flip. Now, in addition to her million dollars, Blonell had the glum satisfaction of seeing Roz try to get a wedding ring from him. Shortly after they met in 1973, bubbly Roz told *Jet* that she and Flip were engaged. Two years later she was still waiting for him to set a wedding date. Meanwhile she threw herself into the role of stepmom, driving David and Kevin to school when Flip opted to sleep in, which was most of the time. She drove them to tapings of Flip Wilson specials. She drove them to Roscoe's for chicken and waffles, and to history lessons with her father, a dean at Shasta junior college who taught black history. Flip wanted his sons to know as much about George Washington Carver and Frederick Douglass as about George Washington and Douglas MacArthur. On weekends Roz dressed up and joined Flip for parties like the ones at Sammy Davis's house, with its circular living room where Sammy let Roz try on a pair of shoes he kept on a shelf, the ruby slippers Judy Garland wore in *The Wizard of Oz*.

More often Flip socialized at home. It was safer. He didn't want some *National Enquirer* snoop snapping photos of him lighting an expertly rolled joint (David and Kevin were back on the assembly line) or dipping his nose to a dollop of white powder. Celebrity guests understood his caution, but was he being practical or paranoid? After a quarter century of drug use, Flip wasn't always sure himself. Leery of anyone he didn't know and of some he did, he accused Roz of pilfering jewelry. He jokingly frisked guests he didn't recognize, and some he did, before leading them on tours of the house. When a music mogul's wife gushed about the place and Flip joked that he was bringing down local property values, she offered to buy it on the spot for a million dollars. Flip acted offended. "This is my *home*," he said. He shook his head when the woman upped her offer to a million and a half. "No." Two million? "Forget it." When she asked if he'd take three million dollars, he said, "Can I get my toothbrush?"

His guests sipped Dom Pérignon—Pryor preferred Courvoisier—and noshed on sushi, still exotic in 1975. There was always plenty of pot, coke, and hashish, plus peyote and the occasional magic mushroom. Redd Foxx was a regular. So were the Davises, Sammy and Miles, Rodney Dangerfield, Gina Lollobrigida, *Fugitive* actor David Janssen, and singers Minnie Riperton and Helen Reddy. One night Bette Davis wobbled through the door on her high heels, clutching Dangerfield's arm.

"*Flippp*," said the doyenne who'd named the Academy Award after her uncle Oscar. "You . . . are . . . brilliant!"

Before then his top encounter with Old Hollywood was Groucho Marx's eightieth birthday in 1970. Groucho had walked him through his den, waving a cigar at an Oscar he dismissed as "honorary" and showing off a prize he preferred, a lapel pin he'd won for a hole-in-one at Hillcrest Country Club. Flip thought tonight was even better, hearing sixty-seven-year-old Bette Davis praise Geraldine.

"Brill-i-ant!" she said. "As Geraldine you remind me of Olivier—with better legs."

He introduced her to Roz, who had the best legs in the house. Flip listened to jazz on the stereo, his guests' laughter, a *clack* from the next room—his sons playing pool with Jermaine and Michael Jackson—and as he clasped Bette Davis's papery hand it occurred to him that this was a miracle. Little Clerow from The Hill was so far ahead of the game that he could keel over dead at this moment with no regrets. Unlike Bobby Darin. Unlike his real pops, Leroy Taylor. Unlike almost every man who ever lived. But he didn't fall over. He sped up. Soon he and Rodney were abusing their nasal membranes in a corner of Flip's den. There, *better!*

The final *Flip Wilson Show* aired on March 7, 1974. Flip's guests included Dennis Weaver of *McCloud* and Buffalo Bills football star O. J. Simpson. In a fit of prescience, Flip and his writers revealed that Simpson was Geraldine's never-before-seen boyfriend—Killer.

There were no tearful farewells. After the wedding skit in which Geraldine finally marries her Killer, Flip took his bows and got out of there. He now had ninety-five shows in the can, just enough to ensure success in syndication. Flip agreed to finish out his NBC contract with four specials to run during the 1974–75 season. The specials paired Geraldine with bumbling cop Peter Sellers and a charm-school principal played by Cher in horn-rim shades and a leopard-print dress. Pryor played pool shark Peoria Stroker to Flip's Willie the Trick. Behind the scenes, Monte Kay explored opportunities with other networks. Flip and his manager were precisely as loyal to NBC as the network had been to them.

Less than six months after NBC's final Flip Wilson special, a new series of specials began on CBS. *Travels with Flip* showed the star sparring with Muhammad Ali, riding horses with jockey Willie Shoemaker, visiting ski country in Idaho and the Grand Ole Opry in Nashville. In one program he popped up in all-black Boley, Oklahoma, where the women lined up to kiss him and the men shook his hand, saying how proud of him they were. "The show suited his love for the road," says producer Paul Cooper. "He'd drive the Rolls to our location and take off after the shoot. When he got tired of driving, he'd leave the car at an airport—drop it at the curb and fly home. He'd stick a note on the dash, *Call Paul Cooper*, with my phone number, and I'd have the car towed back to L.A."

During Flip's year of transition, Richard Nixon self-destructed. Brought down by the Watergate scandal, Nixon helicoptered off the White House lawn in August 1974, leaving Gerald Ford in the Oval Office. The new president described himself as, among other things, a Flip Wilson fan. When he celebrated his sixty-second birthday the following summer, Flip was there to serenade him. Swanning around Ford, Geraldine trilled "Happy Birthday, Mr. President." She called the Republican president America's "main man" and hailed Betty Ford as "first Mama." Somewhere, Richard Pryor and Franklyn Ajaye were wincing. If Flip saw his White House gig as Geraldine's Marilyn Monroe moment, they saw something more like Sammy Davis's hug with Nixon. Flip was photographed schmoozing with billionaire vice president Nelson Rockefeller and Cambodia carpet-bomber Henry Kissinger. Soon he was teeing off with Ford, Bob Hope, and their friends on the PGA golf tour, pointing to the golfers and joking, "He's the pro, I'm the phylactic." Was this fruit salad or a lone Cocoa Krispie in the wrong bowl?

"Would Richard Pryor do that? Flip knew he was losing ground with younger, hipper people," says Roberta Kay, a hairstylist on *Travels with Flip*. After succeeding Diahann Carroll as Monte Kay's wife, she joined Flip's inner circle in 1975. "He was restless. Would he make more specials? Play Vegas? He really did want to raise his children, but I think he had a sort of performer's idea of what that meant. He wanted to be a superhero to his kids, but I'm not sure he had the patience for it."

When a fifty-year storm struck Carbon Beach, triggering mudslides and floods, he hired a bulldozer to build a berm of sand on the beach. He woke David and Kevin. "Come on, we've got to help people out." They pushed a wheelbarrow loaded with buckets and shovels to Burgess Meredith's house and cleared the veteran actor's driveway. They helped *Dallas* actor Larry Hagman sweep sand from his living room. It was after midnight, rain still sweeping the beach, when they joined Linda Ronstadt, unrecognizable in galoshes, raincoat, and a floppy hat, shoveling mud from a neighbor's deck while Rodney Dangerfield sat in a lounge chair nursing a drink, saying, "You missed a spot."

One afternoon the breeze brought feathers into Flip's living room. The boys saw their pops run across the deck in a bathrobe, waving his handgun. "Where's the cat? Where's the cat?"

One of Pryor's doves lay dead on the deck. Flip was apoplectic. He'd read that doves mate for life. "This motherfucker's mate is screwed. Widowed!" Chasing an Abyssinian downstairs to the beach, he fired. One bullet kicked up a puff of sand. Another hit the cat.

David and Kevin helped him bury both animals in the sand. They trudged up the steps to the deck to find the second Abyssinian cleaning itself, a small white feather stuck in its paw.

"Shit," Flip said. But then he decided it was funny. "I bet I'm not the first guy from my old neighborhood who ever shot the wrong cat."

Christmas week 1975: Flip lay on the couch in his sunken living room, rubbing his eyes. Still bleary from last night's party, he was lonely. Lonely and shocked to be lonely so soon after making the right life choice. The spiritual choice had to be the right one, didn't it? Or what was the use of being spiritual?

He reached for his tape recorder, a cassette deck with a microphone attached by a black curly cord. He'd been taping his thoughts, collecting material for a memoir he planned to publish someday, the life of TV's first black superstar. Maybe this would be its low point. He cleared his throat, pressed a red piano-key button on the recorder.

"My lady friend of seventeen years abandoned me," he said. "I'm sitting here in the first house I ever owned, the home I have made for my family. I'm a millionaire, a *multi*millionaire, and I'm sitting here saying, 'What is it for?' Looking for the why."

That day he'd frightened the kids for the first time. He herded all four of them into KILLER—daughters Tamara and Stacey lived with him now, too—and drove into the bluffs east of Malibu. Flip said they must be a hell of a sight, five black heads bobbing up Topanga Canyon Boulevard in a Corniche convertible. They'd probably get arrested before they got to the summit. He stuck a gospel tape into the dashboard deck and cranked the volume, letting Aretha's voice soar.

"Pops, where are we going?"

Pops was hurting, he told them. Pops felt lonesome, but not for people. He felt too far from God. Parking in a turnout at the top of the ridge, he turned his face to the setting sun. "Sit still," he said. "Listen." Now it was the children who were restless, stranded with a father who duetted with Aretha between crying jags, hugging and kissing any kid he could reach. Finally, after twenty or twenty-five minutes, he kicked the parking brake, backed into the road, and aimed KILLER downhill.

"I drove the kids home. I put them to bed," he told the tape recorder, sounding half asleep. The room was dark except for a small red light on the cassette deck. "My energy's drained. I've been having a lot of sex and snorting a lot of coke." Never more than a social drinker, he had been adding Johnnie Walker Red to his usual Heineken. Sometimes he left out the Heineken. "I'm taking megadose vitamins and protein pills to offset the coke and scotch." So why didn't he feel better? Why didn't he feel like writing new material? On the other hand, why bother when prime time motored on, with *All in the Family* and *Sanford and Son* racking up ratings while Jimmie Walker of the sitcom *Good Times* made *"Dy-no-mite!"* America's favorite catchphrase, as if Flip Wilson never existed? It was only twenty months since the last *Flip Wilson Show*. His specials were fresher still: a *Travels with Flip* in October 1975 and a *Flip Wilson Comedy Special* with Carlin and the Pointer Sisters a month later. But it seemed like forever because he was alone. Because his kids, being kids, which is to say solipsists, were already accustomed to life in Malibu, going to school in a Rolls fucking Royce, everything first-class, nobody thinking to thank the one who made it all happen. And the more day-to-day child care he did, the more he believed it was woman's work. "And there's no woman helping me. And I won't find the one I need in a bar."

Again he cleared his throat. "I put the kids to bed," he said. "That was hours ago. Then I went out and bought three thousand dollars' worth of cocaine and a bottle of scotch, and decided to kill myself."

13

Flip Out

He sat in the dark swigging scotch. It was just before dawn. The house was quiet, the children asleep upstairs. Feeling buzzed enough to think he heard their heartbeats from the living room, Flip took a bump of coke. He hadn't eaten. He'd had nothing to drink all day but whiskey. Slipping off the couch to the floor, he patted a couch pillow. He could feel the Walther pistol beneath it. But there was no hurry. He had plenty of time, sitting here in the stillness before another day began, thinking that something about sunrise spoke to his spirit. He could see leaving this world just as the sun entered it, leaving it to people with more tolerance for its thankless bullshit. Of course that would mean leaving the kids.

"Fuck the kids," he said. "Nothing they go through will be worse than what I went through."

The tape recorder was off. He was talking to himself. "Fine. I'm fucked up." He took another drink.

The sky was turning purple and orange. He stripped naked. Stripped off his rings, watch, necklace, everything, and lay naked on his back the way he had on Guam the night he tried smack for the first time. The night he lay speechless on a baseball diamond, looking up at the stars. He wasn't speechless tonight. Tonight he called for his father. Which father, he didn't know. Father in heaven, father sleeping sitting up in a stiff-backed chair, father beside him at a comedy show in Newark in 1942.

"Where are you?"

He shivered and drifted off. When he woke, the sun was up. He wasn't drunk or buzzed, just clear. Rested. He felt younger. To test this new sharpness he drank the last of the whiskey and snorted several lines of coke.

"It had no effect," he told the tape recorder in a later entry, remembering the morning when he saw what his next step should be. "I had about fifteen hundred dollars' worth of coke left in the vial. I flushed it down the toilet. I promised myself I'd never need more than a momentary toot. I wasn't sure what just happened, but it was a turning point."

He needed to perform again. To stare into stage lights and feel the spiky energy of stepping onstage with nothing but a microphone between him and success or disaster. So Monte Kay set him up at Caesars Palace—two weeks for $250,000 plus a comped penthouse suite and a wink from management. Any losses in the casino would be discounted. With his name atop the marquee by the fountains outside, Flip served as headliner on the main stage and loss leader in the casino, his glamour tempting bettors to join him in the pits. Poker was still his game. That had meant five- and seven-card stud or draw during his Air Force days and even later, when he sat in for a few hands with Bobby Darin or Sammy Davis, but now the game was Texas hold 'em. Originally known as Hold 'em and fuck 'em, it called for more patience than Flip brought to the table. Hold 'em ate his chips in no time. Roulette was more his speed. Carrying an inch-thick bankroll of hundred-dollar bills and a pouch packed with black hundred-dollar chips, purple five-hundred chips, and orange thousand-dollar chips called pumpkins, he handed out black chips as tips and saved his pumpkins for big bets. Three out of four nights he lost, but now and then he rode a hot streak until he was up fifty or sixty thousand, surrounded by cheering fans. One night he had

to stop because it was almost curtain time. He paused at the rou-
lette wheel on the way to a private elevator. Leading the crowd in a
chant of *"Win, Flip, win,"* he covered half the board with pumpkins.
As the wheel spun he theatrically checked his watch, popped his
eyes—*It's that late?*—turned and walked away. Listening, and still listening while the wheel clicked slower and slower, he heard the ball
fall . . . and a chorus of cheers told him he was a winner.

He liked the pulse of Las Vegas. He wore a tux onstage, snapped
his fingers, and delivered an hour of Geraldine-free stand-up for
gray-haired audiences. He asked matrons in pearl necklaces if they
were wearing their husbands' gallstones. Working blue-ish for the
first time since his Village Gate and hungry i days, he claimed Indian heritage, saying he was a member of the Fugawi tribe, "de-
scended from Chief Fugawi, who got lost between Africa and
Harlem, and said, 'Where the Fugawi?'" Vegas crowds loved a bit in
which he said he couldn't stand "creepy little midgets" before a
dwarf in a tux barreled onstage to kick, punch, and chew Flip's leg.
Better yet was the night Elvis himself came out of the crowd, threw
his arm around Flip, took the microphone and told how he'd begged
Priscilla's forgiveness for boinking Ann-Margret by quoting Geraldine: "The devil made me do it!" The band struck up "Devil in Dis-
guise" as Flip and the King bowed to the crowd and each other.

After that Caesars gig, Flip headlined at the Sands, the Sahara,
and the MGM Grand before returning to Caesars for double the
money: $250,000 a week. At Caesars a security man would tap on
his door, ride downstairs with him, and walk him through a restaurant kitchen to the showroom, all in less time than it took a leggy
companion upstairs to climb out of his circular bed. Still, with Vegas evolving from its Rat Pack era to a more modern, corporate
mode, even Frank Sinatra bowed to new efficiencies. Sinatra, at
sixty, was playing fewer dates than before, leaving his band idle for
weeks at a time. Management suggested that Sinatra's bandleader,

Don Costa, cut costs by losing a horn or two. Frank had a better idea. He asked his buddy Flip to use Costa's band, too. Not directly—requests from Frank came from guys who were said to know guys—but the message was clear, and Clerow from Jersey City wasn't going to disappoint the pride of Hoboken. Now, instead of a lone piano player, Flip had Costa's seventeen-piece orchestra playing him on and off. Partly to justify its expense he added a Geraldine set to his act, which pleased fans who expected to see her. Prancing in a miniskirt and a feather boa, she sang, "How can I miss you if you never go away? I like beef, but not every day," backed by a band worthy of the Chairman of the Board.

Flip took pride in the fact that his groupies were younger than Sinatra's. Younger and more limber. One night six of them joined him in his suite. Flip's female fans rubbed his back. They fed him grapes. They undressed each other, then undressed him. This was a longtime fantasy come true: half a dozen nude, adoring girls waiting to do his bidding, waiting for Flip to make his move in a penthouse suite overlooking the Strip. He stood beside the bed, taking in the scene, then stepped onto it as if it were a diving board.

"I don't want to see no faces," he said.

When Flip came home from Vegas, he decided to do something useful. He signed on as chairman of the American Cancer Society's 1976 fund drive and threw himself into the role. He sat through long banquets, gave speeches, visited cancer wards, recruited corporate sponsors, and helped break a TV taboo. The taboo breaking was an accident. That August, guest-hosting for Carson for the umpteenth time, he welcomed his friend Minnie Riperton, a frequent guest at his Carbon Beach parties, to *The Tonight Show*. Riperton, then twenty-eight, was known for her vocal range. He was about to ask about her next album and her five-octave range when she startled him by revealing that she had breast cancer. According to news reports, Riperton "admitted" undergoing a radical mastectomy. *Ebony* reported that she "came out of the closet" by speaking about the disease, urging other women to get mammograms. Before dying three years later—survived by husband Richard Rudolph and daughter Maya, who would go on to star on *Saturday Night Live* and launch a movie career—Riperton said she regretted springing the news on her friend. "Flip was really shook up."

Still uneasy with talk of illness and death, he wept after cancer ward visits. Roz and the kids heard him crying after Elvis died in 1977, the King falling dead on the toilet like Lenny Bruce. "We didn't know if he was sad or scared," son Kevin recalls. "We left him alone till he was ready to speak. By then he was Pops again, raring to go."

Like many fathers he related to his sons through sports. David was the first to earn a pool cue by beating his pops on their home table, sinking the eight ball while Flip shouted and pounded his hands on the table to distract him. David got so proficient that his father lured Redd Foxx into his den for "a few friendly games." Flip lost a few hundred dollars to Redd, then dared him to "play my little boy double or nothing." Foxx lost and kept losing until his wallet was as empty as on the day he stiffed Flip for cab fare. After that, he addressed David as Slick. "Hello there, Slick, your daddy lyin' and cheatin' as usual?"

David grew to five-eleven. Lighter skinned and more angular than his father, he got used to hearing Flip joke that darker, chubbier Kevin was his real son. Yet Flip fairly melted with pride the first time David broke 80 on the golf course. No matter how many pro-am events Flip played with President Ford, Bob Hope, and dozens of PGA Tour pros, as a golfer he could be charitably described as a chop. He never broke 90. After David shot 79, the father who'd told his sons they were spoiled, saying they should go to military school, get a little iron in their butts like he did in the Air Force, began talking about sending David to golf school, where number-one son could hone his game in hopes of turning pro.

When the Wilsons went to movies, easily bored Flip liked to re-enact a prank from his youth: tossing Jujubes and Raisinets so that they fell like hail on moviegoers behind him. He considered updating the prank by throwing money, but coins might put someone's eye out, and bills fluttered rather than flew. He solved the aerodynamic problem by folding dollar and five-dollar bills into pebble-sized sixteenths, but they fell unnoticed. That prank pleased nobody but the theater's surprised, delighted cleanup crew.

"He'd rather stay home anyway," Kevin says. "We sat around watching sitcoms—*Laverne and Shirley*, *Hogan's Heroes*, *M*A*S*H*." They were watching TV one evening when the doorbell rang. Flip checked the monitor beside the front door, a closed-circuit screen showing a cab, a driver, and a scraggly passenger ranting that Jesus had sent him to save Flip Wilson's soul. Flip thumbed the intercom. "Praise the Lord and wait there." He went to the garage, returned with a baseball bat, and charged outside. "Jesus told me to beat the shit out of you," he yelled. The soul saver fled on foot. There was no police report. Malibu police seemed more concerned with black motorists doubling the 50-mph speed limit on PCH in fifty-thousand-dollar cars. Kevin recalls zooming along with Jermaine Jackson in a glistening Mercedes 450SEL 6.9 when a cruiser pulled them over. The white cop "handcuffed Jermaine. For speeding. He said he was sick of us. 'You Jacksons and Wilsons with your Rolls-Royces and Mercedes, and then we get off work and get in our Pintos.'" At the police station, Jermaine signed autographs for cops until Berry Gordy's bodyguards arrived to drive him home.

Flip's golf buddy Evel Knievel had the fastest ride of all. The daredevil motorcyclist admired Flip's Corniches, joking that he'd like to get them out on a figure eight—he'd once won a demolition derby driving a nearly indestructible Rolls. Knievel hobbled around on a cane that sloshed when he walked—his hollow cane was stocked with Wild Turkey. He and Flip toasted each other with nips from the cane while Evel showed off the X-2 Sky Cycle he'd ridden into Idaho's Snake River Canyon, barely escaping with his life. "To suck a joint and do that jump," Flip said, mounting the Sky Cycle, "that would be the ultimate."

He claimed to be fighting his drug habit to a draw. Sometimes he stayed clean for a month or more—not counting the cigar-sized joints he chain-smoked—to prove he wasn't addicted. There was no more pretending that drugs were work tools. Smoking and tooting relaxed him and kept him sane, he said, and that was enough. Pryor wanted to freebase with his old friend, but Flip refused, saying, "Smoking that shit will eat you alive." He said he worried about Pryor because Richard was an addict while he, Flip, was not the addictive type. Checking his reflection in KILLER's rearview mirror, he told himself that the handsome devil in the mirror was no junkie, even if he sometimes missed his nose while driving and had to brush white powder off his chest at the next stoplight.

One day Flip parked outside a decaying apartment building in Hollywood. He was jogging across the street to his supplier's door when a black Mercedes with tinted windows and a gold grille cut him off. The car stopped and the driver's window slid down. "Flip, Flip!" cried Michael Jackson, jumping out for a hug. Only in Hollywood, Flip said later, would you have a celebrity meet-and-greet while you're trying to cop.

In Vegas he spilled several grams of coke in his suite at Caesars. The stuff was too costly to waste, but recovering it turned out to be a project. Too much jostling and he'd lose the powder in a forest of shag-carpet fibers. After circling the spot for a minute, he found a straw, crept around the spill on his hands and knees, and sucked a buzz off the top of the pile. Yet he swore he had his habit under control. "I stay on top of it, not the other way around," he said, warning his sons to steer clear of coke.

He wasn't so strict about weed. "You boys know I smoke this shit. It's better if you try it with me," he said, lighting up. David and Kevin exchanged a look. This wouldn't be their first smoke or their twentieth, but why spoil a family moment? From then on they shared Pops's pot. He flicked burning joints at them—smoke it if you catch it—and let them keep the debris left over at the end of the household assembly line, a policy that affected quality control. "We made sure some good stuff slipped through those colanders, not just sticks and stems," Kevin says. Soon they modernized the process: after picking out the stems, they ground the buds in a kitchen blender for a smoother smoke.

Roz flew the coop in 1979. Flip's girlfriend of two and a half years sued him for half his earnings since 1976 plus $12,500 a month. "It's a cheap shot based on that Lee Marvin thing," he told report-ers, referring to the landmark 1977 case in which actor Marvin's live-in lover sued for millions in "palimony." Michelle Triola Marvin lost in court. Flip settled out of court with Roz, as he had with Syl-via and soon would with another girlfriend, dental assistant Kay-atana Harrison, who demanded $7,500 for providing what her lawyer called "wifely duties." Flip's legal team made them all go away for dimes on the dollar. "After Roz, his girlfriends kept getting younger," David recalls. "Every four or five months he'd bring one home and say, 'Treat her like she's your mother.' Well, I'm a teen-ager now, and the girls are getting closer to my age! Pretty soon I was checking out their asses, thinking, 'That's some sexy mama!'"

"Women. Want. Money." Those words introduced Flip's belated sex talk with Kevin and David. He sat his teen sons down, cleared his throat, and, like many fathers, got through it as fast as he could. "They *want* you to knock them up. Then they've got the lock on you," he said.

"It was the birds and the bees as a scare tactic," Kevin recalls. "He was trying to tell us to use protection."

Around that time Flip got permanent protection: a vasectomy. Limping around the beach house with an ice pack in his underwear, he said he couldn't wait for some gold digger to claim he'd gotten her pregnant. "I'll yell, 'Liar! I'm shooting blanks.'"

After his vasectomy, his sons were no longer allowed to fly on the same plane. "He didn't want his line to end. He said he had to keep at least one of us alive till we had a kid. He was joking, sort of," David recalls. When all four children flew, they took separate planes with one son and one daughter on each flight.

He fell for a cocktail waitress in 1979. Thailand-born Tuanchai "Cookie" Davis, described by *Jet* magazine as "a stunning Oriental," bowed to the man whose publicity photo adorned a Reno casino near the Imperial Palace, a Japanese restaurant where she worked. Cookie's bow revealed three things that appealed to Flip: her bust, her smile, and her deference. Unlike black women who argued with him and sued him, Cookie barely met his gaze. "What if we fell in love and got married?" he asked.

"Perhaps we would be happy," she said, playing along.

"But marriages go bad," Flip said. "What if I stopped loving you?"

"In that case I would lose face. I would have to kill myself."

"That's a deal I could live with!"

He invited her to his suite, but Cookie turned him down. "That's not my style, to meet a man in his hotel." His ardor ignited, Flip reached for a keno slip.

"You're playing keno?"

"No," he said. "I'm already a winner." Signing the slip with a flourish, he added, *Would you marry me?*

Cookie thought he was joking. Weeks of nonstop wooing plus a custom-made ring, a filigreed band bent under the weight of what the *National Enquirer* described as "a huge, sparkling white diamond," convinced her that he wasn't. Blonell never got a ring like that. Neither did Sylvia. Roz had dreamed of one, perhaps leading to what Flip considered her unhealthy interest in jewelry. But Cookie was the first woman since Peaches back in the fifties to get a wedding and a ring. She married Flip in the Benihana restaurant at the Las Vegas Hilton on December 14, 1979. Flip's restaurateur friend Rocky Aoki, who owned the place, served as best man.

From the start Cookie was the quietest of the Malibu Wilsons. Nineteen-year-old David, his brother, Kevin, seventeen, sisters Tamara, thirteen, and Stacey, nine, and clusters of friends whirled in and out. "There was a lot of craziness in that house—everybody doing his or her thing," Tamara recalls. When Flip got irked with his sons, he flew them to Miami to stay with Blonell. When he got too busy to drive his daughters around, he hired an English governess to look after them. Meanwhile calm Cookie watched the surf crawl up Billionaires' Beach, waiting for her husband to come home.

Her husband spent afternoons at Monte Kay's house on Curson Terrace in the Hollywood Hills. A private drive led uphill from the gate to Kay's nine-thousand-square-foot home with its commanding view over the city to the sea ten miles away. The Beatles had made this place their California hideaway in 1965 and '66, enjoying its sauna, five fireplaces, motor court with room for twenty cars, practice-shooting range, and sixty-five-foot horseshoe-shaped swimming pool with an underground observation bay. John Lennon likened it to "something out of Disneyland." George Harrison floated a papier-mâché toy, the original yellow submarine, around the pool. Now it was Flip rolling up the blacktop drive through ranks of imperial palms. "He'd honk his horn all the way to say, *'I'm here!'*" Roberta Kay recalls. Flip and Monte discussed Little David

Records and their other businesses, and plotted how and when Flip might return to TV. They often continued their talks at Kay's offices on Sunset. "Flip and George Carlin sat in my office smoking a joint, talking about George's next album for Little David Records," says the label's Paul Cooper. Franklyn Ajaye, another client of Kay's, dropped in to chat. "Flip seemed relaxed. Some performers like Joan Rivers have a desperate need to be onstage, but his take was, 'I made my money. What do I have to prove?'"

Roberta Kay saw a different side of Flip. "He was always volatile. Maybe it was drugs, maybe he just missed the limelight. Maybe it hurt him to see George Carlin and Richard Pryor passing him by. But he wasn't happy, and he blamed Monte." He blamed his manager despite the fact that Monte Kay had advised him to invest—and invested with him—in records, radio stations, office buildings, motels, ranches, and even Brahma bulls, adding millions to Flip's net worth. Thanks in part to Kay, Flip's fortune would more than quadruple in the next fifteen years. Kay also helped manage the Wilson Family Children's Trust, a multimillion-dollar fund designed to support David, Kevin, Tamara, and Stacey through the millennium and beyond. Still Flip, restless and increasingly suspicious, probably high, accused his manager of stealing from him. "It was racial," Roberta Kay says. "Supposedly Monte, of all people, cheated Flip because Flip was black."

Portia Qualls was Kay's receptionist in the Sunset Boulevard office. "I loved Flip," says Qualls, who had enjoyed his spontaneous generosity. "He'd show up with boxes of lobster, chicken, and waffles from Roscoe's. Lunch for everybody! Once he up and flew Mary Moore and me to Vegas. Mary cut Flip's hair—she charged ten dollars a haircut and he tipped a hundred. One weekend he flew us to Vegas for the weekend, put us up at Caesars with meals, show tickets, and everything, all expenses paid. Why? Just to be nice."

Qualls waved hello the day he shouldered his way through the front door carrying three gallons of paint and a brush. "Flip ignored me. He started throwing white paint around—painting our desks white, painting the copy machine, our brand-new Selectric II typewriters, and the paintings on the wall. He was shouting, 'I'm sick of Monte's shit!' I jumped out of his way. Girls were screaming, ducking under their desks and peeping around corners, saying, 'He's crazy!' But I didn't think Flip was crazy. I thought, *The man is royally pissed off.*"

His attack on his manager's office—the whitewash, everyone called it—was a statement. More than firing Monte Kay, he was erasing him. "Monte sat down and cried," Roberta Kay says. "What hurt him the most, I think, is that he'd believed in Flip all those years. He *loved* Flip."

How crazy was Monte's top client? An hour after the whitewash, dropping his paint cans in the garage, Flip gave son Kevin a thumbs-up. His thumb was spotless.

"Do you know what impresses me about what I did?" he asked. "They thought I was crazy, but I didn't get one drop of paint on me."

Flip said he couldn't trust anyone except immediate family. And he wasn't so sure even about them. He sent for nephew Rashon Khan, whose westbound flight from New Jersey was his first airplane flight, to serve as the kids' martial-arts instructor and Uncle Flip's assistant. A teenager steeped in the black-power movement, with an Afro and a don't-screw-with-me attitude, Khan admired his uncle for more than his celebrity. "Flip was never a sellout," Khan says. "He felt he was representing us all. He sent a Rolls-Royce to pick me up at the airport, and when I saw the Malibu house I got so filled up with pride that my skin tightened up, to think it was *possible*." Settling into life with the Wilsons, Khan traded books with Flip, exchanging an African-history text for a copy of his uncle's latest inspiration, Kahlil Gibran's *The Prophet*. "Flip was a mystical cat.

He would tape himself reading from *The Prophet*, reciting and playing it back until he could recite the whole book from memory."

Khan joined Flip on some of his marathon drives. "He liked to do the driving, so I just rode along." They were in Texas, passing a cattle ranch that extended to the horizon, when Flip said he had to take a piss. "He pulled over, got out. We're looking at cows as far as you can see, thousands of cows. And he hops the fence." Watching his uncle pound on the door of the nearest house, Khan had visions of a shotgun-toting cattleman blowing the intruder off his porch. "This big cowboy opens the door, takes one look at him, and *hugs* him. Turns out Flip owned the ranch."

On another trip Khan played bodyguard at a private gig at a Colorado country club, where Flip was surrounded by oilmen and their wives. "There must have been twenty white couples all dressed up, one rich cracker talking about the necessity of apartheid in South Africa. Then somebody clinks a glass. It's showtime. Flip did Geraldine for them. He did Reverend Leroy. Well, I was ashamed. It seemed like shuffling. I wouldn't speak to him on the way out of there. Flip just laughed. He held up a check and said, 'This is my job.' Asking me who won. 'Who won tonight, Rashon?' The check was made out to Flip Wilson for four hundred thousand dollars."

Flip helped his nephew get work as a bodyguard for Pryor, who needed someone to drive him to his psychiatrist's office. Pryor came out of one session looking baffled. "Rich, what's wrong?" Khan asked.

"That mother says I'm a paranoid schizophrenic. Like seven motherfuckers in one."

"So *that's* where your characters come from."

Pryor shot him a look that said *Who's the comedian here?* Then he burst out laughing.

Joining the comedian's entourage for Pryor's 1979 trip to Africa, Khan found himself shaking hands with Zimbabwean tyrant Robert

Mugabe. "A couple years before then I was writing a high-school paper on Mugabe. Now I'm eating cornbread and greens with him." In Kenya the star of *Bicentennial Nigger* and *That Nigger's Crazy* looked around a city square and saw hundreds of black faces but, in Pryor's words, "no niggers." He vowed on the spot to quit using the word. At least in public. In private, Pryor and Flip tossed the word around with glee. "Sometimes you just want to kick back and be a nigger," Flip said. At times like that he and Richard used a common code. Saying "I got a letter from home" was code for "Let's send the white folks home." After a round of handshaking and backslapping cleared the room of Caucasians, Richard and Flip felt free to break out the chicken, biscuits, and grape drink.

They still feuded constantly, leaving Khan to make peace when he could. Khan was with Pryor on a film set, whipping up Richard's breakfast—a bodyguard's sideline—when Flip slipped into Pryor's trailer with a finger to his lips. *Shh.* He and Richard hadn't spoken for months. Flip ducked behind a door, but when Pryor came in he sensed someone's presence. "Who's there?" Flip jumped out. The two men fell to their knees, hugging, saying they'd work together again in the eighties.

It wasn't to be. After an all-night drug binge on June 1, 1980, Pryor spilled rum on himself while freebasing. Neighbors saw him racing down the street with his body in flames. Third-degree burns, skin grafts, painkillers, and the onset of a twenty-year battle with multiple sclerosis dragged Pryor down in his prime.

Flip wept over his friend's misfortune but said it proved what he'd been saying: Richard was crazy to freebase. Coke was safe in moderation, but smoking it could eat you alive.

In March 1981 he and Rashon Khan flew from Miami to Los Angeles. Police officers at LAX, believing that Khan matched a "drug courier profile," stopped them. According to the police account, Flip's nephew made eye contact with a detective on the scene, "eye contact . . . consistent with the behavior of persons he had arrested in the past." The officers told Flip they wanted to search his luggage.

"Sure," he said. "I don't have any drugs that I know of. Go ahead."

They found 2.5 grams of cocaine and a plastic bag that held traces of hashish.

"Mr. Wilson, you're under arrest."

Flip and L.A. mayor Tom Bradley had to cancel their lunch meeting. When news of the coke bust broke, 7UP canceled a series of commercials featuring Geraldine. At that point the prudent business move would have been to apologize. First-time offenders could cop a plea, settle for probation and a few hours of community service. But Flip was spoiling for a fight. Insisting that he and his nephew had been singled out at least partly because they were black, he dubbed himself "No-deals Wilson" and fought the case for two years. He made a holiday of court dates, taking his kids to the courthouse where he nodded and gave a thumbs-up to his lawyer, Paul Moore II, as Moore challenged his arrest as an illegal search under the Fourth Amendment. On return trips to Malibu, Flip treated family and friends to sushi and manicures.

In 1983 the California Supreme Court ruled unanimously in his favor. *Wilson v. Superior Court* set a precedent that still governs police searches in California. The victorious appellant toked and tooted all the way home.

The week he turned fifty he hosted *Saturday Night Live*'s 1983 Christmas show. In the night's best sketch Eddie Murphy played a hairdresser with an overbearing mother: Geraldine. Thicker-waisted than in his heyday, hip-checking and smooching his "son," he got Murphy to break character with tales of "your father, Killer, a war hero. Shot three times in the back . . . he almost dropped his white flag!" (In the *SNL* universe, this made Eddie Murphy the son of Flip Wilson and O. J. Simpson.) During the curtain call under the credits, Flip, sporting a peach-colored suit and bow tie, schmoozed with Joe Piscopo, Tim Kazurinsky, and Mary Gross while Murphy, twenty-two, stood alone in a skintight jumpsuit, all black leather and attitude, the future.

When Flip agreed to host a 1984 reboot of the old Art Linkletter series *People Are Funny*, the producers had him undergo a physical exam for insurance purposes. The star came through with what he called "flying blackness." Making a muscle for producer Don Ohlmeyer, he asked, "What other fifty-year-old motherfucker do you know who looks this good? I'll outlive you all." The show was canceled after four months.

"Television's changing," he said. The craftsman who once spent years honing a routine now left empty legal pads wrapped in cellophane on his desk beside his Emmys, Golden Globe, and 1970 Peabody Award. Times were changing. So was he.

"He loved us. He hated us," says David Wilson. "He'd hug us, then say we were spoiled."

"He'd talk about family, then cut us off," second son Kevin remembers. "I'd say, 'Pops, I'm a man now.' But if I disagreed with him or took too long to cook his breakfast, I was on the outs."

"He'd freeze us out for days. Weeks."

"Finally we called him on it."

David and Kevin demanded a meeting. They told their father they loved him, but he had to "stop shitting on us." Flip nodded, thinking it over. "Then he rolled a couple of fat ones. He opened a bottle of expensive wine and shared it with us. Finally he told us how proud of us he was, and said, 'The bullshit ends now!'"

Not for long. A few days later Flip got angry because David beat him at golf. Or maybe it was because Kevin asked for money. All his sons knew was that some trivial dispute had got them frozen out again. Their father looked right through them. He wouldn't speak to them except through their cousin Rashon, the bodyguard.

"So we sent Rashon back with a message," Kevin recalls. "We said, 'Pops, how can you cut us off? Don't you remember our meeting?'"

They waited an hour. Two hours. Finally Khan returned. Trying not to smile, he said, "You win. Your father says, and I quote, 'Tell Kevin and David they're right. But I reserve the right to be a nigger.'"

The only one in Malibu, by Flip's description. And the longer he lived, the more he enjoyed testing the ways a black man with a grade-school education could spend his time and money. Buying Roscoe's chicken and waffles for everyone in the place, for instance, or watermelon and sushi for himself, as well as African art, Hawaiian weed, and the purest Colombian cocaine. Bowling was a worthy hobby. So was golf with Bob Hope and Gerald Ford. Driving into the desert soothed his soul. So did cruising the world. Standing in the shadow of the Sphinx, he said he was probably the only kid from The Hill ever to see such a sight. "He cried with happiness," Cookie recalls.

Upon their return he took up a sport more exclusive than golf. Joining Rocky Aoki's Team Benihana, Flip became a helium-balloon racer. Piloting a 1,000-cubic-foot balloon lifted his spirits—he called it a new way to get high—and gave him a distinction he figured no other man could match.

After one race, he passed a pretty girl watching the balloons come in for a landing. "They're beautiful, aren't they?" she said.

"Yes, you are." That got a smile out of her. So Flip drew himself to his full height and tried his new pickup line. "Did you know that I am the only black helium balloon pilot in the world?" he asked.

She replied, "What's black helium?"

14

God's Fool

◈ Daredevil Flip piloted several of Rocky Aoki's balloons before buying one of his own, an all-black behemoth labeled HNIC, and began entering balloon races. During one race he spent twenty hours stranded fifteen thousand feet over Mooreland, Oklahoma, peering down into storm clouds, waiting for the weather to clear. Running out of fuel, he executed a perilous nighttime landing in forty-mile-an-hour winds that left him shaken but unhurt.

Cookie wasn't so lucky. Soon after taking up her husband's hobby she crash-landed near the Missouri-Oklahoma border, the balloon's seven-hundred-pound gondola careening through the trees and fences of a wildlife preserve. "We came down fast. I heard the pilot say, 'Oh shit, we are going to die,'" she recalls. "We crash-landed, bounced up, crashed down again. I broke my left leg. My right knee was crushed." During her monthlong convalescence in an Omaha hospital, Flip visited once. "He didn't really know how to be a husband," Cookie says.

She'd never expected fidelity from Flip. Their clear agreement from the start was that Cookie wouldn't complain about his girlfriends as long as he kept them out of their home. What surprised her was her famous husband's constant need for praise. "He was so needy he couldn't stand it if I said something nice about somebody else." Kind words for Bill Cosby, Rocky Aoki, or even his own children annoyed him. "It had to be only for him. He missed the spotlight." Flip beamed the day Cookie ironically asked, "How's the world's greatest husband?" He often slept past noon on the days he didn't spend playing golf, or he holed up in his giant bathroom with his safe full of drugs, phoning downstairs when he wanted something to eat. By the fall of 1984 he and Cookie were living in separate wings of the beach house. They finally parted the following year. Flip liked to joke about the generous terms of their divorce. "I gave my fortune to a Cookie," he'd say. In fact the settlement was a sliver of his still-growing fortune: thirty months of spousal support that added up to $369,000.

Roz Taylor was back on the scene almost a decade after suing him for palimony, but the man of the house was losing faith in almost everyone around him. Convinced that someone was stealing from him, he threw what friends would later refer to as his "paranoid party." During an evening of dining and dancing, selected guests got tapped on the shoulder. They were led to his study, where a polygraph expert administered lie-detector tests.

"Have you ever stolen from Mr. Wilson?"

"Of course not!"

Roz flunked the test. Exit Roz.

The beach house seemed cursed. "Cursed or just crazy," Kevin Wilson says. After foul odors began rising from the sandy soil under the house, Flip hired a construction crew to install a new septic tank. The work site collapsed, burying a workman alive. Flip raced downstairs from his study, but there was nothing he could do. He paid for the funeral and gave the worker's wife a check for $95,000. She thanked him, then sued him.

At a family meeting, Flip told his children he was going to "find out who's who around here." Women never had to doubt that their children were their own, he said, but things were different for men. A man whose wife cheated on him might spend his life raising some other motherfucker's kids. "So I hired a private detective, and the man found some things out. One is that you, David, are not my real son. Your mother cheated on me." Flip promised that nothing would change—they were still family—but David spent weeks reeling from the news.

Flip sought refuge from his family troubles by returning to prime-time TV. While he'd never admit it, he owed his comeback to Bill Cosby.

Their relationship had been fraught from the start. Like Flip, Cosby was a natural entertainer. Unlike Flip, he skipped the years of scuffling it often takes to prove it. Rather than fight his way up, the college-educated Cosby seemed to stroll straight to TV stardom. Three and a half years younger than Flip, he'd never acted before playing a smooth secret agent on *I Spy*, becoming the first black star of a weekly TV drama. Cosby won three consecutive Emmys as Outstanding Lead Actor in a Drama. Meanwhile Flip was making his first *Tonight Show* appearances and a struggling midwesterner, Richard Pryor, three and a half years younger than Cosby, was reading a newspaper article on Cosby, thinking, *That nigger's doing what I'm fixing to do.* Pryor moved to New York and began haunting Greenwich Village clubs—a nervous kid in a suit a couple sizes too big for his bony frame, trying to be cool like Cos.

While Flip honed his act as a headliner and Pryor got his start in Village clubs, often hyperventilating with stage fright, Cosby banked his first million. Rather than exaggerate black characters the way Flip did with Reverend Leroy and Geraldine (and Pryor did later with his junkies and winos, not to mention himself), Cosby mostly ignored race. His wide-eyed kids and flustered dads were 1960s Americans of no particular color, and his timing—cultural as well as comedic—was perfect. As comedy chronicler Mel Watkins observed, "At a time when racial confrontations were escalating in the streets, his relaxed, chatty style and image of a clean-cut, sanguine black man was the antithesis of the menacing figures on the street." Bill Cosby was more than a very funny fellow. He was a perfect fit for the cool, still-young medium of television, a laid-back Negro who got himself invited into America's living rooms. Flip admired him, resented him, and learned from his example.

Activist blacks dismissed him as vanilla, a Negro Pollyanna. But Cosby was keenly aware of his color. The difference between his style and Dick Gregory's was that Cosby made his view of race relations clear without mentioning the subject. "I've never known any white bigot to pay to see a black man, unless the black man was getting hung," Cosby told *Playboy* in 1969. "So I don't worry about how to slip a social message into my act." Not mentioning race was a way of saying that human foibles are universal. We're all equal under the skin. It was what Flip meant when he said the funny has no color.

Still, some guys are forever more equal than others. While Flip survived a failed pilot to scramble his way into prime time, and worked twice as hard once he got there, Cosby seemed to stroll from one triumph to the next. In 1984 his NBC sitcom *The Cosby Show* became a surprise blockbuster. Occupying half of Flip's old Thursday-night time slot, it starred Cosby as well-to-do obstetrician Cliff Huxtable. *The Cosby Show* topped the Nielsen ratings for five years in a row. According to *TV Guide* it "almost single-handedly revived the sitcom genre and NBC's ratings." It proved to be a gold mine for its star, whose ownership stake boosted Cosby's net worth past $100 million (on its way to a reported $450 million by 2012), paving the way for stand-up-star sitcoms from *Roseanne* to Tim Allen's *Home Improvement* to *Seinfeld*. Before *The Cosby Show*, stand-up comics dreamed of killing on Carson and maybe headlining in Vegas. After *The Cosby Show* they dreamed bigger: eponymous sitcoms, endless wealth from syndication, multipicture movie deals.

During *The Cosby Show*'s second season, NBC offered Redd Foxx $35,000 a week to star in a comedy that would air in the golden half hour following Cosby. Despite dire money troubles due to his wars with the IRS—Foxx was allergic to paying taxes—he said no. "I won't be their nigger for thirty-five thousand a week." But when ABC offered $50,000 a week, Redd said yes. "They wanted Redd Foxx because Bill Cosby was rocking on NBC," said producer Rick Kellard. But *The Redd Foxx Show* wouldn't be the only *Cosby Show* clone on the air that year, or even the first. CBS beat its rivals to the punch with a 1985 sitcom called *Charlie & Co.*, starring Flip Wilson.

Flip relished the idea of taking on NBC, his old network, and his friendly rival Cosby. Maybe he relished it too much. He was growing more impulsive as he aged and ingested more grams, ounces, clouds of coke and weed. He knew Cosby had contractual control of almost every aspect of his show, but when contract talks with CBS got down to the last crucial clauses, he was in a hurry to get the deal done. "Fuck it," he said, and ceded control of the show to the network and producer Allan Katz.

The working-class family of *Charlie & Co.* struck many viewers as more realistic than the upscale fantasia of obstetrician Cosby and the Huxtable household. Flip lobbied for what he called "relevant" story lines while Katz and a handful of executive producers, all white, pushed for cheek-pinching scripts that he found unfunny. "They lured him out of retirement to be a Cosby clone," says Jaleel White, who played son Robert on *Charlie & Co.* three years before gaining TV immortality as Urkel on ABC's *Family Matters*. White remembers Flip as his protector on the set. "He spoiled me like a real son. On one of our first days he brought a big bag of toys to work. Flip starts pulling out footballs and remote-control cars, launching them at me. 'Jaleel, catch!'"

Gladys Knight landed the part of sitcom wife Diana on Flip's recommendation. They'd been friends through double bills at the Apollo, her mother Sarah's home-cooked meals in Atlanta, and a Chitlin' Circuit show that devolved into a riot. "I was new to acting, and he helped me," she recalls. "Della Reese, who was on our show, too, used to drive with me to Flip's house to read through the scripts. He'd say, 'No, Gladys, it's funnier if you say it this way.' And he was always right."

After a slow start in the ratings, *Charlie & Co.* sank lower. Each week's Nielsens brought more bad news. Workweeks began with a table reading that often found Flip with his head on the table. He suggested script changes, some as simple as turning "sexy woman" into "hot mama" or "neat" into "funky." Producer Katz rejected them. Then, with ratings shrinking, he had a brainstorm. Katz told Flip to banter with his TV wife in the most popular comic voice of the seventies: Geraldine's.

"They kept pushing him to do Geraldine," White says, recalling reams of critical notes from higher-ups telling Flip how to be funny. "They'd give him lines where he'd mimic Gladys in Geraldine's voice, trying to catch that old ratings magic."

"By then Flip *hated* Geraldine," Knight says. "He felt he'd created a monster. Anywhere he went people were after him to do Geraldine. Now he's got a network program for the first time in ten years, and the four white men running the show want him to do Geraldine. Flip got more frustrated every week."

White remembers a tense atmosphere on the set. "He protected me from the fights, but I could feel the heat rising. I'm nine years old, hearing the grown-ups throwing *shits* and f-bombs around, thinking, 'This can't be good.'"

Flip smoked fat joints to smooth his moods. Driving Gladys Knight to lunch on their breaks, he offered her a taste. "Keep that away from me," she said. "I pay too much for my perfume to go to work smelling like marijuana." Flip, who admired his costar's values as well as her immortal singing voice, let her brush ashes off his clothes before they went back to work. "He'd have holes in his pants from the ash off the joints he smoked." Lucky for him, the holes were too small to show up on pre-HD TV.

Each week brought a new battle with Katz and the network. "I wanted to help, but I had no power," Knight says. "It was Flip against the bosses. He felt that nothing in his life was going right. He wanted to be a great father to his children, but what sort of example was he setting for them, doing drugs all the time? He felt he was disappointing the people who loved him."

Flip gave *TV Guide* a candid quote: "I told CBS, 'My career is going down the toilet, and you're pulling the chain.'"

In 1986, after eighteen episodes, CBS canceled *Charlie & Co.*

When fans asked Flip to do Geraldine for them, he shook his head. "Sorry. She's retired," he said. "Mr. Wilson's going the rest of the way alone." After turning down another series because he'd have no control over the writing, he sped west in KILLER. Seeing the ocean, he raised his fist and said, "Thank you, Lord! Flip's still free!"

He filled his free time playing celebrity golf tournaments, tooling down Palm Springs fairways in a customized $18,000 Rolls-Royce golf cart complete with a color TV, bar, and loudspeakers for heckling other players. He hosted the Black Achievement Awards, and captained an NBC team in *Battle of the Network Stars*, gamely leading Michael J. Fox, Mark Harmon, Vicki Lawrence, and other celebrities in kayaking, tennis, outdoor bowling, a tug of war, and Simon Says. He took his son Kevin on a luxury cruise through the Panama Canal to Aruba and Martinique—Flip would duck out of their first-class cabin to play poker with waiters and bartenders—and treated daughter Tamara to a trip to France. "I was twenty-two or twenty-three," she recalls. "He'd been flirting with a woman there, but I guess it didn't work out. I went into his suite and found a note. *Elvis has left the building. See you back home.* He'd taken his wallet and headed for the airport. That's my father for you. He traveled light."

In 1991, CBS tried the *Charlie & Co.* formula again, this time with Flip's old mentor Redd Foxx as a mailman. Originally titled *Chest Pains*, the show aired as *The Royal Family.* Creator-producer Eddie Murphy cast *Charlie & Co.* veteran Della Reese as Foxx's wife. Flip stopped by the set to smoke and joke with Redd, but he wasn't around the day Foxx clutched his chest while rehearsing a scene. Everybody knew this stunt, a reprise of his famous fake heart attacks on *Sanford and Son*, when Redd would wince, roll his head back, and cry, "I'm coming, Elizabeth!" An amused *Royal Family* producer called for a camera—he didn't want to miss this. Then, as Reese told Foxx biographer Michael Seth Starr, "Redd reached for a chair and did what we thought was a pratfall. And we all stood there laughing while he was laying on the floor." Foxx, sixty-eight, died of a heart attack.

Reese, Gladys Knight, Slappy White, Mike Tyson, and hundreds of others attended Foxx's funeral in Las Vegas. The mourners included a man resembling Flip Wilson—an impostor who talked his way in by claiming to be Flip. The real Flip, who still didn't do death, mourned in private with his friend Stanley Nathanson, lifting a drink and a joint in Redd's honor. Flip said he'd been thinking about reincarnation lately, but it wasn't for him. "I'm not coming back," he told Nathanson. "Why would I? I had a hit show in this life. I made millions, sailed around the world, and fucked six girls at the same time. How am I gonna beat that? So if I die and you see a cockroach, go ahead and step on it, 'cause it ain't me."

Flip rallied his dwindling inner circle around a new passion. "He went wild for motorcycles," Kevin recalls, "so we had to be bikers, too."

Pack leader Flip rode a 1,300-cc Harley-Davidson Softail with forked handlebars and fringed leather saddlebags. Dismounting for a *Jet* photographer, he touched a leather-gloved fist to his chest and said, "If I could marry my motorcycle, I'd roll her right up to the altar." He had a local artist paint *God's Fool* on both sides of his bike's gas tank, a reference to a Kahlil Gibran character who comes out of the wilderness to "gaze with awe and wonder at the temples and towers and palaces" of a great city. In Gibran's tale the authorities arrest the poor fool and parade him through the city to be mocked by festive, laughing crowds, but God's fool is happy. He thinks they love him.

Flip marched his sons into a Harley-Davidson showroom in Marina del Rey. He bought motorcycles for David, now thirty-one, and twenty-nine-year-old Kevin, and outfitted them in leathers. They emerged from the store looking like a three-man biker gang, tall David between shorter, darker Kevin and Flip. On the way home they sped past a couple of Malibu police cars, and the cops let them go. Flip said he knew why. He said he'd paid his dues—and taxes—long enough for the town's only nigger to grow into a more mature role. "I'm Malibu's elder nigger now."

Elder son David wasn't so sure about his pops's latest passion. "My passion was golf, and golf's not a biker kind of game," he says. While Flip zipped around unencumbered, David had to balance his golf bag on his back while riding from course to course or else ship his sticks to each course he played. "Pops, I need a car," he said. "A car with a trunk."

"The bike's a gift," Flip said. "I like riding with my sons. You want a car? Get a job and buy one."

David stuck to motorcycles. He couldn't work a steady job and hone his golf game at the same time. And so in March 1993, David rode a 600-cc bike down Wilshire Boulevard to join his brother and sisters for the Museum of Radio and Television's salute to his father.

* * *

The tribute opened with a reel of *The Flip Wilson Show* highlights. Standing in shadows beside a movie screen, Flip peered up at his younger self. The spry comic on-screen clowned with Richard Pryor, delivered goofy news with George Carlin, danced with Aretha Franklin, and, as the unshrinkable Geraldine Jones, berated a hapless psychiatrist played by Perry Como. The audience laughed but Flip, twenty years older than the performer on-screen, with thinning hair and a downturned mouth, didn't. He nodded when punch lines drew laughs from the others. He knew each laugh was coming, because a good joke works whether it's 1973 or 1993. What pleased him most was seeing his children in the audience. Beside David and Kevin sat Tamara, twenty-seven, and Stacey, twenty-three—both as pretty as models, their proud pops thought. Like everyone else they were watching the screen, laughing as Flip made a face at Michael Jackson, saying, "I'm not jivin', shorty. Don't think I won't crack your nose."

Flip remembered every skit. He remembered sitting at the piano with Ray Charles as Geraldine, singing just badly enough to be funny. He remembered playing straight man for Don Rickles and Don Knotts, and dancing around Aretha while she did note-perfect impressions of Diana Ross, Sarah Vaughan, and Dionne Warwick. Watching his younger self with Aretha, he could still feel the dance moves in his feet.

"And now, ladies and gentlemen, Mr. Flip Wilson."

The announcement jarred him from his reverie. With a wave to the crowd, he stepped onto the stage and bowed. Still fit in his sixtieth year, he wore a tan suit and matching loafers. His eyes hung deeper in their sockets, as if worn out by years of bug-eyed mugging.

Seven of his *Flip Wilson Show* colleagues took turns praising him.

Director Tim Kiley lauded Flip's efficiency. He always knew his lines, never broke character, never played to the wrong camera. Producer Bob Henry recalled manager Monte Kay's reaction to the second-season debut costarring Lucille Ball, Ed Sullivan, and the Osmonds. "Monte said, 'Great, but there's nobody black on the show.' Flip said, 'What the hell am *I*?'"

When Henry told how Bing Crosby did a double take at the sight of Playboy Bunny Geraldine, fifty-nine-year-old Flip piped up with her answer: "You better believe it, 'cause you ain't gonna see it!"

Flip opened his remarks by thanking his old colleagues. "My only regret is, they're getting old, and I'm not." Recalling the hard work of creating an hour of entertainment with a laugh built in every twenty to thirty seconds, minute after minute, week after week, he said he'd felt the weight of the task as he and his coworkers wrote, rehearsed, rewrote, blocked, lit, and performed *The Flip Wilson Show*. "I thought that if twenty million people watched, that's twenty million hours they're giving me." More than two thousand years of viewer-hours each week. "That's an investment of trust." Taking his fans' trust seriously, he tried to be worthy of it. He tried to outwork everybody else in show business, he said, but all the while he was missing something.

Nodding toward the front row, he said, "My son David is here in the audience." Acknowledging David as *my son* was Flip's attempt to make amends for the freeze-outs, the private detective, maybe even his refusal to buy his golfing prodigy a car. It meant so much to him that he forgot to introduce his other kids.

Blinking tears, Flip recounted phone calls to Florida on Thursday nights in the seventies. "Did you like the show?" he'd ask his boys. At first they always said yes, but by the second season their story changed. As often as not they said they'd missed it. "I said, 'Damn, how can you miss my show?' Finally I got the story. Kevin said, 'I like your show, Pops, but David likes *The Waltons*. Every week we flip a coin, and you've been losing lately!'"

When the laughter died down, Flip got serious again. For years, he said, people wondered why he abandoned his top-rated show after four seasons. "I stopped the show because I wasn't seeing my kids," he explained.

This wasn't quite true, as his kids knew. It made a nice story, like his frequent claim that *The Flip Wilson Show* had been number one in the ratings, when in fact it topped out at number two and was sinking fast in its final season. He quit before NBC canceled him. Only then did fatherhood become his mission, but over the next twenty years he told the fatherhood-first story so many times he'd come to believe it. "These kids had to be raised," he declared at his tribute, extending an arm toward David, Kevin, Tamara, and Stacey, who shifted a bit uncomfortably in their seats. "I'd been a hero to *your* kids. It was time to be a hero . . ."

He paused, pointing to his heart.

". . . to mine."

The hall filled with applause. Flip bowed, his sunken eyes shining.

The next day, David Wilson climbed onto his motorcycle and headed back to Palm Springs. He was practicing for the PGA Tour's annual qualifying tournament, in which top performers earned the right to join Fred Couples, Greg Norman, and the rest of the game's elite on the pro tour. He knew the tour was a three-hundred-yard long shot for a three handicapper like him, so he was also studying country-club management. One way or another he was going to make a career in golf.

On March 17, 1993, five days after the tribute at the Museum of

Radio and Television, David spent a couple of hours drinking at Flaherty's Pub. It was St. Patrick's Day. He recalls peeling out of the parking lot that afternoon. Perhaps his drinking slowed his reflexes. Maybe he rode a little faster than usual to prove a point. *I'm a risk taker like you, Pops.* Maybe he just hit a patch of gravel.

"The next thing I remember, I was lying on the ground."

No one knows exactly what happened behind the Palm Springs Marriott that day. The most plausible account goes like this: David's Yamaha fishtailed. The bike went sideways while he kept going straight, sliding ten to twenty feet across gravel-strewn pavement toward a curb behind the Marriott. If not for his leathers he might have lost the skin on his back and shoulders, but may have stopped short of the curb. Instead he skidded into it.

Looking up at the desert sky, knowing he might have a broken arm or leg, he wondered why nothing hurt. What luck—a painless motorcycle crash. "I tried to get up," he says. "Nothing happened. My arms were just lying there. That's when I got scared."

Kevin Wilson's phone rang. "David's in trouble," he heard his father say. "I'm not shitting you, we've got to get a limo to the Springs *now*." They rushed to Palm Springs, where a surgeon took Flip aside.

"Mr. Wilson, it doesn't look good."

"He's a golfer—"

"Your son's spine is broken. It's unlikely he'll walk again."

Flip was quiet for a minute. The doctor started to say something else, but Flip held up his hand. Kevin saw his father's fist trembling. When he found the strength to speak, Flip couldn't find any words.

Tall, athletic David was paralyzed from the shoulders down. Flip spent tens of thousands of dollars on postoperative care at a rehab center near L.A., including more than $30,000 for a customized wheelchair with electronic controls David could operate by blowing through a straw. Flip was a frequent visitor at first, pushing David around the grounds in his wheelchair, reading Gibran to him. *The deeper that sorrow carves into your being, the more joy you can contain.* Once, as David lurched and swerved down a hallway while he learned to use the high-tech chair, his father said he was lucky he never had a car. "David, you never could drive!"

"Pops said he was proud of me for following my passion for golf," David recalls. "He said he loved me."

Before long, however, he noticed Flip's attitude shifting. Flip asked whether David had been wearing a helmet on St. Patrick's Day.

"Of course I was."

"Then where's the helmet?"

Flip kept asking. At first his sons were sympathetic. They knew he felt guilty about buying them bikes in the first place and for refusing to buy David a car when he asked for one. "That was eating him up," Kevin says, "and he got obsessed with the helmet. Because if he wasn't wearing a helmet it was David's fault, too. Pops accused me of lying about it. *'You're just following David's script!'*"

Within three months of the accident, Flip's sons were on the outs again. Flip never entirely gave up his suspicion that David was lying about the helmet, and never learned that the Palm Springs police had kept David's helmet after the accident.

That December, nine months after David's crash, a few friends and family members gathered in Malibu to help Flip celebrate his sixtieth birthday. If he did feel guilty about putting his sons on motorcycles, it didn't show. He still dressed in leathers and rode his *God's Fool* bike everywhere. His birthday cake, emblazoned *Happy Birthday You Devil You*, showed Geraldine on a Harley of her own.

With David lying in the rehab center, relying on nurses to keep him alive, with Cookie long gone and Kevin, Tamara, and Stacey pursuing their own lives, Flip spent more and more time alone. He fought his black moods with recreational drugs that seemed to help less and less.

"He was an introvert who hated being alone," says Gladys Knight. "I tried to buck him up. I said, 'Look at your life. You had a precious gift you shared with millions of people who loved you.' But he didn't feel the love."

"Flip had all the money in the world, but he lost himself," Bob Henry said. "He was lonesome to the point of tears."

He had one more grand gesture to make toward his children. In 1997 he sold syndication rights to *The Flip Wilson Show* to Viacom. Here was the last big payoff for his ownership stake in the show. Viacom paid a reported $10 million for the right to carry reruns of his ninety-four episodes on its TV Land cable channel. "This sets the groundwork for my comeback," he told *USA Today*. Privately, in separate conversations with his children, he said, "You won't have to worry about money when I'm gone."

That fall he promoted the reruns on Howard Stern's radio show. Now sixty-three, Flip let Stern quiz him about a "medical proce-dure" he'd heard about. The host's leering questions and Flip's hun-ger for attention led him to make an odd boast. "I had a pump implanted in my penis," he said. Flip swore he wasn't impotent, just sexually overworked. "So many women, so little time."

Stern asked one of his producers to help test the device. Flip dropped his pants and underwear. Producer Robin Radzinski was less than impressed with the size of his penis. She pumped. As his penis stirred, Flip said this particular pump was a replacement. His first implant, which cost $35,000, made his penis crooked, so he got a new one at the same price. "I've got a seventy-thousand-dollar penis!"

One night, sitting alone with his tape recorder, Flip said, "I'm ready to go again. People will be surprised to find that I stopped my show on psychic advice, and I could start again at any time. The years I performed were like going to a great university, developing my craft and myself. And now I feel a fresh flow of ideas. I feel that the flow is endless, and the best is yet to come."

He had a year to live.

15

Naked in the Wind

◈ In the summer of 1998 Flip noticed his pants getting looser. First one, then two notches in his belt pulled past the buckle. He was pleased to be losing weight. At the age of sixty-four he'd shed the spare tire around his middle. He felt fitter than he had at fifty.

Then he felt the first ache in his gut. A pinched nerve, he thought. But it didn't go away. The ache started low and crept upward, the pain growing sharper until he couldn't stand up straight. A doctor said the trouble might be liver stones caused by excess cholesterol. But no treatment helped. He still felt gut-shot. After a week of agony, he saw a specialist, who told him he had a tumor. "Liver cancer," the doctor said.

"Get it out. Cut it out of me," Flip said.

Second and third opinions confirmed that surgery would not make him well, but might kill him. His cancer had metastasized. The patient was stoic about the news. Stocking up at his favorite liquor store after another grim set of tests, he shrugged when the owner asked how he was doing.

"Dying of cancer," he said. "They're giving me two or three months."

"Ha!" The clerk thought he was kidding. "See you later."

"Let's hope."

The pain mounted until he could no longer tolerate a motorcycle ride, even on his smooth-riding Softail. The Harley gathered dust in the garage while Flip stretched in bed, trying to find a comfortable position. He sent Kevin to fetch his dope from the local Wells Fargo branch. Trailing a gray-haired matron into the safe-deposit room, Kevin used Flip's key to open a box stocked with Saran Wrapped bricks of hash-laced pot. They were wrapped loosely enough to give off a pungent scent that wafted into the lobby as he slipped past a security guard with his fragrant shopping bag. But the errand did Flip no good. Weed only made him obsess over the disease that was whittling away at him. Coke sometimes dulled the pain, sometimes doubled it. Hallucinogens were out of the question. His dreams were scary enough already.

He found a surgeon willing to try to cut out the tumor. "We're gonna roll the dice," Flip said. His operation was scheduled for October 2, 1998, at St. John's Health Center in Santa Monica. Flip, still plotting a TV comeback, invited the *National Enquirer* to cover his last-ditch operation. "This has been the most terrifying ordeal I've ever faced. But I'm ready," he said, giving an *Enquirer* photographer a thumbs-up.

Before they carted him to surgery, a nurse rolled another prone patient into his room.

"Wouldn't you know it?" Flip exulted. "Wouldn't you know my boy would find a way to come to my side on the day I need him the most?"

David had arranged to be trundled into an ambulance for the hour-long ride to Flip's side. They couldn't embrace, not with the pre-op patient plugged into monitors and IVs while quadriplegic David could do no more than turn his head. Flip felt like dancing. He settled for narrating the moment for the *Enquirer*. "My eyes filled with tears when I saw my David. That's when I knew God is with me," he said. "That big guy upstairs is giving me one more chance."

Between the photo op and the operation, he and David had a moment to themselves.

"He said he was going to beat the cancer, and then he was going to bring me back into his life," David recalls. "To make things right between us. I thought, *No, you won't. It's too late.* But I believe he wanted to try." Before they parted, father and son had the closest thing to a handshake that their plights allowed. "He reached out to me. Somebody picked up my hand and put it on top of his hand." David couldn't feel his hand, of course. He could only see it lying on his father's trembling hand. "Then they rolled him away."

The man who didn't do death dreamed about dying. In one dream he was a jet pilot at long last. "I kept flying straight up at the sun, getting closer and closer to God, until the plane disintegrated," Flip confided to his tape recorder. In another dream, "I was onstage with the whole world in front of me, telling my funniest story, and while everyone had their heads thrown back in hysterical laughter, I would die."

He gave some of his African art to Frank and Barbara Sinatra. He gave his last Corniche to Don Costa, the bandleader he'd shared with Sinatra. He made lists noting who should get which of his possessions, and as 1998 slipped away he spent sleepless nights reciting Gibran to himself. *For what is it to die but to stand naked in the wind and to melt into the sun? And what is it to cease breathing, but to free the breath from its restless tides that it may rise and expand and seek God unencumbered? And when the earth shall claim your limbs, then shall you truly dance.*

"I don't want to die in a hospital," he told Kevin. "Take me home."

In his last days he weighed ninety-eight pounds. There was no more need to eat, he said, not while his guts were eating him. Pain, too, was a thing of the past. When Kevin offered a joint, Flip said he'd found something better.

"Morphine," he said, "is really good shit."

Flip lay on a gurney in his sunken living room, his head propped on two or three pillows, channel-surfing. He saw faces of all colors and ethnicities. Too weak to play golf, he watched Tiger Woods on TV. Flip considered Woods a bit of a phony. He had laughed when the half-black, half-Thai golfer denied being black when he turned pro in 1996. "With those lips, he says he's not black? Wait till Nike gets him. He'll be black then." His prediction had come true when Woods made his proudly black "Hello, world" Nike ad later that year.

Now he watched a new generation of black comics prowl comedy stages on network and cable TV. Eddie Murphy, Whoopi Goldberg, Jamie Foxx, Chris Rock. "Before I came out," Murphy said, "you had Richard Pryor and Bill Cosby and Flip Wilson and Redd Foxx. Now you see millions of niggers telling jokes!" Martin Lawrence, Arsenio Hall, the Wayans brothers, Sinbad, Cedric the Entertainer, Steve Harvey, Bernie Mac, Dave Chappelle, Tyler Perry, Robert Townsend, and others became stars while the comic who'd transformed television in the seventies watched from his bed in his opulent beach house, feeling forgotten. Except for the occasional rerun on TV Land, Flip *was* forgotten.

Stepdaughter Michelle moved into the beach house to look after him. "Toward the very end, his pain got really bad," she recalls. His doctors were reluctant to give him still more morphine; there was talk of the perils of addiction. Flip struggled to speak. When he could, he begged Michelle to end the pain. Nodding toward his pain pills, he asked her to feed him the whole bottle, one pill after the other. To stop the pain and let him go. One of his last words, she says, was "please."

"I didn't know what to do. I was scared. I mean, I wasn't even a blood relative. What if they did an autopsy and found out? Would I go to jail?" In the end, she says, "I didn't have the guts to do what he wanted."

Sometimes he hallucinated. One night, half starved and high on morphine, he was sure he was dying. Lifting a bone-thin arm, he said, "The angels are here."

Sometimes he watched tapes of his old shows and specials. One of the specials was a children's cartoon he wrote and voiced at the height of his career. In *Clerow Wilson and the Miracle of P.S. 14*, a Jersey City schoolteacher tells her boisterous students that they're such a no-account bunch that the Statue of Liberty turned her back on them. If one of them ever made a mark on the world, maybe Lady Liberty would notice.

At the end, the statue peeks over her shoulder and winks at little Clerow.

Back to the Beach

◈ Flip died on November 25, 1998, the day before Thanksgiving. He didn't want a funeral. His kids remembered how he used to joke about the subject. "If you motherfuckers get an invitation to my funeral, don't go, because I won't be there, either." But he said they might still hear from him after he was gone. A bell might ring just when they thought of him. A gull might crap on them and laugh, just to remind them that Pops still had his eye on them. Or they'd trip on the stairs—him again. But there was to be no funeral. "I hate that death shit," he said.

Some of his old coworkers arranged a service anyway. Along with his ex-wife Cookie, Rocky Aoki, and several family members, they gathered at Pierce Brothers Funeral Home in Westwood at noon on December 10, 1998. A television monitor showed clips from *The Flip Wilson Show*. The show's producer, Bob Henry, now seventy-eight, provided opening remarks and a eulogy. A former NBC publicist gave a reading from Kahlil Gibran. There were Bible readings, New Testament benedictions for a man who didn't dig mainstream Christianity and hadn't been to church in years. Oddly enough, the Wilson children weren't included in the program. They sat and listened. "The whole thing was bizarre," Rashon Khan recalls. "It was hastily put together. It didn't do him justice."

"Here was a man who was the top comedian on TV," says Kevin Wilson. "He deserved a big send-off."

Instead, TV's first black superstar stepped off life's stage almost unnoticed. There was no farewell TV special, no candlelight vigil by Flip fans, no star in his honor on Hollywood's Walk of Fame. And as time passed he would only slip further from view. Johnny Carson and Bill Cosby would be hailed as TV icons while Flip Wilson was barely a footnote. Richard Pryor and George Carlin entered comedy's pantheon while their old boss faded to black. Pryor in particular inspired the next generation of comics. Eddie Murphy, whose fame and wealth surpassed that of every other contemporary comedian, called Pryor his hero. When Murphy sided with "motherfucking Richard" against Jell-O-shilling Cosby, Flip didn't merit a mention.

"Flip's show was a step in the evolution of TV and comedy," says Lily Tomlin. "It was the step that won over middle America to the idea that a black host was okay. He was more conventional than Richard, but who wasn't?"

Flip set ratings records and helped bring dozens of worthy performers, many of them black, into the American mainstream at a time when other variety hosts played it safe. A newcomer of his own making, Geraldine Jones, spent a couple seasons as the most-quoted "woman" in the country. Geraldine amused and influenced comedians from Whoopi Goldberg, who says she sometimes "channeled Geraldine" onstage, to a slew of drag kings, including Tyler Perry, Martin Lawrence, RuPaul, Jamie Foxx, John Leguizamo, maybe even Dustin "Tootsie" Hoffman and Robin "Mrs. Doubtfire" Williams. Yet when was the last time Tyler Perry tipped his tiara to Geraldine?

"Show business has a short memory," Tomlin says.

In the decade after Flip's death, reruns of his show—without the era-defining musical numbers—turned up occasionally, if at all, in cable TV's dustiest corners. With *Seinfeld* earning more than $2.7 billion in syndication after leaving the air in 1998, the year Flip died, Flip's $20 million estate looked puny by comparison—especially to his children, who settled for $375,000 apiece after weeks of wrangling with their pops's lawyers and ex-girlfriends who threatened to leave them with nothing. The Wilson kids scattered, with Kevin, Tamara, and Stacey settling in and around Los Angeles. Stepdaughter Michelle moved to Negros, a volcanic island in the Philippines, to help look after David, her paralyzed half brother. David had relocated there because the round-the-clock medical care he needs is cheaper in the Philippines. Due to the settlements Flip's kids accepted after he died, they got no cut of any revenue his show generated, not that there was any revenue to speak of. By 2011, DVDs of *The Flip Wilson Show* highlights were selling for pennies on eBay.

But there were signs that Flip wouldn't be forgotten. In summer 2012 Magic Johnson's fledgling cable channel, Aspire, began rerunning *The Flip Wilson Show*. A new boxed set of DVDs was due out that fall. Comics who came of age long after Flip's heyday sometimes invoked his memory. Cedric the Entertainer and Wayne Brady called him a hero. *30 Rock* star Tracy Morgan hung a painting in his house—a version of *The Last Supper* that had Pryor, of course, as Jesus, with Carlin and Flip in attendance.

"Flip's hip. He always was," says Whoopi Goldberg. "Back in the seventies it was amazing that he got his own show. It was mesmerizing to see black people on TV because it still was so new, and he was the big star. He had a big impact on me. I remember when I first imagined being an entertainer, thinking, *Who in Hollywood do I look like?* Well, it wasn't Cher. It was Flip. I looked like Geraldine!

"Then all of a sudden he was gone," Goldberg says. "George Carlin went on to do a bunch of specials. Richard had specials and movies. Eddie, too. But Flip didn't make movies. He wasn't an actor. The business was shifting, too. Geraldine seemed naughty in 1970 or '71, but comedy got edgier. Dirtier, you could say. And he wasn't going there."

You could say that Flip was the first and last of his kind. Like Jackie Robinson he was brave and talented enough to break a color barrier, patient and likable enough to do it without scaring white America out of its wits. Then, just as suddenly as it arrived, his moment passed. Pop culture was shifting so quickly that the slightly naughty nice guy who rocked prime time in 1970 seemed a bit dated four years later. "He was a pioneer," Goldberg says. "But it's hard to be the first at anything. Other people come along and build on what you've done."

Mel Watkins, who wrote Flip's obituary in *The New York Times*, cited his "likable personality, seemingly effortless delivery and joyful depiction of the language and mannerisms of black street life." Noting that Flip arrived at a key point in comedy history, a crossroads between old and new, Watkins wrote that he "invested his characters with the broad, boisterous humor of older black circuit comedy and combined their portrayal with the thrust of the new stand-up comics."

In short he was a man of his time who changed his time. When Flip hit prime time, it was still something special to see a black performer on TV, much less a black host who got millions of Americans to tune in every Thursday and quote his best bits the rest of the week. This was the brief, heady time Gladys Knight calls "a huge, wonderful, surprising event." Of course it couldn't last. By 1974, due largely to *The Flip Wilson Show*, nobody blinked when Gladys Knight and the Pips, Richard Pryor, or another black act took center stage in prime time. The battle was won. Whatever else you might call Clerow Wilson—self-made millionaire, Emmy and Grammy winner, mentor, talent scout, doper, faithless husband, flawed father, spiritual seeker, or world's only black helium balloonist—he was one of a handful of pioneers who integrated prime time.

After the memorial service in Westwood, Flip's survivors filed out into noonday sun, wondering what to do next. Stepdaughter Michelle held a pale blue urn full of his ashes. A mortuary worker had handed her the urn as well as a plastic bag that held Flip's dental bridge, a set of false teeth that wouldn't burn.

Flip had said he wanted his ashes cast into his favorite canyon in Arizona, but nobody was sure how to find it. He'd always gone there alone. Nephew and bodyguard Khan suggested spreading the ashes in the ocean. Flip had loved the Pacific from the moment he got over his seasickness on his first ride on a troop ship in 1950. Decades later he'd spent long hours watching the waves from the deck of his Malibu mansion, and spent his last days lying in his sunken living room with the doors open wide, listening to the surf. "We agreed on the ocean. But we weren't prepared to charter a boat," Khan says. Time was short. They would go their separate ways the next day. So off they went to Zuma Beach.

This, they thought, would be Flip's true farewell, not some staged Hallmark moment at a funeral parlor. Khan set the tone by playing African djembe drums. First a *lamba*, a healing song, and then a song of celebration, a *ninjane*, to guide the spirit's crossing to a new plane of existence.

Someone took a stick and drew a circle in the sand around them. Five people—Khan, Michelle, Tamara, Stacey, and Flip's longtime assistant, Angie Hill—overdressed for a beach outing, each one alone with his or her thoughts. Until Stacey spoke, recalling happy moments with her pops, and then Michelle spoke, and then Khan. When Tamara's turn came, she took a long breath. "I loved you," she told her father. "I still love you."

That's when it hit her. What's wrong with this picture?

What was wrong, she thought, was that everybody from Bob Henry to her siblings was acting like a posthumous publicist. Flip had after all been a man, not a saint. Not even a hero, at least to his children. "It just hit me—we were acting out the grieving-family parts we'd seen in movies," she says. "And I decided to be honest."

Nobody recorded her words, but they all remembered the heat in

Tamara's voice as she spoke to the urn Michelle held. They remembered the gist: Why weren't you a better father? Did you love us as much as we loved you? Who *were* you? As Khan drummed an African requiem, Michelle offered the urn to Tamara, who recoiled.

"What am I supposed to do? Just reach in?" she asked. "With my hands?"

Nobody had gloves. Tamara held her breath and pulled a handful of ash from the urn. She carried it down the beach. She tossed the ashes into the air. It was the season of Santa Ana winds, offshore breezes that carried Flip's ashes toward the shining sea. The others took their turns until the urn was almost empty. By then their impromptu memorial service was drawing unwanted attention. A bunch of black people on a nearly all-white beach, sending up puffs of smoke—even in 1998, they were asking for trouble.

"I was the lookout," Michelle recalls. As the one who had signed documents taking charge of the urn, she knew that they needed to be three miles offshore to legally dispose of human remains. "I was the one who could get nabbed." And in the quiet between Tamara's outburst and Khan's last tap on his drum, Michelle watched a pair of pale beachgoers approach a lifeguard, pointing at the Wilsons. She watched the lifeguard hop down from his whitewashed chair, climb onto his fat-tire three-wheeler and rev it up. "He was heading our way. I said, 'Okay, let's wrap this up!'"

She upended the urn, casting the last ashes toward the surf. They all grabbed their belongings as the lifeguard approached. Juggling the urn and her flip-flops, Michelle quick-walked up the beach. She stuck the plastic bag that held the dental bridge into her back pocket, and as her weight shifted, Flip's false teeth poked her.

Just like him, she thought. *Two weeks gone and he's biting me on the ass.*

◈

ACKNOWLEDGMENTS

◈ This book belongs to Kevin Wilson as well as to me. Flip's son opened his life and heart to me without ever trying to control what I wrote. In the course of our two years together he became a friend and an ally. From one Kevin to another, thanks.

Readers who play golf should know that Kevin, who never matched his brother, David, as a golfer, has caddied at some of the most exclusive courses in Southern California. If you want proof of his expertise, I have photographic evidence. David Wilson, still chatty and upbeat twenty years after the motorcycle accident that left him paralyzed, was a vital source. A far better golfer than the rest of the chops involved in this project, he's a major champion to me. Readers who would like to contact David—perhaps even help with his ongoing medical expenses—can reach him at David@ meetdavidwilson.com.

Hollywood pro David Hopwood teed up our project. Consider this a shout-out to "Hopperwood" and Mark Canton, who may one day bring Flip's story to the screen. Roberta Kay gave me several interviews as well as a transcription of the notes Flip recorded for a memoir he hoped to write. I'm deeply grateful to Roberta for helping me bring Flip's voice to this account of his life.

The warm, wonderful Cookie Mackenzie was a great help to my work. Thanks, Cookie. Rashon Khan, Tamara Wilson, and Michelle Zacharias, my guide and great friend in the Philippines, aided my efforts. (Michelle, I hope we'll have another San Miguel beer sometime.) So did my heroines Gladys Knight and Lily Tomlin, along with Whoopi Goldberg, Jaleel White, Franklyn Ajaye, Stanley

Nathanson, Bob Schiffman, Tim Conway, Portia Qualls, Franco Basile of On Golden Pond Films, Winston Moss, Bubba Knight, Paul Cooper, Sidney Miller, Bill Bateman, the staff at the Paley Center for Media, and Neal Brunson at the Jersey City Afro-American Historical Society.

Big thanks to editor Rick Kot, who remembered Flip, believed in *Flip,* and made the book better. Thanks also to the sharp, reliable, essential Nick Bromley, and to Kyle Davis, Michael Burke, Carla Bolte, Ben Petrone, and Rick's other colleagues at Viking, as well as to my agent, David Vigliano, and his associates Anthony Mattero and David Peak at Vigliano Associates.

My work got grassroots support from Ken Kubik of New Jersey's Grass Roots Inc., as well as Liz Halsted, David Barnes, Arthur Kretchmer, Steve Randall, A.J. Baime, Chris Carson, Doug Vogel, Luis Fernando Llosa, Christina Bloom, and Allison Burnett.

Here's where I tip my cap to the home team: Forever thanks to Lily Lady and her big brother, Cal, for being the people they are, and to their mom, Pamela Marin, whose *Motherland* is one of the best books of our young century.

◆ Kevin Wilson would like to thank "first and foremost, my mother, Blonell Teresa Pittman; my lovely wife, Frances Copeland-Wilson; my siblings David, Tamara, Stacey, Michelle Zacharias; Marcus Daniels, Rashon and Linda Khan, Portia Qualls, Roberta Kay, Mark Canton, David Hopwood, Rob Friedman, Jim Burkus, Ari Emanuel, Jerry Abrams, Wayne and Janet Gretzky, Jermaine Jackson, Keith Davidson, Jim Hale, Stanley Nathanson, Lance Smith, Chris Kaczke, Paul Hopkins, Stan Smith, the Millett family, Irving Azoff, John Burack, Josh Luwark, Herschel Boone, and Lola Allen.

Flip's son Kevin Wilson (left) on the course with a noteworthy golfer.

SELECT BIBLIOGRAPHY

Bianculli, David. *Dangerously Funny: The Uncensored Story of the Smothers Brothers Comedy Hour*. New York: Touchstone, 2009.

Branch, Taylor. *At Canaan's Edge: America in the King Years 1965–1968*. New York: Simon and Schuster, 2006.

Branch, Taylor. *Parting the Waters: America in the King Years 1954–1963*. New York: Simon and Schuster, 1988.

Branch, Taylor. *Pillar of Fire: America in the King Years 1963–1965*. New York: Simon and Schuster, 1998.

Carlin, George. *Braindroppings*. New York: Hyperion Books, 1997.

Dangerfield, Rodney. *It's Not Easy Bein' Me*. New York: HarperCollins, 2004.

French, Kenneth. *Jersey City 1940–1960*. Charleston, SC: Arcadia Publishing, 1997.

Haggins, Bambi. *Laughing Mad: The Black Comic Persona in Post-Soul America*. New Brunswick, NJ: Rutgers University Press, 2007.

Hine, Thomas. *The Great Funk: Styles of the Shaggy, Sexy, Shameless 1970s*. New York: Farrar, Straus and Giroux, 2009.

Hudson, James. *Flip*. New York: Scholastic Book Services, 1971.

Lauterbach, Preston. *The Chitlin' Circuit*. New York: W. W. Norton & Company, 2011.

Littleton, Darryl. *Black Comedians on Black Comedy*. New York: Applause Theater & Cinema Books, 2006.

Malcolm X. *The Autobiography of Malcolm X*. New York: Grove Press, 1965.

Starr, Michael Seth. *Black and Blue: The Redd Foxx Story*. Milwaukee: Applause Theater & Cinema Books, 2011.

Sutherland, Meghan. *The Flip Wilson Show*. Detroit: Wayne State University Press, 2008.

Watkins, Mel. *On the Real Side: A History of African-American Comedy*. Chicago: Lawrence Hill Books, 1994.

Williams, John A., and Dennis A. Williams. *If I Stop I'll Die: The Comedy and Tragedy of Richard Pryor*. New York: Thunder's Mouth Press, 1991.

Zoglin, Richard. *Comedy at the Edge*. New York: Bloomsbury USA, 2008.

INDEX